Library of
Davidson College

GROUP PREJUDICES
IN
INDIA

A SYMPOSIUM

EDITORS
Sir MANILAL B. NANAVATI
C. N. VAKIL

GREENWOOD PRESS, PUBLISHERS
WESTPORT, CONNECTICUT

Originally published in 1951
by Vora & Co., Publishers, Ltd., Bombay

First Greenwood Reprinting 1970

Library of Congress Catalogue Card Number 79-98783

SBN 8371-3132-4

Printed in the United States of America

PREFACE

The importance of the subject of Group Prejudices in India has been explained at some length in the Introduction. All thinking people would agree that the early removal of the prevailing group prejudices in the country is an essential preliminary for moulding free India into a united, strong and democratic nation. With a view to focussing public attention on the many aspects of this important problem, we decided a few years ago to approach eminent persons in different walks of life to record their experience and ideas each on some aspect of the wider problem. In order to help contributors an outline scheme indicating different types of prejudices was circulated to a large number of specialists in different fields of knowledge and experience. In spite of their sincere desire to co-operate with us, some of the eminent persons whom we approached could not spare the necessary time to send their contributions on the subject. We are glad, however, that as many as twenty-eight contributions have been received from outstanding thinkers in the country. These have been classified and put under appropriate headings. It is hoped that this effort will stimulate thought on this vital problem and lead to further intensive work on the subject with a view to finding an appropriate solution for it. We welcome the recent efforts of the Government of India in co-operation with the UNESCO to encourage intensive research in this problem.

It is unfortunate that due to a variety of circumstances, over some of which we had little or no control, the publication of this Symposium was delayed. We must apologise to our contributors for this unfortunate delay. We have, however, every hope that their valuable contributions will help in the better understanding of the problem. We take this opportunity to thank Mr. M. K. Vora, the Publisher who undertook to publish this work on his own in spite of pressure of other work.

In the work of classifying and editing contributions as well as in preparing the Introduction and subsequently in seeing the book through the press, we received valuable help from Dr. A. R. Desai.

Bombay,
May 10, 1951.

M. B. NANAVATI
C. N. VAKIL

INTRODUCTION

I. The Basic Problem in Free India

The partition of India followed by mass massacres in certain parts of the country as also the assassination of Mahatma Gandhi and the revealations made at the trial of the murderer and his associates have naturally set people thinking regarding the deeper causes which have led to these unfortunate events. We are painfully aware of the many fissiparous tendencies in Indian life. Among the various forces which may be responsible the chief place may be given to what may be described as "Group Prejudices" or what are sometimes termed "Group Tensions" which exist in the country in diverse forms, at different levels and in varying degrees and shades.

The present volume represents a pioneer effort to focus the attention of the people of India on these group prejudices which are sapping the foundations of our very existence. The method adopted is to present the viewpoints of several eminent thinkers in India on different aspects of group prejudices which are rampant in Indian society today. We are experiencing at present one of the gravest crises in our history. The difficult historical processes through which we secured national independence have unleashed numerous suppressed and semi-suppressed forces. A host of group antagonisms born of group prejudices have rent Indian society at a time when we need the united efforts of all for stabilising our freedom on the one hand and for progress on the other.

We have achieved juridical independence. The basic task confronting us is to transform this juridical freedom into real freedom, i.e. into higher forms of material and cultural existence. Even after achieving independence, the multitude of group prejudices and resultant group tensions and conflicts are undermining the unity and strength of the nation and are obstructing free and rapid national advance. Successful overcoming of all these disruptive forces requires from those who are at the helm of affairs, great qualities such as a catholic outlook, clear thinking and above all a broad vision to correctly trace the real causes of these forces and evolve an effective practical programme for dissolving them without delay.

II. What are Group Prejudices?

Let us consider the nature of group prejudices.

Prejudice means distorted perception. It means prejudgment about a person or a quality of a person based on a previous bias in the mind of the observer without correlating it to the actual situation. For example, when we attribute certain characteristics to individuals as representative of a group, we expect in advance certain behaviour of them. In doing so, we also have in mind a certain idea of values, good or bad, superior or inferior regarding the parties. Such preconceived beliefs about others involving certain types of evaluation constitute group prejudices."*

* Robin. M. Williams jr.: "The Reduction of Intergroup Tensions" p.35.

This distorted vision about the other group and its behaviour is one of the major causes of misunderstanding and conflict among the various groups and communities. For example, the Hindu may presume certain generalised traits among the Muslim; the high caste Brahmin may imagine certain clusters of traits among the low caste Hindu; the North Indian may evolve a stereotyped picture of the South Indian; the Maharashtrian may attribute a certain set of qualities to the Gujarati and *vice versa*, which may not exist at all among the group as a whole. In spite of this, attitudes are formed and actions taken on such prejudgments and assumed favourable or unfavourable pictures of the other groups. The misunderstanding goes on increasing on the basis of such biased practice, and a fertile soil is created for the emergence of hostilities and active conflicts. It is now being increasingly realised that the effects of such group prejudices permeate almost every sector of life, in the country.**

In India such wrong attitudes of men towards men, such incorrect notions prevalent among various groups, such irrational prejudices made by different groups and members of a group in mutual social transactions, such hosts of suspicions, jealousies, false judgments and misevaluation of motives of others which are rampant in Indian society are the direct causes of group discords and social disharmony. Their roots lie deep in the hoary history of the Indian people. To comprehend properly the sources of these group prejudices, it is necessary to have a proper understanding of the forces that have influenced the entire life of the people in this country.

III. India's Complex History

Indian Society is perhaps the most complex society that has emerged in history. It presents a fascinating and at the same time a baffling problem.

Firstly, the geographical environs in which Indian Society emerged and developed have been unique. The geographical environs play an appreciable role in moulding the life of a people and their social structure. India is a vast country, almost a sub-continent. Its territory extending from the mighty Himalayas to the Cape Comorin is a rich pattern of zones with varied, even contradictory climatic conditions, topographical features, thick forests, vast deserts, big and small rivers, diverse types of flora and fauna. Such a peculiar geographical structure was bound to influence the character of the Indian people and their social organisation in all phases of their history. Their past history can, through archaeological research, be traced to the hoary times of Mohenjodaro and Harappa, where civilisation flourished even before the

** cf. The Annals of the American Academy of Political and Social Science, March 1946, p.167.

> They "extend to all aspects of group living and personal-social relationships in methods of bringing up children, in manners of training, in food habits, in differential standards for men and women, in preferred forms of leadership, in the way in which a factory or organisation is run—in these and innumerable other areas, distorted social perceptions or prejudices play a significant role. The close inter-dependence of perception and conduct points to the very practical and consequential role of prejudice in social living."

Vedic time. Archaeologists and anthropologists have reached the conclusion that modern Indian society can be traced back to still earlier paleolithic and neolithic phases of social existence.

Thus civilized social existence in India commenced centuries before it emerged in the life of most other human communities. India has been an ethnic laboratory in the past. The people of India exhibit a mixture of numerous races, indigenous as well as foreign, through a process of complex ethnic combinations. The ancient history of India is the history of long drawn out struggles of the Aryan invaders and the Dravidians, Naga, Dasyu and other races—the original inhabitants of the country. Subsequently the Scythians, the Mongols, the Huns, the Greeks, the Persians, the Muslims and finally the Europeans came to India. It should be noted that unlike the Europeans, all other groups referred to above were domiciled in India. The contemporary Indian people are thus the result of the assimilation of these groups. The process of amalgamation of diverse races through mutual contacts and even collisions brought about decisive alterations in the structure of Indian society and explains the great diversity of social forms within contemporary Indian society.

The cultural history of the Indian people can be traced through various stages of evolution, such as phases of magic, animism, polytheism, and the emergence of philosophic Hinduism embodied in the Upanishads in the ancient period. India has been the birthplace of the two great religions of the world, Hinduism and Buddhism. India became also an arena of great religio-philosophical movements such as the Sankhya, the Bhakti cult and others, which though based on Hinduism, gave rise to a number of cults and social sects around them. Muslim invasions of India which occurred in subsequent periods resulted in the conversion of millions of Hindus to the Muslim faith; these constitute mainly the Muslim section of the Indian population today.

In the same way, the invasions of the country by the Christian nations of Europe resulted in the conversion of a section of the Indian people to Christianity and today there exists in India a large number of Christians. Thus, the Indian people came to have a multi-religious social composition. The Indian nation is comprised of Hindus, Muslims, Christians, Parsis, Jains and others. No nation in the world has such a heterogeneous socio-religious composition.

A unique type of social organisation was evolved in India in the past, the caste system. This was the product of the peculiar historical development of the Indian people. It was the offspring of diverse causes, economic, ethnic and cultural. Some castes or sub-castes were the result of the ossifying of the functional economic groups into rigid social groups. Some were the consequence of the incorporation of vanquished social groups into the social organisation of the victorious Aryans as subordinate social groups. Further, the various religio-philosophical movements referred to above based on different interpretations of the early idealistic monistic Hindu philosophy, gave rise to a number of sects which also became social castes or sub-castes. Thus, the Hindus, themselves a component part of the Indian people with a multi-religious social composition, came to be divided into a number of castes and subcastes. The social and religious conflicts between the various communities and castes and sub-castes have influenced and still influence the development of Indian society.

The political history of the Indian people presents also a fascinating study. Indian history starts with the tribal existence of the primitive population inhabiting India. The next stage of political development brings into being Gana-Rajyas on Sapta-Sindhus during the Vedic period. Subsequently, great kingdoms spreading from Gandhara (modern Afganistan) to Ceylon spring into existence. The rise and fall of a number of Hindu and Buddhist empires mark the next stage in the political history of India, which in turn is followed by the rise and fall of the different Muslim Empires. The emergence of the Maratha Empire and the advent of the British come next. The political unity of the country is brought about for the first time under the British regime. The most recent phase in the political evolution of the Indian people is the partition of India into two independent states of India and Pakistan. This demonstrates how the political history of India has had a varied complex pattern, a long series of political upheavals which also determined its economic and social institutional structure as also the cultural life of the people.

Different types of social institutions also emerged in India in her long history of many centuries viz. matriarchical and patriarchical systems of tribal organisations; self-sufficient village communities with their Panchayats, the unique caste institution of the Hindus and their Joint Family system, family systems based on polyandry, polygamy, monogamy and others.

India has thus been the arena of conflicts of various cultures Hindu, Buddhist, Muslim and modern European. Further, various linguistic groups evolved their own cultures. There have emerged variants of the same cultural groups in different territorial zones that constitute India. The modern European culture with its doctrines of liberalism, democracy, recognition of the liberty of the individual and concern for his personality and rationalism came in sharp conflict with the indigenous Hindu and Muslim cultures based upon religio-authoritarian principles.

Thus a complex heterogenous and belligerent social and cultural life is incessantly flowing within the framework of the very complex social structure of contemporary Indian society divided among a multitude of social groups. This gives rise to group prejudices, tensions and conflicts. To counteract such Group Prejudices which arise in such a society with such a varied culture, a comprehensive, scientific and systematic study of Indian society as it exists today and as it developed in its present form due to a long historical evolution is urgently called for.

IV. Group Conflicts in Contemporary Indian Society

We shall briefly enumerate the principal Group Tensions in order to locate the correct remedies.

(a) *Religious Conflicts*: First in order of importance come religious conflicts among which that between the Hindus and the Muslims is deep-rooted and bears a pernicious character. The scale and the ferocity of Hindu-Muslim collisions in recent years have been staggering. Entire provinces became transformed into battlegrounds of these clashes. Tens of thousands of Hindus and Muslims were killed. Millions were uprooted from their homelands and became refugees. The colossal refugee problem which both the states, India and Pakistan, have been facing today, is the consequence of this communal warfare.

Further, no means were considered too barbarous and inhuman in this warfare. Arson, rape and torture profusely characterised it. Sometimes even the sinister slogan of total annihilation of the adversary religious group was shouted. Even after partition, communal riots born of irrational communal prejudices did not stop. There have been periodical outbreaks even till recently. This proves how deeply rooted religious prejudices are in the consciousness and social life of the Indian people.

(b) *Regional Conflicts*: Regional conflicts constitute another outstanding type of group conflict from which Indian society is suffering. In South India, Malayalam, Tamil, Telugu and Kannada speaking zones are the theatres of this species of group conflict. The State of Bombay is increasingly becoming the hot-bed of sharpening friction between the Maharashtrians, the Gujaratis, the Kannadigas. Bengal, Assam and Bihar are not still harmoniously adjusted to one another. The newly merged States are still smarting under real or imaginary humiliations and injury due to the merger process. East Punjab has become a storm centre of Sikh-Hindu conflict.

The social gulf and the psychological hiatus between different regional groups have been deepening in the post-independence period. The urge for reconstruction of existing state units on linguistic basis among different linguistic groups has engendered inter-regional animosities. These animosities tend to retard national consciousness, national unity and collaboration of various social groups comprising the nation.

(c) *Political Conflicts*: In addition to the above mentioned communal and regional tensions and conflicts, Indian society is rent also with tensions and conflicts of a political nature. A perpetual political warfare is going on in the country between numerous political parties representing various group interests. The struggle between the Indian National Congress, the Socialist Party of India, the Hindu Mahasabha, the Forward Bloc, the Communist Party, the Workers' and Peasants' Party, the various political parties of different communities like the Sikhs and others, not to speak of the host of small political groups which have recently had mushroom growth in the country have kept the Indian people in a state of political turmoil. These political organisations carry on a ceaseless struggle among themselves through continuous press and platform propaganda. Some of them have even built up volunteer organisations to back up their agitational work. The atmosphere is surcharged with hostile political passions sometimes transforming political warfare of these groups into physical clashes. Though the Congress party is in power and dominates the field, it is obvious that it is slowly losing its hold in some degree to some of the other parties.

(d) *Economic Conflicts*: Conflicts between various socio-economic groups also eat into the vitals of our national life. The cleavage and conflict between labour and capital have been intensifying, in recent years, in our country. This is reflected in the phenomenal growth of strikes, and frequent lockouts. In fact there is a growing tendency on the part of labour and capital to organise themselves into two distinct belligerent camps. It is, however, heartening to observe that these struggles have been reduced in recent times partly due to the machinery for the settlement of industrial disputes now in operation in the country.

In the agrarian area, the conflicts between the landlords and tenants, the money-lenders and peasants, rich peasants and landless labourers, are becoming more and more acute. In some areas the conflicts have assumed even violent character. The evil consequences of such economic conflicts are obvious.

(e) *Social Conflicts*: The social life of the people is also affected by prejudices and torn with resultant conflicts. Conflicts are growing and becoming increasingly acute within castes, communities and even among members of joint families. It looks as if old forms no longer correspond to living contemporary realities. These conflicts are increasingly shaking the entire foundations of Indian social structure and create major problems in the field of social reorganisation.

(f) *Cultural Conflicts*: Our intellectual and cultural life is also poisoned by an under-current of group prejudices and influenced by group hate complexes. The press and literature in India on the whole is not free from partisan passions and prejudices. They in the main become exponents of communal and caste biases. Sections of the educated class squabble over educational and cultural facilities for their own social groups. Even some of the scholars and ideologists of repute exhibit narrow provincial or communal biases. Those who think and feel in terms of cultural advance on a national basis and on democratic lines seem to be in a minority.

We have only enumerated the more pernicious of group tensions and conflicts from which Indian society is suffering. There are rampant a multitude of minor tensions and conflicts which also play a disruptive role in our national life.

The rhythm of unity, the music of social harmony and the exuberance of solidarity, and fraternal collaboration in solving complex and baffling problems confronting the nation almost seem absent among the people. There is a danger of a complacent denial or under-estimate of group conflicts affecting our national life.

The present volume is an attempt to survey these group prejudices which prevent the growth of harmonious relations between citizens of sovereign free India. It also shows how these group prejudices have their roots in the hoary history and vast complexity of Indian society, and how they obstruct the emergence of a right approach to such problems like poverty, ignorance and unequal opportunities from which an important section of the people is suffering. Indian society, as these authors very ably point out, is plagued by innumerable prejudices. There are rampant in it religious prejudices, racial prejudices, regional prejudices, linguistic prejudices, social prejudices, also prejudices born of distinctions of caste, rituals, customs, dress and diet.

V. Urgent Need for the Study of Group Prejudices

Such group prejudices, as we have seen, are very subtle and tenuous. They cloak themselves in various disguises. They also get nourishment as we have seen from social and ideological forces which are difficult to trace. Not only for the progress but even for the survival of the nation it is vitally important to analyse these prejudices, to study their sources and discover appropriate remedies for their extermination.*

VI. Lessons from the U.S.A.

Though the subject of group prejudices is being studied all over the world, since all societies suffer from the cancer of group prejudices of varied types in varying degrees, it is in the U.S.A. that a systematic comprehensive and multisided study of this ugly social phenomenon has been organised. Numerous organisations, both national and local have sprung up there. Millions of dollars are spent and thousands of people are giving their energy and talent to the study of this subject. Lessons from the experience of the U.S.A. can help us to approach scientifically the problem of group tensions in India without repeating the errors committed there. Though the Americans have organised their work of investigation into the sources of group prejudices and carry out campaigns against them on a vast scale, they recognise that the study of group prejudices presents tremendous difficulties.

VII. Difficulties in Studying Group Prejudices

Among the difficulties encountered by the student of prejudice we may mention the fact that the data necessary for understanding the problem combine the disciplines of psychology, sociology, anthropology, and economics. The formulation of the problem is therefore no easy task. It also presupposes correct concepts regarding the problem and requires a detached outlook and willingness to translate scientific results into practical remedies.

VIII. Need for Organised Research in India

In India an organised, systematic and scientific study of the subject of Group Prejudices has not yet been made. Only sporadic reflections on group prejudices, group discriminations and group conflicts are to be found in the studies published by some scholars and research institutions. There is still no literature embodying a theoretical analysis of group prejudices, advancing scientific practical programmes to remedy them. Whatever work has been achieved in this direction has been perfunctory and on a small scale. Reflections on group prejudices and suggestions made for their removal have been more the by-product of some other pursuits rather than conclusions derived from a planned study of the subject of group prejudices itself. Considering that group prejudices gnaw at the very vitals of Indian society a carefully planned study of these, which alone can help to find correct remedies, has become an urgent necessity for establishing social harmony, guaranteeing fruitful social co-operation of various groups and thereby assuring national progress. A study of the subject must be made in a concrete and objective manner which would demand a historical sense, a sociological and economic background and capacity for psychological analysis on the part of the research worker.

* Messrs. Lippit and Radke observe, "The need for an understanding of the dynamics of prejudice has no equivalent in importance in the social sciences. In no other aspects of interpersonal and intergroup relationships is there a more urgent need for social sciences to get out and do something'." (Ibid. March 1946 p.167)

IX. Trends of Thought

We shall now briefly indicate the trends of thought on the subject which are reflected in the contributions of the various writers who have contributed to this symposium.

Mr. K. G. Saiyidain, Mr. P. G. Shah, Dr. B. H. Mehta, Dr. Tara Chand, and Mr. and Mrs. Kodanda Rao, point out how Diversity is confused with Discrimination, and how the individual's misconceptions, are rooted either in unreason, wrong reason or conflict of interests. They emphasise the necessity of a properly developed spirit of tolerance, selflessness and appreciation of the viewpoints of the opponents as some of the effective means of liquidating one's prejudices.

Dr. R. C. Majumdar, Mr. P. C. Diwanji, Mr. A. A. A. Fyzee, Mr. S. K. George, Rev. Principal Kellock and Yogi Suddhananda Bharatiar, give valuable information and evaluation of the ideologies of various religions extant in India. They also point out how misrepresentation of the tenets of religions, together with hostile criticism of ritual patterns of different religions, engender prejudices and antagonism among the people and obstruct the growth of harmonious social relations among them. Further, they have clearly shown how various religions, however widely they may differ in philosophical principles or ritual patterns, possess a basic common ethical principle viz. that of human brotherhood, which they preach in an almost passionate chorus. All religions exhort men to live in fraternal relations with one another irrespective of regions, races, nations, religious or social groups. Some of them have also stressed the arch-need of a synthesis of all religions or atleast the peaceful coexistence based on the recognition of the basic principles of humanism characterising all religions.

Dr. G. S. Ghurye. Dr. G. Narang, Mr. G. K. Mashruwala and Dr. V. S. Agrawala present a vivid picture of the evolution of Indian society from its hoary past down to the present and have shown how the social organisation of the Indian people has always been dynamic, pointing out some of the causes that led to its cultural and institutional degeneration. Dr. Ghurye urges the necessity for the creation of culture disseminating national centres like Nalanda and Taxila which existed in ancient times, and which trained scholars who subsequently instilled through educative work cultural values among the people all over India. Dr. Narang, Mr. Mashruwala and Dr. V. S. Agrawala give a thought-provoking analysis of the caste structure of Hindu society and suggest methods to eradicate prejudices and conflicts resulting from hierarchically graded caste-stratified Hindu society.

Mrs. Hansa Mehta explores another region of social prejudices, the world of women. She traces the causes of Group Prejudices among women to their conservatism and fear psychology arising out of their role as mothers. Sir Manilal Nanavati surveys rural society and enumerates and analyses the multitude and varieties of prejudices rampant among the rural population. He considers a close study of the structure and life processes of rural society as the indispensable prerequisite for liquidating these prejudices.

Dr. Pattabhi Sitaramaiyya, Sir S. V. Ramamurthi, Sir V. T. Krishnamachari, Mr. Ashoka Mehta and Professor M. Venkatarangaiyya examine the group of political prejudices rampant in India, which due to their decisive role in all spheres of our national life have a tremendous baneful effect. They also try to locate the genetic causes of these political prejudices. As principal causes of the origin of these political prejudices they mention the *Divide et Empera* strategy of the British rulers; the caste division of the Hindu society; fomenting of communalism among the mass of the ignorant people of different communities by vested interests; division of India into administrative provinces which were not based on common language, culture and economy and hence generated inter-provincial animosities; the existence of the reactionary princely order for a long time; the undemocratic regime and factionalism in various political parties and others. Prof. Venkatarangaiyya has vividly portrayed the significant role of the New Constitution in removing, through democratic means, the conditions which gave rise to many of the political, social, religious and cultural prejudices.

Rev. Dr. V. Gracias, Sir R. P. Masani and Justice Khosla have discussed the problems of minorities viz. the Christians, the Parsis and the Sikhs respectively. They have evaluated the position of these communities in the present historical phase. They have suggested the ways which would assure cultural freedom to them enabling them to develop their own life freely.

Mr. Durgadas gives a concrete account of the rise of the communal press in India, and the efforts made to combat the pernicious effect of such reactionary instrument of mass suggestion.

Sir Lakshmipati Misra brings out how railways, running regularly, carrying millions of persons from one place to another and silently mingling peoples and cultures of varied regions are playing a tremendous role in overcoming Group Prejudices. He also points out the necessity of its proper development as a great cultural force.

Mr. V. V. Giri explores the world of the poor, labouring, illiterate and exploited sections of the Indian people. He asserts that poverty, illiteracy and the low standard of living are the main breeding causes of the prevalence of prejudices among them. Improvement of the material and cultural conditions of the life of the masses, he remarks, will prove a potent weapon to weaken and liquidate prejudices among them.

Dr. S. D. Mahant and Dr. S. S. Bhatnagar also consider the appalling poverty of large sections of the Indian people as the principal cause of the prejudices which they are suffering from. This appalling poverty which is the cause also of the cultural backwardness of the people can be removed, they observe, only if science is utilised in a planned manner in our country. Application of science to such problems as public health upon which labour productivity mainly depends, industrial expansion and agricultural development, will result in economic prosperity and elimination of mass poverty of the people.

X. Prejudice—Its Analysis from Many Angles Necessary

Prejudice, which in the broad sense of the term is an all-pervading feature of Indian social life requires to be closely scrutinised. Besides considering the various causes of the prejudices, we have to analyse them from different angles for example, whether they are mild or violent, whether they are directed against groups with which they have no contact or against those with whom contact is intimate, whether they are 'all based on comformity to the social customs of a group' as against 'those which are anchored in deep aggressive needs in the personality, which may persist even in the face of group pressure' or whether they emerge out of 'economic and political opportunism often calculating and impersonal, in contrast to fanaticism of the religious or cultural zealot.'

The task of making a scientific diagnosis of these prejudices, major and minor, and of evolving effective realistic programme for their cure is a task demanding consummate scientific knowledge and skill on the part of competent persons. It demands great vision, political insight and profound knowledge of research methods in social sciences. Governments with their decisive powers and enormous resources, political parties with their many adherants and instruments of propaganda, trade unions with their live contact with the daily life of the people, the press which shapes the thoughts and feelings of the people through the medium of the printed word, universities and academies with their rich knowledge and learning as also specialists in social problems, film producers who possess the mighty art organ of mass ideological and emotional appeal and also all responsible citizens will have to combine and collaborate in a huge constructive effort if the hydra-headed monster of Group Prejudices which threatens to disintegrate Indian society is to be controlled and eliminated.

XI. Conclusions

It is here that we can properly learn from Mahatma Gandhi, who was the greatest crusader against group prejudices in India. His martyrdom in fighting against communal prejudices, his heroic and systematic struggles against caste and sex prejudices and his fundamental crusade against intolerance, narrow-mindedness and snobbery which permeate every facet of society have to be deeply appreciated and understood to evolve proper remedies to combat group prejudices. Mahatma Gandhi who scrupulously propagated tolerance, who insistently preached respect for human personality irrespective of sex, age, caste, religion and nationality, his consistent practice in creating harmony amidst diversity, and his personal sacrifice for the cause of group harmony stand as a permanent beacon light for Indians and even humanity as a whole for evolving the right methods to combat and eliminate group prejudices among mankind. It is also a very heartening fact to note that the great principles that were upheld, preached and practised by Mahatma Gandhi have found concrete expression in the constitution framed for the Indian people. As Professor Venkatarangaiyya has pointed out, the new constitution strikes at the root of the group prejudices viz. fear and suspicion. We will reproduce here a few relevant sections of the new constitution embodied in its preamble and its section on Fundamental Rights to show how a new era has begun in the life of the Indian people :—

We, the people of India, having solemnly resolved to constitute India into a Sovereign Democratic Republic and to secure to all its citizens :

Justice, social, economic and political ;

Liberty of thought, expression, belief, faith and worship ;

Equality of status and of opportunity ;
and to promote among them all,

Fraternity assuring the dignity of the individual and the unity of the Nation;

In Our Constituent Assembly this twenty-sixth day of November, 1949, do Hereby Adopt, Enact and Give to Ourselves This Constitution.

Part III :- Fundamental Rights

RIGHTS OF EQUALITY

14. The State shall not deny to any person equality before the law or the equal protection of the laws within the territory of India.

15(1) The State shall not discriminate against any citizen on grounds only of religion, race, caste, sex, place of birth or any of them.

(2) No citizen shall, on grounds only of religion, race, caste, sex, place of birth or any of them, be subject to any disability, liability, restriction or condition with regard to :-

- (a) access to shops, public restaurants, hotels and places of public entertainment; or
- (b) the use of wells, tanks, bathing ghats, roads and places of public resort maintained wholly or partly out of State funds or dedicated to the use of the general public.

(3) Nothing in this article shall prevent the State from making any special provision for women and children.

RIGHTS TO FREEDOM OF RELIGION

25(1) Subject to public order, morality and health and to the other provisions of this Part, all persons are equally entitled to freedom of conscience and the right freely to profess, practise and propagate religion.

(2) Nothing in this article shall affect the operation of any existing law or prevent the State from making any law :

- (a) regulating or restricting any economic, financial, political or other secular activity which may be associated with religious practice;
- (b) providing for social welfare and reform or the throwing open of Hindu religious institutions of a public character to all classes and sections of Hindus.

Explanation I—The wearing and carrying of kirpans shall be deemed to be included in the profession of the Sikh religion.

Explanation II—In sub-clause (b) of clause (2), the reference to Hindus shall be construed as including a reference to persons professing the Sikh, Jain or Buddhist religion, and the reference to Hindu religious institutions shall be construed accordingly.

CULTURAL AND EDUCATIONAL RIGHTS

29. (1) Any section of the citizens residing in the territory of India or any part thereof having a distinct language, script or culture of its own shall have the right to conserve the same.

(2) No citizen shall be denied admission into any educational institution maintained by the State or receiving aid out of State funds on grounds only of religion, race, caste, language or any of them.

30. (1) All minorities, whether based on religion or language, shall have the right to establish and administer educational institutions of their choice.

(2) The State shall not, in granting aid to educational institutions, discriminate against any educational institution on the ground that it is under the management of a minority, whether based on religion or language.

The function of the constitution is to provide a climate which will determine the norms of social behaviour for the individuals. The new constitution, as we have seen, provides such climate. However, it is one thing to adopt principles, it is another thing to put them into practice. Eternal vigilance is the price for successful implementation of what has been propounded. It is here that the role of the administration acquires significance. An impartial, efficient, strong and incorruptible administration is absolutely necessary, if the rights granted to the people are to be successfully safeguarded. The services, police and the army are the heart of the administration. A conscious and careful endeavour to eradicate the legacy of inefficiency, corruption and partiality, which have taken deep roots in our administrative apparatus has to be made, if the fear and discrimination which different groups of people are suffering from are to be really removed. We are glad to note that the Constitution itself removes a number of factors which led to favouritism, discrimination, regional, communal, racial, caste and economic prejudices, which prevailed and played havoc with the administration. The present tendencies, however, have to be properly studied, and a very thorough effort should be made to make government what it ought to be. Some of the efforts made for reforming the army and the police, and the administration are really praiseworthy and should be more effectively pursued.

XII. Growing Awareness in India

It is encouraging to note that all over the country there is a growing awareness of the seriousness and urgency of studying and controlling this menace of group prejudices which corrodes the very vital existence of Indian society. It is also a healthy sign of the times that the Government of India is taking a lead in making a serious and systematic study of this problem.

The Ministry of Education issued a circular some time ago outlining suggestions for research on group tensions, to all Universities and requested them to systematically organise the study of this problem. Some of the Universities have actually submitted schemes of research projects on group tensions and group prejudices.

It is necessary in this connection to recognise the significant role of UNESCO in stimulating and organising studies on group tensions in various parts of the world. In fact it is making an effort to organise on an international scale a systematic exploration into this most baffling problem of contemporary life. At its various conferences it has outlined schemes and has also deputed experts to launch such projects. At the request of the Government of India, Dr. Gardner Murphy, the eminent social psychologist, was deputed for a period of six months to give an impetus to such studies in this country.

Dr. Murphy arrived early in August 1950 and held an informal meeting with some eminent scholars at Delhi. It was resolved after some discussion to organise pilot studies on social tensions in several selected centres with the Hindu-Muslim tension as the central theme. The results of this work when ready will, it is hoped, pave the way for more systematic work on similar lines.

The Government of India are considering the desirability of giving an impetus to this work. They have appointed a special Committee for the purpose and have set apart some funds to help research workers. It is likely that UNESCO will also help in furthering this work in India.

OUR CONTRIBUTORS

MR. K. G. SAIYIDAIN, B.A., M.ED. (Leeds)

Outstanding educationist. Educational Adviser to Bombay Government, 1947-1950. At present Educational Adviser to Government of India. India's delegate to UNESCO Conferences. Member, UNESCO Consultative Committee on Adult and Fundamental Education. Author of various books in English and Urdu like "School and the Future", "Education for International Understanding," "Education of National Character".

DR. B. H. MEHTA, M.A., Ph.D.

Professor of Social Welfare Administration, Tata Institute of Social Sciences, Bombay. As a sociologist he has specialised in the study of community life, and has spent several years doing research work amongst the aboriginal tribes of Gujarat and slum communities of Bombay.

MR. P. KODANDA RAO, M.A.

Member of the Servants of India Society, Carnegie Scholar, Department of Race Relations, Yale University, U.S.A., 1934-35. Member of the Government of India Deputation to Malaya, 1946. Vice-President, Indian Council of World Affairs, 1950-51. Author of various books like, "Malabar Tenancy Problem", "East versus West, Denial of Contrast", "Culture Conflicts, Cause and Cure"

MRS. MARY C. RAO

Secretary and later President, National Council of Women in India, Nagpur Branch. Vice-President, Nagpur Women's Home. Lectured on Education in America, India and America, etc. in India, Canada and the U.S.A.

MR. P.G. SHAH, M.A., B.Sc.

After a brilliant academic career entered Indian Audit and Accounts Service and retired as Accountant General, Bombay. At present a member of the Bombay Public Services Commission. Vice-President, Gujarat Research Society of Bombay. President, Anthropological Society of Bombay.

DR. TARACHAND ROY,

Eminent Scholar. For last many years attached to the cultural section, Indian Embassy, Berne, Switzerland.

DR. R.C. MAJUMDAR, M.A., Ph.D.

Some time Vice-Chancellor, University of Dacca. At present Principal, College of Indology, Benares Hindu University. Also President of All-India, Oriental Conference and Indian History Congress. Author of "Corporate Life in Ancient Indian Colonies in the Far-East", (Three Volumes), "Outline of Ancient Indian Culture and Civilization". Joint author "The Vedic India". Editor: New History of Indian People, Volume VI, etc.

SHRI P. C. DIWANJI, M.A., LL.M.

Member of the All-India Oriental Conference and Indian Philosophical Conference. Chairman of the History and Culture Sub-Committee of the Gujarat Research Society. Contributed a number of scholarly articles and papers in various journals. Author of a number of books like "Sidhantabindu", "Indian Political Riddle", "Prasthana Bheda", etc.

MR. A. A. A. FYZEE, M.A. (Cantab.), Bar-at-law.

A Scholar and a sportsman. Principal, the Government Law College, Bombay from 1938-1947. Founder and Honorary Secretary of the Islamic Research Society. Member of the Indian Delegation to UNESCO Session held at Beirut in November 1948. At present Indian Ambassador to Egypt. Author of " Outlines of Muhammadan Law ", " Islamic Culture ", etc.

MR. S. K. GEORGE

Belongs to the Ancient Syrian Christian community of Kerala. Having been influenced by the personality of Mahatma Gandhi has dedicated his life to the blending of Christianity and religious life of India. Was in charge of Deena Bandhu Bhavana in Shantiniketan for four years. At present on the staff of Wardha College. Author of " Gandhi's Challenge to Christianity ", and " Jésus Christ ".

REV. PRINCIPAL JAMES KELLOCK, M.A., D.D.

Joined Wilson College as Professor of Economics and Philosophy. At present Principal of Wilson College, Bombay. President, Bible Society of India, Pakistan and Ceylon ; President, Bombay Representative Christian Council. Author of " Mahadev Govind Ranade, Patriot and Social Servant ", " Foundation and Growth of the Christian Church ", etc.

YOGI SHRI SUDDHANANDA BHARATIAR

A famous poet, mystic and yogi of South India. Under the influence of Mahatma Gandhi he took to village welfare work. At present he is residing at Pondicherry. Author of numerous books like " Heart Beat ", " Communion " (in French), " Atma Shodhan ", etc.

DR. G. S. GHURYE, M.A., Ph.D. (Cantab.)

Professor and Head of the Department of Sociology, School of Economics and Sociology, University of Bombay. President, Anthropology Section, Indian Science Congress, 1935 ; President of the Ethnology and Folk-lore Section of the Oriental Conference, 1937. Author of " Caste and Class in India ", " Aborigines— So-called and their Future ", " Culture and Society ", " Occidental Civilization," " Indian Costume," etc. (the present contribution was written on 8-4-1949).

SHRI KISHORLAL MASHRUWALA, B.A., LL.B.

Joined Gandhiji's movement in 1917. President, Gandhi Seva Sangh, 1935-40. Editor, Harijan Weeklies since 1948. Author of " Practical Non-violence ", and numerous works in Gujarati.

DR. GOKUL CHAND NARANG, M.A., Bar-at-law.

Lecturer, D.A.V. College, Lahore from 1901-1907. Practised in the Lahore High Court upto 1930. Minister, Local-Self Government and Industries, the Punjab, 1930-37. Member, Punjab Legislative Council, 1924-26. Vice-President, the Akhil Bharat Hindu Mahasabha. Publications : " The Message of Vedas ", " Transformation of Sikhism and Real Hinduism ", etc.

DR. V. S. AGRAWALA M.A., LL.B., Ph.D., D.Litt.

Interested in religious history, folk culture and history of modern Indian languages. Curator, Mathura Museum, 1931-1939 ; Curator, Provincial Museum, Lucknow, 1940-45 ; at present Superintendent, Central Asian Antiquities Museum, New Delhi. Author of " Prithviputra ", "Mathura Terracottas ", " Gupta Art ", etc.

SHRIMATI HANSA MEHTA, M.A.

Active worker during Congress Civil Disobedience Movement. Member, various women's associations. Member, Bombay Legislative Council 1937-45 and again since 1946. President, All-India Women's Conference, 1945. Member, Constituent Assembly, 1946-50. India's representative on various U. N. Commissions. Vice-Chancellor, Maharaja Sayajirao University, Baroda, since 1949. Works: "Women Under Hindu Law of Marriage and Succession", "Tracts on Post-war Educational Reconstruction and Civil Liberty", etc.

SIR MANILAL B. NANAVATI, Kt LLB.

Engaged in Baroda State Service from 1904 to 1935. Appointed Deputy Governor of the Reserve Bank of India in 1936. Member of the Famine Inquiry Commission, 1944. President of the Indian Society of Agricultural Economics. Author of "Indian Rural Problem" and several other publications.

SHRI PATTABHI SITARAMAIYYA, B.A., M.B.C.M.

Outstanding Congress leader. A member of the A.I.C.C. since 1916. Member of the Working Committee of the National Congress. President of the Indian National Congress 1948-50. Author of several works like "History of Congress", "Gandhi and Gandhism", "Constitutions of the World", etc.

SIR S. V. RAMAMURTHY, M.A. (Cantab.), D.Litt. (Andhra)

Joined the Indian Civil Service in 1912; served in various capacities from District Officer to Chief Secretary and Adviser to the Governor of Madras. Acted as Governor of Bombay for a short time in 1947. Now Regional Commissioner for Agricultural and Food Production, South India.

SIR V. T. KRISHNAMACHARI, K.C.I.E.

After being connected with the Madras Civil Service, became Dewan of Baroda in 1927. Acted as delegate at the Round Table Conferences, the Joint Parliamentary Committee and served as member of the Federal Structure and Finance Sub-Committee, and the Reserve Bank Committee. Delegate to the League of Nations, 1934 and 1936. Delegate to the U.N. Conference 1945. Vice-President, Constituent Assembly, 1946-49. President, Fiscal Commission, 1949-50. Member, Planning Commission, Government of India.

PROFESSOR M. VENKATARANGAIYYA, M.A.

Head of the Department of Politics, Economics and History, Andhra University, Waltair from 1931-1944. Principal, W.G.B. College, Bimavaram, 1945-46. President, Andhra Teachers' Federation. At present, Head of the Department of Politics, School of Economics and Sociology, University of Bombay. Editor, "Educational India". Author of a number of books in English and Telugu like "Fundamental Rights of Man", "The Case for a Constituent Assembly for India", "India's Draft Constitution", "Fair Elections", etc.

SHRI ASHOKA MEHTA

Active in student and youth movements from 1927-32. One of the founder members of the Socialist Party of India. Edited the Socialist, the party's organ from 1935-39. Till recently was the General Secretary of the Hind Mazdoor Sabha. Now General Secretary of the Socialist Party. Author of "The Communal Triangle in India" (along with Shri Achyut Patwardhan), "Indian Shipping", "1857: The Great Rebellion", "Who Owns India", etc.

RT. REV. DR. VALERIAN GRACIAS, D.D., M.Agg.

Secretary to the Archbishop (1929-39), and Chancellor of the Archdiocese, since 1929. Was appointed Rector of the Pro-Cathedral of the Holy Name in December 1941. Was elevated to the Episcopate by his nomination as Titular Bishop of Tannis, and Auxiliary Bishop to his Grace the Archbishop of Bombay,

16th May 1946. Now the Archbishop of Bombay. Publications; "Features of Christian Life", "Heaven and Home", "The Vatican and International Policy".

SIR RUSTOM P. MASANI, M.A.

After a distinguished academic career, joined the Bombay Municipality where he became Deputy Municipal Commissioner. Secretary to the Provincial Banking Enquiry Committee. Identified himself with several institutions devoted to educational, cultural and welfare work. Former Vice-Chancellor, Bombay University. Member of the Central Board of Archaeology, and Indian National Commission for Co-operation with UNESCO. Chairman of the Indian Institute for Educational and Cultural Co-operation. Author of a number of books in English and Gujarati, viz. "Evolution of Local-Self Government in Bombay", "Court Poets of Iran and India" and others.

JUSTICE G. D. KHOSLA.

Member of I.C.S. since 1926. Appointed as High Court Judge in November 1944. Author of "Stern Reckoning" and "Our Judicial System". Also author of a number of short stories.

SHRI DURGA DAS, B.A.

From 1918-1937 was Parliamentary Correspondent and Editor of Reuters and Associated Press of India at New Delhi and Simla. Was President of the U.P. Press Conference, 1946; Secretary, Press Association, New Delhi, from 1943-47, and Vice-President, 1948-49. One of the two representatives nominated in December 1948 by the All-India Newspaper Editors' Conference to represent the Indian press on Inter-Dominion Press Consultative Committee to improve relations between India and Pakistan. At present Joint Editor of the Hindustan Times, New Delhi.

SIR L. P. MISRA

After having a distinguished career in the Railway Service, retired as Chief Commissioner of Railways, Government of India, in 1945. Has been working as General Manager, Hindustan Motors Ltd., Calcutta. Author of Reports and Notes on various aspects of the problems of railways in India.

SHRI V. V. GIRI

Trade Union leader for many years. General Secretary and President of the All-India Railwaymen's Federation. Twice President of the All-India Railwaymen's Congress. Delegate to various International Conferences. Member of the General Legislative Assembly for many years. Minister for Labour and Industries, Madras Government in 1937-39 and in 1946-47. High Commissioner for India in Ceylon from July 1947. Alternate Leader of the Indian Government Delegation to the Asian Regional Conference of the I.L.O. in January 1950.

MR. S. D. MAHANT, M.Sc., Ph.D., F.R.I.C.

Possesses a wide experience of research and administration both in Government and in Industry. At present Industrial Economist and Research Development Officer, Council of Scientific and Industrial Research. Has published several papers on Physical Chemistry and other scientific subjects.

SIR S. S. BHATNAGAR, D.Sc., F.R.S.

A distinguished scientist. Was Professor of Chemistry, Benares Hindu University. University Professor of Physical Chemistry and Director of University Chemical laboratories, Lahore. Dean of University Instruction, Punjab University. Director, Council of Scientific and Industrial Research, Government of India. At present Secretary to the Government of India, Ministry of Natural Resources.

CONTENTS

	Page
PREFACE	3
INTRODUCTION	4
OUR CONTRIBUTORS	17

Section I CULTURE AND PREJUDICES

THE CONFLICT BETWEEN CULTURE AND PREJUDICE	K. G. Saiyidain	25
THE SOCIOLOGICAL BACKGROUND OF PREJUDICE	B. H. Mehta	34
CRITIQUE OF GROUP PREJUDICE (WITH SPECIAL REFERENCE TO HARIJANS)	P. Kodanda Rao and Mrs. Mary C. Rao	45
SUBLIMATION OF GROUP FEELINGS	P. G. Shah	56
INDIVIDUAL AND GROUP PREJUDICES AND UNITY	Tara Chand	64

Section II RELIGIONS AND PREJUDICES

HINDUISM, A RETROSPECT AND REVIEW	R. C. Majumdar	71
RELIGIOUS PREJUDICES AS A CLOG ON NATIONAL UNITY	P. C. Diwanji	78
ISLAMIC LAW AND CUSTOM	A. A. A. Fyzee	85
RELATION OF CHRISTIANITY WITH OTHER RELIGIONS SPECIALLY (a) HINDUISM, (b) ISLAM (c) OTHERS	S. K. George	90
CHRISTIANITY IN INDIA	James Kellock	96
INDIA'S UNION	Yogi Shri Shuddhananda Bhartiar	108

Section III SOCIAL PREJUDICES

INDIAN UNITY: A RETROSPECT AND PROSPECT	G. S. Ghurye	115
THE HINDU SOCIAL ORDER	K. G. Mashruwalla	124
HINDU SOCIAL ORGANISATION	Gokulchand Narang	130
GROUP PREJUDICES IN INDIA: SOCIAL AND RELIGIOUS	V. S. Agrawala	135
WOMEN AND GROUP PREJUDICES IN INDIA	Hansa Mehta	144
GROUP PREJUDICES IN RURAL INDIA	Manilal B. Nanavati	147

Section IV POLITICS AND PREJUDICES

GROUP PREJUDICES IN INDIA	B. Pattabhi Sitaramaiyya	157
GROUP PREJUDICES IN ADMINISTRATION	S. V. Ramamurthi	163
GROUP PREJUDICES AND POLITICAL PARTIES	Ashoka Mehta	167
INDIAN STATES AND THEIR FUTURE	V. T. Krishnamachari	173
THE NEW CONSTITUTION AND THE REMOVAL OF GROUP PREJUDICES	M. Venkatarangaiyya	176

Section V MINORITIES AND PREJUDICES

THE POSITION OF CHRISTIANS IN A SECULAR STATE	V. Gracias	183
PARSEES IN INDIA	R. P. Masani	188
HINDU-SIKH RELATIONS	G. D. Khosla	196

Section VI MISCELLANEOUS

INDIAN PRESS AND ITS INFLUENCE	Durgadas	203
GROUP PREJUDICES IN INDIA	Lakshmipati Mishra	209
GROUP PREJUDICES IN INDIA	V. V. Giri	213
PLACE OF SCIENCE IN BUILDING OF A UNITED INDIA	S. D. Mahant and S. S. Bhatnagar	219

Section I
Culture and Prejudices

THE CONFLICT BETWEEN CULTURE AND PREJUDICE

K. G. SAIYIDAIN

Group Prejudices, Obstacles to National Unity

In some circles in India there is a feeling that, with the establishment of a national government, the main difficulties in the way of achieving a national and cultural unity have been removed. I am not inclined to share that undue optimism. So long as we were engaged in a grim struggle for our political freedom, the struggle itself provided a rallying point, so much so that at some stages we were able to achieve complete unity of effort and outlook and, even when there were lapses, due to the provocation of communal feelings, they did not—except in the recent tragic years—materially affect the powerful drive of the political movement. It was not that differences and prejudices did not exist—they were there, some dating back to the distant past like the problem of untouchability, others more recent like the Hindu-Muslim tension which had been fanned by political motives as well as economic factors. But they were held in check; for, generally speaking, people realized that their energies must be primarily devoted to the over all objective of achieving national freedom. Now that that freedom has been won, the unity forged on the anvil of a common opposition has broken down and all kinds of regional, provincial, sectarian, communal, linguistic and cultural conflicts and prejudices have come to the forefront. If we are to guard the treasure of our freedom and to use it for building up the 'good life' in our country, it is essential for us to reconcile and transcend these conflicts, to resolve these prejudices and thus ensure that all elements of our people and all strands of our thought and culture are enabled to contribute to the material progress and spiritual enrichment of the country.

Diversity, No Bar to Social Harmony

It is perhaps necessary as a background to this discussion to state a few fundamental propositions clearly. To some people, whose thinking has not become warped and distorted by the psychological poison released by recent happenings, these may appear almost self-evident; to others they would appear to be entirely unacceptable and out of date. Our problem is really to win back the latter to reason and sanity and it is to them really that this analysis of Prejudices is primarily addressed. Let us see, what would be a sensible starting point for our approach to this problem.

In the first place, we should recognize, frankly and without mental reservation, that there is nothing wrong or criminal or shameful or weak in a nation having people with different languages, forms of dress or types of food or belonging to different religions or races. Variety, under proper conditions, is a source of strength and enrichment, not of weakness or poverty and one of the greatest problems facing the world, and big countries like India, is to work out a mental reorientation and the technique of social and political life which would stop these perfectly healthy differences from breaking out into conflicts and antagonisms. The unity that we want to achieve does not mean uniformity, a levelling-down or ironing out of all differences such as a totalitarian regime aspires to do. No, it is to be a unity-in-diversity, a pattern of many shades and textures, a music of many different notes. On the intellectual plane, it is always the clash and contact of different ideas that leads to new developments; on the cultural plane, it is the confluence of different traditions in arts and crafts and literature and music that enriches culture and creates new forms; on the social and political plane, it is the spirit of experimentation, of accepting new ideas and ways of life, of trying new theories derived from different sources that ensures progress. So, any attempt to stifle differences, whether in art or literature, of forms of social and political life or religion and philosophy is treachery to the future of the country as also the future of the human race.

Assimilative Genius of India

In the second place, we must realise that, historically, the genius of India at its best has been assimilative and receptive. Its tradition has been that of the open mind, welcoming whatever contributions have come to it from different races and religions or regional and cultural groups. From the time of the Aryans to the days of the British, it has tried to assimilate within its culture and civilization elements of value that have come within its reach from the four corners of the world. In fact, as some of our great writers and thinkers have pointed out—Tagore and Gandhi and Radhakrishnan and Iqbal and Azad and Jawaharlal to name only the moderns—it is only when Indians have kept the windows of their hearts and minds open that they have been most creative and progressive and whenever they have tended to become exclusive, dominated by prejudice and intolerance, those have been periods of national decadence and decline. So, in advocating this open hearted and receptive approach in cultural as well as socio-political life, one takes not a revolutionary or heretical value but one that is in harmony with our national genius and the trend of our historical development. The people in the dock are really those who advocate or indulge in dreams of an exclusive cultural revivalism which would intolerantly reject the great gifts which, say, the civilization of Islam or the civilization of the West has brought to India and hanker after an ancient and exclusive "Hindu" way of life which is gone beyond recall. Likewise, people in Pakistan, who wish to reject the rich contributions they have received from a thousand years of contact with the Hindu element in Indian civilization and culture, are trying vainly and foolishly to reverse the historic process—an effort which would be harmful to their own development. It is not only the genius of Indian culture and the genius of Hinduism and Islam which revolt against such a mentality but the entire trend of modern history is against it. No group or nation can afford to withdraw itself into a tower of seclusion, for the forces that are shaping and moulding our life are universal in their scope and cannot be ignored and, to the extent that any people may succeed in ignoring them and not benefiting from them, they are only working for their own impoverishment.

Communalism, the Arch-problem

In the third place, we must clearly realize that a number of things have happened in India in recent decades which have made the situation very critical and acute. The foreign government tried, as any other government would have done, to see that communal differences were kept alive. It is a tribute to their manouvering skill—but none to our intelligence!—that we fell an easy prey to these machinations and actively contributed to the object that the government had in mind. The growing conflict amongst the various communities, particularly the Hindus and Muslims, culminated in the demand for Pakistan and the final partition which cut the organic unity of the country into two and reversed a centuries' old historic process. If this partition had solved the Hindu-Muslim problem and established cordial and co-operative relations between the two newly created dominions, perhaps partition would not be too high a price to pay for it. After all, Canada and U.S.A. exist as friendly and co-operative nations and they are none the worse for being separate nations. But this hope has not come true. Partition had a blood bath at its very birth and the rioting, disorder and migrations that followed, on a scale unprecedented in the history of the country, led to such an accentuation of bitterness and deepening of prejudices that to-day, in some parts of both dominions, it is almost impossible for people of certain communities to live with any sense of security and freedom. The refugees of both dominions, who have suffered untold privations and sorrows, have created a psychological problem of great gravity not only as between the two dominions but also for the new countries of their adoption. Many of them acquired a distorted outlook, based on misunderstanding and prejudice, which not only colours their own judgments but also affects by contagion the ideas and behaviour of their countrymen. It is no use blaming them for they are the victims of circumstances over which they had little control and the blame for a great national disaster like this should rest not on any one group or section but on all of us, without exception. The fact, however, remains that this unfortunate conjunction of instances has created for us - teachers, thinkers, writers, administrators, social workers, in fact every one with a social conscience - an extremely difficult and urgent situation which should not be allowed to deteriorate further. We must either fight intelligently and resolutely against all the widespread individual and group prejudices or these will overwhelm and embitter our national outlook and endanger the maintenance of our freedom.

Gandhiji, Crusador against Prejudices

Gandhiji, with his unerring instinct for what was basic in every complicated situation, had divined and diagnosed this situation correctly and he had devoted himself as earnestly to this **educational** problem as he had done, for three decades, to the **political** problem. He fought against Prejudices - which is another name for intolerance and narrowness and snobbery - on every conceivable front and laid bare their inroads into every nook and corner of our national life. In its most aggressive and obvious mood, it had assumed the form of communalism and Gandhiji's whole life was a crusade against it and his martyrdom was the triumphant vindication of his life-long stand on this issue. Within the framework of Hindu Society itself, there was that age-old prejudice against the "untouchables", those children of God whom an unjust social system had deprived of the most elementary basic human rights. Again, there were amongst all classes of people, what I can only describe as sacrilegious prejudices against all religions other than their own. Gandhiji proclaimed boldly the ancient truth that all great religions are one in their ultimate objective — love of God and service of man — that their great teachers and scriptures are worthy of our respect and that they represent different ways of leading to the same goal. He was not content merely with stating this dynamic truth but actually made a reverent and sincere study of the Quran, the Bible, the Granth Sahib and other Holy Books and insisted on the recitation of passages taken from them at his evening prayer meetings. Some people are apt to feel surprised at his almost obstinate insistence on this ritual and his reverting to this question over and over again during his Delhi broadcasts. They fail to realize that he was fighting for one of the greatest of human freedom—the freedom to welcome and respect truth and cultivate tolerance—and was concerned with safeguarding the dignity and decency of the spirit of man against the onslaught of irreligious fanaticism. Again, he carried on a magnificent crusade against intolerance on the language front and his advocacy of Hindustani as a common language was a declaration of his faith in a composite, many-sided culture and a composite language as an expression of that culture. All those who have been raising the slogan of cultural revialism in India or of a common language which would harken back to Sanskrit and refuse recognition of the enrichment and simplification which it has received from Persian and Arabic and Urdu and English and the many spoken dialects of the masses are trying to set back the hands of the clock of time. They will not be able to arrest the flow of time but it is quite likely that they will do great mental damage to themselves in this process of reaction. Gandhiji was, likewise, a believer in Indian unity and he completely rejected the claims of regions and provinces to restrict his loyalty—he never lent his support to any movement which sponsored a Bengali or Panjabi or Maharashtrian or South Indian patriotism as against loyalty to India and her true genius as a reconciler of differences. Through his whole life and more specifically through his scheme of Basic Education, he sought to break down the prejudice against manual labour and to bring about repproachment between manual and intellectual workers. Thus, one by one, we see the various idols of prejudice being shattered by the iconoclastic tolerance and humanism of Mahatma Gandhi.

I have referred to his achievements in this field because these are precisely the problems which we have to tackle. He wrestled with them all his life but his countrymen were so preoccupied with the political issue and he had so many problems on hand that he could not bring about that psychological revolution which was always near his heart. And then the happenings, to which I have referred above, menaced to undo a good deal of the great work he had done. When people talk of Gandhiji's constructive work, they refer mainly to his practical schemes like Charkha Sangh, Talimi Sangh and Kasturba Trust activities but, to my mind, his most significant constructive work lay in the domain of the human mind where he was anxious to liquidate prejudices and build up a new set of attitudes and values which will centre round the concept of the dignity of man and reject the discriminations made amongst human beings on grounds of caste or creed or race or language or sex, and Brahmin and Harijan, Hindu and Muslim, Indian and British and Punjabi and Bengali, Hindiwalas and Urduwalas, men and women, would all be welcome as members of one great human family. The fight against Prejudice is a fight to bring about this urgent but difficult mental transformation.

Linguistic Prejudices, Illustration

I do not know whether many of us have a clear idea of how deep is the hold that blind prejudice has got on our minds. Take, as one instance, the question of language. Those who have any knowledge whatever of the history of languages in India, know that Urdu is one of the richest languages in India and in some branches of literature like poetry, it can hold its own, in quality, with any language of the world. And it is just as truly and genuinely Indian as Sanskrit or Bengali or Hindi or Malayalam. But, as Urdu had developed during the Muslim period and languages like Persian and Arabic had contributed to its enrichment, many people who were caught up in the political conflict between Hindus and Muslims extended their hostility to the Urdu language also. They have been trying their best to impoverish the country culturally by denying all support and patronage to this language by even denying—believe it or not!—that there *is* such a language as Urdu! And prejudice is so blind that such stark ignorance passes for scholarship and is welcomed in some circles. In their uncritical partisanship of an untenable thesis, they forget that not only Urdu but Hindi and Bengali and many other Indian languages developed a great deal during the Muslim period, that like them it is spoken without discrimination by Hindus, Muslims, Sikhs, Christians and others, that not only Urdu but Gujerati and Marathi and Hindi and Bengali also have been enriched by an admixture of Arabic and Persian words to varying degrees, that in Urdu forty two out of fifty five thousand words are Hindi words or words of Sanskrit origin! All this they do not see or hear or acknowledge—a new version of "see no evil, hear no evil, speak no evil"! There is a kind of witch-hunt for words of "foreign" origin and a reversion to old and obsolete forms of current words. Now, all this is a source of literary impoverishment, a kind of cultural suicide which only stark prejudice can present in the garb of patriotism or cultural renaissance. I am not referring now to the question of the common language and the controversy which went on between the advocates of Hindi and Hindustani about the name and the contents of the common language. I am citing this as an example of how prejudice can make us deny to a language of the country the support and status which is due to it as a language and as a part of the cultural heritage of the nation. And what applies more emphatically to this particular controversy applies in a lesser but no less unpleasant degree to the other controversies on the language front—say, between the North and the South, or between the regional languages in the provinces of Bombay and the Punjab and Bihar. There was also the recent and, to my mind, undignified controversy over the numerals which almost wrecked the unity of the greatest political party in the country! I refer to these language controversies at some length because they mirror the absurdity as well as the menace of Prejudices most clearly. There is no division of spoils or property here, no real political or economic issue, no clash of class interests—one would have thought that it was the most obvious thing in the world to give groups of people the freedom to speak and write and generally use their own languages, to give the greatest encouragement to them to learn other languages and not to use any kind of veiled or unveiled force to deprive even a single person of what is literally his birth-right. But even this most elementary and elemental human right has given rise to furious controversies and these will not be set to rest till we cultivate tolerance and breadth of mind and regard every single language as a tributary to the wealth of our culture and literature. This would not imply any loss of unity, only possibly a loss of uniformity which is an entirely different thing ! A common national language exists in a basic form and it will grow and develop, not at the point of the constitutional bayonet but as a result of the intermingling of groups and peoples, of the multiplication of contacts, of the mutual interpretation of their several languages. Let the common language be taught in schools by all means but not so as to supplant the mother tongue or regional or provincial languages. Let it make its way into people's hearts through its growing literary power and influence and through love. Let it gradually find its place into services and administration but without undue hurry so that no part of the country may feel that it has been deliberately handicapped. Let it wend its way into the Universities, gently replacing English by stages but without lowering standards or creating academic confusion. But, in any and every case, force is to be avoided which is evil in politics but suicidal and immoral in the field of culture; for, bending and breaking the mind is infinitely worse than bending and breaking the body ! And we should remember that so much prestige attaches, almost inevitably, to the State language and the language of administration that the objects which its advocates have in mind—unity, facility of inter-provincial intercourse, development of a common outlook—will be achieved irresistibly in due course.

What I have said about a common language applies to the other possible common features in a nation—common food and dress and music and ways of life. At least, the underlying principle is the same. If these things develop naturally and spontaneously, as a result of a certain common system of education and a growing common outlook, they have certain advantages. But I would not dream of prescribing common food or dress or music as the means for achieving a common nationhood or removing prejudices. In the first place, is it in the interest of developing a rich and interesting pattern of life to have all people eating the same kind of food, wearing the same kind of dress, singing the same songs, speaking the same language and reacting to various every day situations in an identical manner ? Frankly, I should find such a pattern of life dull and uninviting in the extreme. But there is a deeper reason still why we should not subscribe to the view that common food and dress, etc., are essential for a common nationhood. People advocate them because they think that without these props the differences and conflicts which exist amongst various groups and communities will not disappear. To me, it is a very superficial view, negating that true tolerance which accepts and transcends differences instead of trying to abolish them. It amounts in effect to saying, "If people look alike and dress alike and behave alike and their differences are at least not apparent, they will tolerate one another." But that is no true tolerance, for tolerance is always tolerance of some thing *different*, whether in details or in fundamentals. It is knowing that the other person has a different religion—Hinduism or Islam or Sikhism— or speaks a different language—Hindi or Gujerati or Urdu or Telugu— or belongs to a different caste or group—Brahmin or non-Brahmin or Harijan—or has different political views, socialist, capitalist or communist or liberal—it is knowing all this and respecting these differences; it is knowing all this and getting on without malice or rancour or even passive dislike towards them; it is knowing all this and realizing that the bond of a common humanity which unites all of us is greater and deeper than these differences and that, in spite of them, there are certain standards of conduct and certain attitudes of sympathy, co-operation and decency that we must extend to all of them. It is only when such attitudes become ingrained in us that prejudices will really disappear —otherwise we shall be only tinkering with the problem.

Remedies

It is easy to say all this—though I know how recent phychological perversions of the national mind are making it difficult for many people to say so and for some groups to accept this position even in theory— but difficult to bring it about, difficult even to say *how* it can be brought about. But one thing is quite clear. No single all-powerful, short-cut, *recipe* can be suggested for this purpose. Prejudices are often tenuous, intangible things like the spider's web with their ramifications into the dark labyrinths and chambers of the human mind and emotions. They often begin quite unconsciously in infancy as a result of the home environment and atmosphere, are strengthened by contacts in school and on the playground, are carried further in adult life by the pernicious influence of the press, the political parties, the cinema and all other media of mass communication. It is against this powerful array of forces that we have to pit our strength. We cannot obviously defeat or demolish these influences—we have to win them over to our side. Since they have created all these prejudices they must combine to undo them.

What are the factors which favour their growth? There is firstly, ignorance in the darkness of which prejudices flourish like a rank growth and we should do all we can to dispel ignorance of one another's culture and traditions and ways of life. We often know little of religions other than our own or of other provinces and regions. In our schools and colleges, there should be arrangement for the sympathetic study of the great truths taught by different religions and the special cultural traditions and contributions of different groups and communities. This will, at least, ensure that we know something of the best that they have to offer and shall not depend on hearsay or the suggestiveness of a poisoned atmosphere in judging a great religion or a community or a literature. All men and women of prejudice are neither malicious nor unfair. Many of them are only poor, deluded, ignorant creatures who know no better. More knowledge should be able to improve their outlook.

It is not, however, knowledge passively acquired that will do the trick—knowledge must irradiate our thinking and feelings and thus control our actions. This postulates that, not only in schools and colleges but also in what may be broadly called "Adult Education" we must make use of all the effective techniques of intelligent propaganda —discussion and study groups, co-operative activities, common celebrations, through which they shall not only learn to understand points of view different from their own but train themselves for intelligent and co-operative citizenship as adults through the comradeship of effort in behalf of common causes. A very interesting account of an organized and successful experiment to liquidate prejudices that had embittered the life a mixed American community—which comprised of Jews, Catholics, Protestants, Negroes and others—has been published by Barnes and Noble under the title of "The Story of the Springfield Plan" and it shows how schools, colleges, clubs, municipality and the radio, theatre and cinema can be mobilized for such a campaign. The study of this experiment should prove to be not only interesting but heartening for educators in India who are sometimes apt to be depressed by the enormity of the task that confronts them in this field.

It is well to recognize, however, that even active knowledge will not be enough to liquidate prejudices, for ignorance is not their only source. Prejudices sometimes cloak deep lying economic or political differences e.g. the clash between the Brahmans and non-Brahmans is not a religious clash for both belong to the same religion but primarily an economic issue between those who have and those who would like to have positions of vantage and power. But the political game is always apt to call all kinds of allies into its service and present issues wrapped up in red rags which may easily provoke anger. Wherever prejudices are of this kind, they cannot be liquidated either by honeyed words or by increased knowledge; they can only be liquidated by removing the root causes of the conflict e.g. by establishing a more just social order which will, in fact, ensure equality of opportunity to all groups of the people. And that is part of the statesman's headache—in fact, the whole of it!—and the teachers and writers can only try and popularize this idea even if they cannot do anything directly about it.

Another factor which can help us in this work is the generation of a strong public opinion against the existance of such prejudices—a public opinion that will not extend its countenance to those who indulge in them. At present people often demonstrate, in their individual and group behaviour, the most stupid and undignified prejudices towards other individuals and groups who differ from them in religion or language or social traditions or even the latitude of their birth! They can express them with impunity in their own groups and get away with it, because the others either approve of them or are too cowardly to show their disapproval. Now, it is not much use psychologically if a Hindu or a Muslim or a Sikh or a Punjabi or a Madrasi protests when his group or community or way of life is attacked by some one else—he is apt to be dismissed as a partisan. What is much more effective and essential is that there should be, in each community or group, some persons of integrity and impartiality who will not hesitate to take members of their own group or community to task and express public disapproval of them when they indulge in unworthy sentiments against any other group. It is only the constant exercise of the capacity for self-examination which can keep a group—or a nation—morally and socially healthy. When this spirit of self-criticism is dead and the beam in one's own eye appears to be negligible in comparison with the mote in the neighbour's —in fact, even if the *mote* in one's own eye is complacently ignored—

it is time to ring the bell of alarm. In this work, editors, writers, dramatists, people who produce plays and films, political leaders, social workers, as well as teachers at all levels—can play their part by helping to generate a public opinion intolerant of prejudice. There is no reason, in the nature of things, why society should object more to a petty thief, caught in stealing some petty article, than to the man who would openly deny to others that human dignity and consideration which is their birth right and which they cherish more than their money or their clothes which is all that the ordinary thief can steal! And such persons can themselves form the nucleus of the critical group which will serve its own community by insisting on high standards of integrity, rectitude and tolerance on the part of its members. This does not, of course, mean that they should not exercise their full rights as citizens to appreciate or criticise all that is good or blameworthy in the life of the country as a whole irrespective of any group affiliations. But, in the present state of our national mind, when group prejudices have run amok, we will do well to recognize and accept this special group responsibility. The categorical imperative of the Quran:

> "There should be amongst you a group which will (always) call the people to that which is good, instruct them to do that which is noble and refrain from doing that which is unworthy."

And in all religions, in the teachings of all great teachers of mankind, in all humane systems of philosophy and in the rationalism of modern Science, it is Prejudice that is unworthy and false and Tolerance that is noble and true.

THE SOCIOLOGICAL BACKGROUND OF PREJUDICE

B. H. MEHTA

Group Prejudices in India

The whole world has become a tragedy of group prejudices that result in conflict, preventing the ordinary man from living his normal span of life in happiness, contentment and creative action. India is no exception to the world phenomena, though each country is facing problems that are results of lack of right relationship pertaining to ideas, persons, communities and properties.

In India, several basic prejudices and consequent conflicts are self-evident, whilst others operate in narrower surroundings, or are for the time being latent. Communalism, provincialism, ideological difference, class conflict, cultural antagonism, prejudice between nation and nation, urban-rural conflict, inter-community and inter-family prejudice and conflict based round leadership, organisation, parties and vested interests affect almost every citizen without exception.

The chain of prejudices and conflicts seems to grow rather than diminish as civilisation advances, communications widen, and educational facilities are extended to the entire population. Many of the ills, conflicts and problems of India were easily explained away in terms of our lack of freedom to handle the problems, and many problems even originated in our political subjection.

The country is now free and independent. Yet it has to face problems both within and without the country. It is generally believed that problems are solved by action, that conflicts are resolved by aggression or conciliation, and prejudice is removed by education. However, very often actions create more problems and prejudice; aggression never pays the aggressor or the victim; conciliation, unless it is based on a complete resolution of a problem, gives only a brief respite; and education of a mere objective and informative character leads to greater confusion and mental conflict.

Group Prejudices: Need to Study

The solution of human problems, therefore, requires a detailed understanding of the whole process of living. Prejudices require to be analysed and studied in terms of cause and reaction. Human beings are constantly making and breaking communities. Contact and interaction between individuals and groups lead to conflict and co-operation. Eventually there is a process of assimilation of separate and divided units. The assimilated groups again come into conflict with other assimilated groups, and fresh divisions take place.

It can be generally stated that anything that separates, segregates or divides is creating prejudice, or is the result of prejudice. The world, in order to escape conflict, prejudice and division needs to lend its weight to integration and cohesion of such a substantial character, that divisions become impossible. The term 'love' has been used by prophets, seers and true leaders of mankind as the only real binding force. Love can be defined 'as that which holds together.' But love fails where there is prejudice. Love becomes a meaningless feeling when there is no understanding. Mental understanding is easy, but understanding fails to stand the test of events and circumstances. When events happen that cannot be understood, they cause the usual chain of fear, prejudice, aggression and separation.

In recent years, India has experienced a continuous effort at peace and construction, followed by frustration and defeat. Communalism has become bewildering. Everyone seems to condemn and practise provincialism at the same time. The conflict between Communism and Capitalism abroad, only creates confusion at home. The conflict between Pakistan and India is almost accepted as a permanent phenomenon, and as Pakistan is naturally accepted as always the guilty and the aggressive party, there is hardly anything to do to solve the problem except War. The conflict between Capital and Labour is built upon confirmed prejudices and convictions on both sides. Even the effort to eradicate drink is considered to be a mere conflict of prejudices.

No sociologist can suggest that he understands problems and their roots, and that he has remedies to solve the problems. But the sociologist has a better understanding of the process of life and living, and man and communities; he can, therefore, perhaps understand and interpret human behaviour, and indicate fundamental social concepts, conditions of social organisation, and nature of personal development where conflict and prejudice may be minimised, if not totally eradicated.

Group-Prejudices: Sources

The important causes and sources of prejudice and conflict are; (1) the relationship of man and communities to the physical environment, (2) the content of a people's history, (3) the nature of religious belief and forms of worship, (4) the content of the economic life, (5) the nature of social organisation, (6) the nature and content of the culture of human groups, (7) the nature of mind and thought as it has come to be as the result of life experience of the group and the individual. All the above factors do not operate singly, but they act and react on each other, creating social forces that operate so powerfully in certain cases that it becomes difficult for man and human groups to work against prevailing social trends. The human personality is little developed, the complex pattern of human existence has made self-expression very difficult, and education is not a process which enables man to understand, interpret and work against prevailing group prejudices and react intelligently to social forces, but rather education is itself a part of prejudice, and it is shaped within the cross-currents of the operating social forces. Under the circumstances, prejudices continue to multiply, they are strengthened by life experiences, and they become infectious with the extensive development of communication and means of thought expressions like the radio, the newspaper, the cinema, etc. The vastness of the world with which the individual is in contact to-day, the bewildering rapidity of events and the reactions to these events, and the presence of leadership and other factors that prevent the individual to react individually, and to determine the cause of his own life in terms of his personal life experiences, have led to the formation of layers of stratified prejudices which are like prison walls within which the individual and groups carry on their blind attempts to escape from problems that to-day almost suffocate them.

The Environment

The environment: The extent of the physical environment is not determined by geographical maps and the various frontiers that have come into being in the course of history. Let us try to imagine the state of our own country some two to four thousand years ago. There must have been groups of people occupying the physical area. These groups were small communities. The communities had their economic life, their language and social organisation, their recreations and their cultural patterns. Did they have frontiers? If the frontiers were there, they were limited to the needs of the groups, and thus the communities became tribes. The simple life of the community and tribe had its prejudices. Communities and tribes had their prejudices, differences and conflicts with their neighbours. There were aggressions, conquerors and conquests leading to the fusing of tribes and the expansion of physical boundaries. The world of the tribe gave way to kingdoms, kingdoms were conquered, conquests created prejudices, and continuous shifting of physical boundaries.

Physical boundaries, political boundaries and natural barriers created national frontiers; these were also frontiers of prejudice and cause of conflict, aggression and war. There were times when natural and political boundaries were not identical. This phenomenon caused fear and insecurity. The natural boundaries of India are unique. There are Nature's walls created by seas and mountains. The barriers can be crossed, but not with ease. There are natural fears and prejudices against those who are likely to even think of crossing the natural barriers.

Political frontiers have caused national patriotism. Patriotic feelings are examples of great elations. They lead to love and creativeness. But patriotism can develop within each political frontier only. Consolidated patriotism becomes national prejudice against other competing and neighbourly patriotisms. The clash of patriotisms lead to combustion and war. National frontiers and patriotism are eventual barriers against world understanding. The community frontier is real; it is the limit of personal and group life experience. The national frontier is emotionally, educationally and mentally developed. The mind further makes such a frontier sacrosanct and unalterable unless it is to mean an expansion and a trespass against the frontiers of other nations. The political frontier has become the cause of prejudice and fear; it is an obstacle to the quick realisation of a World State.

History

History: The history of nations is the story of shifting frontiers, deeds of leadership, and emphasised event. Stories of the struggle of communities in their small environment that are the little experiences of the human race are neither treasured nor remembered, and the fruits of these experiences do not remain to educate new generations in the arts of living. Thus only the shifting, shrinking, widening frontiers, the ideas and deeds of the few, and experiences that were sensational, are remembered. The memories help to create prejudices out of the pages of history. Memories of wars, conquests, destructions, dominations are powerful and full of the resentments and frustrations of a suffering people. They may cause righteous indignation. But when these become memory, then a vicious circle of suffering, hatred, struggle for the achievement of strength, aggression and reprisal begins, which releases a chain of conflicts that last for centuries. The most harmful are the wounds that have healed, but whose memories remain in the pages of history to condemn and invite reprisal. If the world desires to live in peace, then the histories of many nations should be rewritten, and the tragedies of the past should either be forgotten, or analysed to trace the cause, nature and consequence of improper relations between human groups.

Religion

Religion: It is generally believed that India is a land of great religious tension and turmoil. The population is made up of several religions, the most important of which are the Hindus and the Muslims. The Christians too become somewhat important since it was the religion of the ruling races for the last few hundred years.

From the religious point of view, India is the most ancient and the most important land. We have already spoken of the tribes and communities that must have lived in the vast continent. The so called aborigines, that to-day number about 25 million, are examples of such communities inhabiting the long belt of land stretching from the Arawalli Hills in the West, through Khandesh and C. P., Bihar, Orissa and Bengal into Assam and even Burma. Before the Vedic times, the ancestors of these aborigines had their religious beliefs and worship of Nature, which summed up their Animism. The Vedas contain sufficient evidence of prejudices of this very wise, ritualistic and philosophical people. At that time the Dravidians too had a highly evolved Polytheism. The acceptance of the Atharva Veda, the total religious beliefs and worships of the masses, as one of the Vedas, shows the understanding, tolerance and powers of assimilation of those wise Aryans.

The Muslims came as outsiders, invaders—a political enemy who came for economic advantage and exploitation. The coming of the foreigner brought the Aryans, the aborigines, and the Dravidians closer together, though fundamental prejudices may have remained amongst them. Any foreigner, who clashed with the religious beliefs and worships of a conquered people, would enforce his religious characteristics upon the conquered, and would set into motion a chain of prejudices which are bound to develop as vital differences.

The aggressive and dominating self-assertion of Islam, and its forthright condemnation of other religions is well known. This lack of understanding of the true nature of religion led Islam into serious conflict even with the Christian world. Both Islam and Christianity may be called a particular type of organised religion with fixed notions about God, a prophet who is renowned, a Holy Book, definite notions of salvation and the spiritual life, an organised church, and a congregation which created a religious community, which cut across its past social and political patterns.

Hinduism is not a religion in the sense in which Christianity, Islam and Zorostrianism are religions. Hinduism, like other religions, is animistic in its foundation, and has evolved a great polytheism from which the notion of a supreme deity has evolved. The concept of Brahman, the concept of one God, and even the belief in no God are permitted in the various philosophies of Hinduism. Indeed Hinduism has never failed even to welcome, revere and worship the Gods of others as the Vedic Aryans in their great wisdom had accepted the great animistic spirits of the Atharva Veda as worthy of man's worship.

Amongst the great prophets of Hinduism are Sankracharya, Buddha, Mahavir, Ramanuja, Guru Nanak, and even others upto Mahatma Gandhi. If Hinduism can be called a religion, then it is the only fortunate one whose stream of spiritual life was constantly fed and enriched by teachers whose philosophies reached perhaps the highest summits of man's interpretation of the life divine.

A religion which knew many prophets naturally will have few prejudices about prophets of other religions, and Indian history is a testimony of the reverence, regard and even love that made Guru Nanak approach Islam with understanding, or which led a great son of Bengal to create the Brahmo-Samaj to weave the true teachings of Christ into the great mosaic of Hindu spiritual thought and philosophy.

Hinduism, with its many great and noble prophets, not only draws its truth and wisdom from Holy Books like the Ramayana, the Bhagvad Gita, the Grantha Sahib and others, but has the rich treasure of the Vedas, the Upanishads, and the spiritual experiences of men like Vivekananda, Swami Rama Tirtha and Mahatma Gandhi to continue the eternal search for Truth. And have not Hindu teachers and scholars explained with anxious desire the pages of the Quoran and the Bible to admire and appreciate the truth they contained? And this love of Truth, the thirst of spiritual knowledge, and the exposition of philosophy have not been reserved for a few great and good men, but even the humblest masses and the Kabir Panthis in the working class have showed their veneration for all that is sacred in other religions.

Hindus, through the ages, have sought their salvation in many ways. The Gnyan Marga, the Path of the Karmayogi, the Bhakti Marga, Shakti Worship—all these lead to the Holy Grail, and in the search of the Ultimate and the Eternal, no prejudice or narrowness ever existed to condemn the path that was trodden by another Bhakta.

The Hindu in the course of history has worshipped in hypoethral shrines open to the sky; sometimes there was only the holy altar marked by stone; the 'deri' was a little temple hardly 24 inches high whilst temples grew in size, importance and divine significance according to the economic level, mental understanding and interpretation of spiritual values by the worshippers. Except when prejudices of others awakened their emotional wrath, the Hindu has never desecrated the Holy Shrine of another, be it a mosque or a church; and the Parsi Fire Temples that have preserved the sacredness of the Holy Fire of a people for one thousand and three hundred years are a testimony to the lack of prejudice, great tolerance, and feeling of reverence for anything that may be sacred to others.

Hindu churches have never created a congregation in the Muslim or the Christian sense. With rare exceptions, Hindu religions have not exploited political and economic life for the material gain of religious groups. If Hinduism had played the role in Indian Feudalism that the Christian church played in Europe, the history of India would have been different.

The writer of the article is not a Hindu. To a sociologist religion merely appears to be an important phenomenon that results from the mind's reactions to the environment, and man's spiritual insecurity. Prejudices there must be in religion, but prejudices act and react on each other. If other religions sought to interpret Hinduism without understanding, if then prejudices created fears and a contempt for aggression in the most sacred aspect of human existence, and if these created prejudices, they can be easily understood. There have been religious conflict, aggression and prejudices the world over. The history of many a nation has been strewn with blood because of religious prejudice. Organised religions, as apart from the teachings of great prophets, sometimes played ignoble roles in the political and economic life of countries. Fortunately the days of worst religious strife are over. If religious strifes exist to-day, they are merely a pretence to cover up the political and economic causes or motives that lie behind them. If there are religious prejudices in the world, the history of Hinduism shows how Dharma can exist without the narrow conflicts of blind dogma. The conflict in India between the religions, or within Hinduism itself, these are not due to religious prejudices, but to economic and political conflicts.

Economics

Economics: The history of man is a struggle for survival, and a competition for profit, gain, and success. Even the economic life of the small self-sufficient community was perhaps not free from the conflict that arose due to natural inequality of skill and prowess, and the desire to promote personal and family ends. Such conflicts lead to prejudice. It is doubtful if the long history of the economic life of the hunter, the fisherman and the cultivator, projecting into the first chapters of land possession, property and feudalism, moving into the insecure life of the nomad with his cattle wealth, passing into the commerce and travel minded age of trade and discovery and culminating in a most complex, speedy, extensive, industrial life of machine and electricity of the present century, can be said to create only prejudice. The economic misdeeds of selfish men, communities and nations have produced consequences which are the root of most human ills, conflicts and suspicions. The origin and spread of slavery in one form or another, the practised arts of exploitation of the many by the few, the organised systems of social injustice and unequal opportunities, the crafty dangers of statecraft that kept autocracy and oligarchies in power have been the distinies of dumb, helpless, ignorant millions; all these have created patterns of human behaviour that have produced fears, antagonisms, suspicions and prejudices that demand complete and radical change in the socio-economic structure of states and societies. These fears, antagonisms and prejudices have crystallised into hatred and organised rivalries that aim at the capture of power, the destruction of oligarchic authority, and the creation of a millenium, which in practice is difficult to reach. All these have created local, national and international organisations, associations, institutions and movements that work against each other, creating powerful prejudices, fears and antagonisms, using all the paraphernalia of modern publicity to hypnotise and deceive man.

The development of communications, the march of science, the creation of tremendous energy for production, the development of chemistry and the discovery of synthetic malinds have widened the gulf between competing economic groups. Science and technical progress has outstripped man's social, political and psychological development. The present crisis of civilisation, needing the control of the very forces man himself has created, brings him on the verge of a precipice. Natural barriers are unable to withstand the tremendous force that is generated by a world economy. The unchartered and erratic evolution of Capitalism with its implied inequalities and injustice, the ruthlessness and violence of Imperialism, the basic antagonism and ideology created by Socialism of one type or another, and the unscrupulous exploitation of science for the benefit of militarism have produced a world situation which is bound to baffle a less developed, and upto now subjugated country like India. The bewildering strength of cold realities can be prevented if old prejudices do not stand in the way, if the impossibility of absolute national sovereignty is realised, and the possibility of planned co-operation for a world economy are explored to the fullest extent.

So far as India is concerned, capitalism has not taken deep roots. We are not so tragically industrialised that we are faced with deep economic crisis. Our class antagonisms, hatreds and prejudices have not evolved so much as they are in the industrialised West. The new economy of India needs to be coolly planned after determining sound philosophical foundations. Man does not attain happiness by multiplying his wants, piling up gadgets, and mechanising the free processes of routine life. Extensive industrialisation, unbridled growth of urbanism, centralisation of economic development and political authority, are the several ways to create complicated socio-economic structures that hold within themselves the seeds of eternal conflict, prejudice and antagonism.

Let human life be simplified, evolve powerful communities that will live co-operatively, decentralise society, liquidate and decentralise unwieldy industrial areas, industrialise rationally, keeping alive the basic arts and skills of man, and a new economic security can be created without urban-rural competition, basic class conflicts, and unbearable inequalities of concentrated wealth. Even a partial elimination of prejudices is not possible, till man attains economic maturity and evolves a sane system of production and a balanced understanding based on true values of what he calls 'standards of living.'

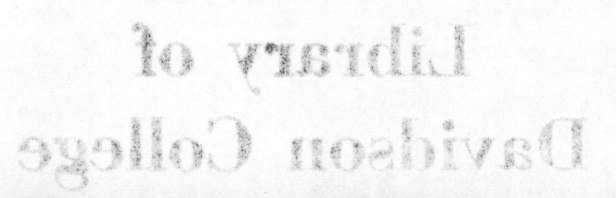

The presence of an hierarchy of standards of living creates room for powerful prejudices. The poor, the middle class and the rich, all have their respective prejudices. A rational levelling of life in happy and creative communities, greater equality of opportunity, and the maximum scope for the expression of skill, art and talent in the economic life of man will give to India a new glory. She will be a proper lesson to the West with its insane lust for profit and industrialisation, excessive development of power, mechanisation of life, production of an endless mass of cheap goods and gadgets, creating leisure in the midst of a moral vacuum, and eventually creating a culture of gadgets and gold that lacks the true dignity of man and a stamp of the spirit of his race.

Society

Society: Indian society and Indian social institutions are products of a long history. Besides, they are products of assimilation of innumerable factors and racial types. In the course of this assimilation, Hindu society may have lost a good deal of charm, dignity and pride of attainment that we have noticed in reference to Hindu religion and philosophy.

The early communities of India were organised in terms of blood relationship. They were fairly large endogamous groups, occupying tribal territories, speaking their own dialects. They were descended from a common ancestor and cherished the memories of their history and the animistic spirits and gods they worshipped as they carried on their struggle for existence as hunters, fishermen or primitive cultivators. They developed their distinctive cultural patterns, as their dialect developed and their arts and crafts flourished in the environments in which they lived.

Such communities were independent, and inter-dependent. They had their conflicts, and in face of danger, they developed forms of co-operation that led sometimes to fusions and assimilated patterns of culture. Almost all primitive communities were strictly endogamous. Whilst marriage was a free and transient unit, a violation of tribal endogamy meant even death. Thus they maintained their distinctive existence, and the same kind of distinctive existence continues even to this day. Primitive endogamy does not seem to be the result of prejudice against 'stranger groups'. Marriage amongst the known was desirable, and selection was preferable within the sufficiently wide circle of the whole tribe.

With the growth of economic inequalities within the endogamous communities, the social organisation took a different turn. The laws of endogamy and exogamy continued to exist, but the institution of marriage developed by custom, religion, and law came to determine marriage relationship according to wealth, land possession, privileges, and social prestige. When communities evolved on the basis of these new marriage groupings, prejudice was bound to arise, and these became worse as property possessing groups became more and more exclusive.

These developments are not peculiar to Hindu society alone, and Muslims, Christians and others have sought to prevent intermarriage in regional communities on grounds of religious taboo and legal and political disabilities, based on economic considerations.

The march of world history, the growth of nations, the development of communications, the technical development brought about by science, the spread of education, the birth of political consciousness and many other factors have made impossible the existence of small, endogamous, exclusive groups living behind their thick walls of social prejudice.

In the course of history, small communities are not found to continue their solitary existence. Even before the Aryan invasion, the Dravidians in the South had evolved more complicated patterns of village communities. It is now generally accepted that the caste system originated with the Dravidians. Not only their social life was organised, but they had economic organisations. Economic organisation very often cuts across social organisation, and the single community with its blood clans is vivisected into competing economic groups.

It is very important to note how, why, and under what circumstances different communities come together, and what is the process and consequence of this coming together. Two community groups, living in two different environments, come together in physical contact. Mental contact as we now have at the present day due to developed communications, was probably not so evident in the past. The first contacts lead to interaction. When two strange groups meet, there is fear, suspicion and a desire to maintain the individuality of each group. Where competition for survival is evident, or where there is aggression for domination, or where there is a design on the women of one community by another, the first inter-action leads to conflict and war. These conflicts create prejudices, and prejudices continue to multiply even after the conflict is resolved. If the conflict is resolved by conquest, it is but natural that prejudice and psychological antagonism should develop. And these embrace every aspect of the mutual life including religion, language, economic life, social system, and cultural patterns.

The long history of India, like China, has known and experienced this process of contact and conflicts for centuries. Not only did large regional groups come into conflict with their neighbours, but there were a series of incursions into the country, migrations and conquests by people and races who came from unknown and distant lands for motives of conquest, or in search for survival and peace.

Let us carefully note the chief of these. The aboriginal belt, with the race often called Kaularian, had tribal cultures. The Dravidians too are found well settled in their homelands in the south, and on the eastern coast. In the early days there were incursions from the northwest; these included the Vedic Aryans, and successive waves of Aryan communities including the Rajputs. Then came the Mulsims, the Tartars and the Moghuls. There were incursions and intermingling from the eastern borders too, from Tibet, Burma and China. The Bengalee group developed its distinct characters. From across the seas, from the west coast particularly entered the Portuguese, French and English.

Each wave of migration and conquest brought a new people with their own history, language, religion, economic experience and motives, social organisation and art of Government, cultural pattern, educational system, arts, crafts and philosophies. The conflict that followed are well known to all students of history. It was not merely a contact of armies and Kings, the intrigues of Ministers and aristocracies, but there was a coming together, a contact, invisible conflicts, fears, loves, and understanding between different groups of people.

The sociologist is aware of the manner in which assimilation, the most important of all sociological processes, takes place. Assimilation is easy after contact has taken place, painful or peaceful, if there is Receptivity. Assimilation is difficult if there is Resistance.

When two different groups from different environments meet in a common region, where one is an outsider and an intruder, the group with a dominant culture, more powerful in arms, and possessing the means to impose authority succeeds to dominate, suppress, and claim the submission of the conquered group. The apparent advantages sought are political domination, and economic exploitation. The effect is resistance, the result is prejudice. And when conflict is apparently over, when the conquest is believed to be complete and reconciliation is effected, the resistance really continues if the conquered group had strong characteristics in terms of its own religions, belief, language and economic, social and cultural patterns. It is also possible for two different groups to meet without apparent conflict or war. When this happens the dominant group may seek to impose its pattern peacefully. Thus there is receptivity and not resistance. The meeting groups evolve a common political pattern and achieve economic co-operation.

Whatever may have been the conflicts within the many and varied groups that make up Hindu society, they are found to assimilate the basic philosophical concepts that help to create a hardly visible integration. This integration, though least apparent, is very real in terms of basic cultural patterns that have evolved in the course of hundreds of years of history. These cultural patterns include the day-to-day details of human life including language, food, habits, dress, architectural concepts, recreations, arts, celebrations, the details of economic life, and the elements of social life including ceremonies and marriage customs. Culture evolves regionally, culture is very much a product of proximity. Differences, however fundamental, cannot stand against the continuous blending and intermingling of life patterns of individuals, families and small communities brought close together in the immediate environment. Within the regional community, receptivity prevails and resistance is broken down.

Assimilation is brought about by living together. Living together implies a continuous process of sharing group experience. Religious differences, class barriers, social exclusiveness, mental conflicts—all these seem to disappear as human beings share the day-to-day struggles and joys, face together the problems of life, and learn to appreciate and understand each other's point of view. The worst conflicts in recent years have proved the above statement time and again. But this process of 'living together' is mentioned here in the sense in which tribes and communities lived together. The cities and urban mores produced individualism; the intellectual life bred isolation. Modern conflicts and prejudices are primarily the creation of the urban middle and upper classes who used prejudices and fostered differences in order to maintain their class privileges and bolster up their political authority. The middle and upper classes provide that 'leadership' which creates 'prejudice patterns', emphasise the differences in thought, ideas, beliefs, customs and behaviour, and create fears and defence mechanisms, that eventually lead to aggression and conflict. They point out the advantages of individualism and the importance of maintaining group superiorities to continue to enjoy economic advantages. Thus they give shape, form, substance, and colour and importance to prejudice.

The way to end prejudice is to yield and be receptive to the forces of assimilation. The consciousness of separation and individualism are barriers created by the mind, disturbing the process of assimilation that is ever present in all human societies. Co-operation fosters assimilation. The practice of co-operation is easy and natural in regional community groups as against artificial communities that owe their allegiance to religious beliefs and class privileges. In the end assimilation always prevails, and worst conflicts lead to complete reconciliation and assimilation after suffering the consequences of physical and psychological warfare.

Conclusion

This brief article has attempted to understand the causes of prejudices and the process of their functions and elimination. Understanding leads to the disintegration of prejudice. In modern world existence, the greatest creator of prejudice is the desire for economic gain and profit. Religion and nationalism are the tools used to foster prejudice, create competition, emphasise individualism and maintain power through aggression. The forms and substance of prejudices are the products of leadership. The masses are the tools by which leaders attain their objects of group, class and national domination. True culture is synthetic and develops integrated patterns. Leadership, by an artful analysis and misinterpretation of culture, succeeds in emphasising differences, eventually creating prejudices and conflicts.

The world is, therefore, in need of right leadership that will seek to organise integrated and harmonious communities, living together in their day-to-day co-operative economic activities. Such communities without creating political frontiers, will successfully create larger and larger communities, federating or evolving into a World State. The weapons of prejudice—property, organised idea patterns, nationalism, and organised religion—will have to be ultimately discarded in the interest of World Peace and Human Happiness.

CRITIQUE OF GROUP PREJUDICE

(*With Special reference to Harijans*)

P. KODANDA RAO

and

MARY CAMPBELL RAO

Introduction

Prof. John Dewey is reported to have remarked that the words of Jesus Christ, "Judge Not", should be taken quite literally, unless it was intended "to do something about it". Apart from historical curiosity, no good purpose is served by listing, analysing and publicising group prejudices and discriminations in India or elsewhere unless it is intended to secure the necessary data for rational and effective action.

The Individual and the Group

What is a "group"? In nature there are only individuals. In so far as a number of them have something in *common* they constitute a group. In the language of Dr. Seba Eldridge, a group is based on *common or concordant experiences and interests* that are differentiated from *other* experiences and interests. (1) The determinants of common experiences and interests may be geographical location, race, sex, language, religion, vocation, social status, disabilities, intellectual pursuits, ethical ideals, organisations, etc. They may roughly be classified under the geographical, the biological and the cultural. A number of individuals may have in common a country like Asia, and they form the group of Asians. Some individuals may have certain racial characteristics in common and they constitute the Jewish or the Negro or the Nordic group. Some may have a religion in common like Hinduism or Christianity, and they constitute the Hindu or Christian group. Some may be members of a Rotary Club, and they form a Rotary group. A number of individuals who were persecuted and had to flee from their homes and countries form the Refugee group. Some individuals who have Communism in common constitute the Communist group. Each determinant, whether geographical or biological or cultural, creates a group in so far as it is common to a number of individuals, few or many.

At the same time, each individual is a member not only of one group but also of several groups simultaneously. For instance, one and the same individual may be an inhabitant of Asia and be a member of the Asian group along with others who also live in Asia. At the same time, he may be Hindu by religion and be a member of the Hindu group, and may be a Communist and be a member of the Communist group, speak

1: Davis and Barnes, An Introduction to Sociology. P. 906.

Hindi and be a member of the Hindi group; may be a manufacturer and be a member of an organisation of manufacturers, and so on.

Thus, *each determinaint cultural or other, is common to several individuals who constitute a group but only as far as that particular determinant is concerned and no other. And each individual has several determinants and is a member of as many groups simultaneously.*

The Census operations offer an analogy. Each Census Table groups the individuals according to one particular determinant they have in common, like age, sex, vocation, religion, language, civil condition, etc. And every individual is enumerated under several determinants, like age, sex, etc. But it does not follow that all these who have a religion in common and constitute a Census category have on that account a common language or vocation also. In so far as an individual is a member of several groups, he is not a coordinated unit. He may have conflicting loyalties to different groups of which he is a member. If he is a member of the the Communist group along with other Communists all over the world, and at the same time a member of the Indian National group along with all other Indians, his loyalties to the two groups may conflict.

It is, however, commonly held that there are a comparatively small number of groups in the world, the determinants of which are primarily place or race, and that each such group has a coordinated and organic combination of secondary cultural determinants like language, religion, political set-up, sports, economic system, and character, and that each individual is a member of one such primary group and has in common the culture-pattern of his group. For instance, it is often held that an individual, who is a Jew by religion, is on that account, crafty in character, undesirable as a companion, unscrupulously rich, etc; that an individual who is Chinese by nationality is concurrently wise, artistic, hard-working, and so on; and that a citizen of India is concurrently a Hindu by religion, a vegetarian, a yogi and palm-reader, undesirable as an immigrant, a cooly, etc. As a matter of fact, there is no such correlation between any two sets of determinants. In the world there are individual human beings and individual group-determinants. In the world there are individual human beings and individual group-determinants, geographical, biological or cultural, and an infinite number of permutations and combinations of individuals and determinants. Sometimes, but not necessarily, a varying number of individuals have more than one determinant in common. For instance, they may all be Hindus, vegetarians, palm-readers and coolies. But it is a coincidence and not a correlation.

Reason and Prejudice

What is "prejudice"? It is pre-judgment, an attitude or action not based on reason. It is generally indentified with the "irrational" or "anti-rational" in attitude and action.

The United Nations Sub-Commission on the Prevention of Discrimination distinguished between the "rational and irrational components" of "prejudice." It observed:—

> On the one hand, prejudice may result from the experience of an individual with some real defects of behaviour of individuals

belonging to another social group; on the other hand, such dislike, which might or might not be justified on account of real experience, is irrationally generalised towards all the people belonging to that social group.(2)

It may well be urged that in so far as a particular experience was based on real factors and was justified, it was rational judgment and not irrational prejudice. If a person touched an exposed live electric wire and get a shock, it would not be prejudice, but rational action, for him not to touch it again. If an individual had been guilty of cheating, it would be good reason, and not a "rational prejudice", if he is not trusted again wihout proof of a change in his character. Indeed, "rational prejudice" seems to be a contradiction!

It is possible, however, that what was rational at some place and time may be irrational at other places and times. When an Englishman wears heavy woollen dress in cold England it is rational, but when he does the same in hot India it is irrational. Even in Science, which is *par excellence* rational, the rational of yesterday may be irrational today. It was rational some decades ago to hold that atoms were the indivisible ultimates of matter; it is irrational today. Many a rational certitude of a century ago has been invalidated by a subsequent one, which, in its turn, may be superceded by yet another, as knowledge advances. Nobody is more certain than Dr. B. R. Ambedkar, the present "Untouchable" member of the Government of India, that "Untouchability" is irrational. And yet he sought to find out the *rationale* of it in his *The Untouchables*. It would seem a contradiction to postulate a *rationale* of the irrational. It only means that what is undoubtedly irrational today was rational when it originated, according to then pervading state of knowledge and experience.

Indeed, it is reasonable to presume that every culture-trait, the product of human activity, was rational in the circumstances of its origin, even though it has since become irrational. Every culture-trait must have been originated by some one, at some time, at some place. It acquired social significance when it was adopted by other individuals besides the originator. It is reasonable to presume that the originator and those who deliberately adopted it from him found it reasonable to the best of their knowledge. Ptolemy's astronomy was reasonable to him and many others of his time. So was the astronomy of Copernicus to him and many of his contemporaries and successors. It was reasonable for Lamarck to propound the theory of the inheritance of acquired characters; it was equally reasonable for Darwin to propound the theory of the survival of the fittest. The horrors of the Inquisition were reasonable to the perpetrators thereof; they were not sadists, but elderly men of God, high dignitaries of the Church of the merciful Christ, pious to a degree. In the Judicial courts of today, it is reason that informs the judge of the lower court in forming his judgment, and it is reason again that persuades the appeal judge to reverse it. *Reason is relative and dynamic*. It is irrational to judge the past from the changed circumstances and standards of the present. It is more rational to presume that everything was rational when it originated, though it may be irrational today.

While prejudice is never rational, it is not necessarily irrational. It may be just *unreasoned*. Both unreasoned and irrational attitudes are

2. United Nations Sub-Commission On the Prevention of Discrimination E/CN. 4/Sub. 2/40. p. 14.

prejudice in so far as they are not rational. When a person avoids another with an infectious disease, his action is rational; when a Brahmin child, following the pattern of his parents, avoids an Untouchable, his action is unreasoned; when however a Brahmin adult is convinced that Untouchability is irrational and yet avoids an Untouchable, his action is irrational. Thus, human actions may be rational or prejudiced; the latter may be unreasoned or irrational.

What are the roles of the rational, the unreasoned and the irrational in the affairs of individuals or groups? Inevitably and eternally reason has a tiny part in the life of the individual and the group, while prejudice, unreasoned or irrational, has the bulk. It is impossible for each and every individual to base his attitudes and actions on his own reasoned judgment. If one were to commence cooking his first meal only after a rational enquiry into the physics, the chemistry, the physiology and the psychology, etc., involved in it, he would not be there to cook his dinner, much less to eat it! Even after a long life devoted to reason, no individual knows the reasons for all his attitudes and actions. At best, he may know the reason for an aspect of an aspect of his actions. Most others have to be content with unreasoned attitudes and actions for the most part of their lives.

Further, no individual has a chance to order all his life on the basis of reason, even if he wished to. Every body is born into the culture of his parents and is shaped by it long before his reasoning faculties come into play. The individual has been given an outfit of attitudes and behaviour long before he can reason about them. He is "conditioned" and "polarised", as it were, before his age of reason dawns. His attitudes and actions have become automatic and almost instinctive, and do not compel the play of reason. Even the most scientific researchers apply their reason to the particular and tiny fields of their investigations, and for the rest are content with unreasoned or even irrational conformity to current inherited pattern. Of icebergs, it is said that the portion above the water-level is a small fraction of the portion below it. It is also said in psychology that the conscious mind is a fraction of the sub-conscious. Even so, it is in the nature of things that the area of reason is a tiny fraction of the area of prejudice. All people are born into a social environment and are conditioned by it. Most stay put, as it were. Only a few apply reason, and even so to a small fraction of their lives. None can be individually rational in all matters and at all times. It is irrational to expect it.

Most of the attitudes and actions of most people are just unreasoned, rather than reasoned or irrational. But even when an individual is convinced that an unreasoned action of his is irrational, it is not always that he gives it up at once. There is generally a time lag due to sheer inertia or some deterrent sanction, like the disapproval of his family and friends. It is a mighty task for those who are emancipated from the unreasoned and the irrational to emancipate others. The task becomes much more difficult if the current irrational acts are included within the range of religious belief and consequently put out of the reach of reason.

Nevertheless, it is necessary to maximise the range of reason and minimise the range of the unreasoned and the irrational. It is essential that as many individuals as possible should continually test each and every one of human attitudes and actions by the latest standards of knowledge and experience, and install reason in the place of prejudice, whether the latter is passively unreasoned or actively irrational.

Discrimination

Prejudice is a subjective mental attitude. Its objective expression is "discrimination", which is departure from equality. But not necessarily in every case. If men are excluded from the women's ward in a hospital, it is not discrimination due to prejudice. It is rational differentiation. In the opinion of the United Nations Sub-Commission on the Prevention of Discrimination, which may be considered the latest and the most authoritative pronouncement on the subject, discrimination is

> any action which denies to individuals or groups equality of treatment, which they may wish.(3)

The last qualifying clause is significant. Differences in treatment which are either accepted or desired are not discriminations. As long as women acquiesced in the denial of the political franchise or exclusion from the armed forces, it was not discrimination. But when they desired equality with men in these respects and were denied it, it became discrimination. The determinant is the wish of the people concerned.

If men wished to be admitted to the women's wards in a hospital and were denied their wish, would it be discrimination in the sense of inequality of treatment due to irrational prejudice? In what circumstances does inequality become discrimination? Since the concept of equality, like reason, can vary with each individual and group, it is necessary to seek a fundamental and philosophic and impersonal basis for it. The U. N. Sub-Commission on the Prevention of Discrimination sought to define discrimination and equality in as precise terms as possible. It said that "equality" referred only to

> moral and juridical equality as proclaimed in the Universal Declaration of Human Rights; that is to say, it is equality in dignity, formal equality in rights, and equality of opportunity, but not necessarily material equality as to the extent and content of the rights of all individuals. (4).

According to the Sub-Commission, the philosophical basis for equality is the ethical concept of the "dignity of human personality". From this concept flowed two principles: Individual freedom and Equality of all human beings before the law.

According to the Sub-Commission:

> Discrimination includes any conduct based on a distinction made on grounds of natural or social categories, which have no relation either to individual capacities or merits, or to concrete behaviour of the individual person. (5)

---

3. United Nation Sub-Commission on the Prevention of Discrimination. E/CN. 4/Sub. 2/40. p. 4.

4. United Nation Sub-Commission on the Prevention of Discrimination. E/CN. 4/Sub. 2/40. p. 33.

5. U. N. Sub-Commission on the Prevention of Discrimination. E/CN. 4/Sub. 2/40. p. 33.

In as much as prejudice is a departure from reason, the consequent discrimination is also a departure from equality, which amounts to privilege or deprivation. Both are discriminations. But generally speaking, discrimination is used to emphasise the latter than the former. It means less than equality, rather than more; "devaluation" rather than appreciation.

Group Prejudice and Discrimination

Group prejudice and discrimination are the attitude and behaviour of the individuals of one group towards the individuals of another group, without individual justification. Bassanio had good reason to dislike Shylock, but it would be group prejudice if all Christians disliked all Jews on the ground that Bassanio was a Christian and Shylock was a Jew. Mr. Winston Churchill is a member of the British nationality group and also the group of imperialists. The late Mr. C. F. Andrews was a member of the British nationality group. It would be reasonable for an Indian nationalist to dislike Mr. Churchill's imperialism, but it would be a prejudice to dislike all Britishers, and Mr. Andrews among them. It would be a prejudice to generalise the imperialism of Mr. Churchill and attribute it to all Britishers, including Mr. Andrews. Group prejudices arise from the unwarranted generalisation from the particular. They are formed by the "process of projection and by association of ideas, experiences and emotions which have been formed casually under the influence of particular or accidental facts." (6)

Group prejudice leads to group discriminations. Human history is full of such prejudices and discriminations; as for instance, Hindus against Muslims, Muslims against infidels, Christians against Jews, white people against the coloured, Brahmins against non-Brahmins, Catholics against Protestants, etc., etc.

Problems and Solutions

Prejudice is a matter of the mind and is subjective. It can be remedied only by indirect rational education and not by coercion. Discrimination, however, being objective action, can more readily and generally be controlled by coercive action, though even here rational education is necessary.

Corrective education and action must however be appropriate to the nature of the prejudice or discrimination. The solution must fit the problem; the medicine must be appropriate to the disease. Both the problem and the solution must belong to the same determinant. If, for instance, the problem is one of race, a racial solution is appropriate, and not a religious, economic or language solution. If it is intended to prevent miscegenation of different races in a country, it is appropriate to exclude the immigrants of alien races and prohibit sex-relations, within or without marriage, between races already in the country. If it is intended to prevent adding to the pauper population of a country, it is appropriate to exclude the immigration of alien paupers and fix a minimum living wage in the country itself. It is, however, inappropriate and irrational to exclude the immigration of aliens by race in order

---

6. U. N. Sub-Commission on the Prevention of Discrimination. E/CN. 4/Sub. 2/40. p. 14.

to safeguard the economic standards within the country. It is irrational to exclude all Asiatics by race, including Pandit Jawaharlal Nehru and the Aga Khan, in order to keep out paupers. Racial solutions for economic problems are as irrational as economic solutions for racial problems. Administrative problems need administrative solutions and not linguistic or religious ones. Similarly, in matters of prejudice and discriminations, solutions must fit the problem.

Summary of Principles

The human world consists of individual human beings. A number of individuals, few or many, constitute a group in so far as they have common factors or determinants, whether they are geographical, biological or cultural, but only in so far as they have factors in common. Each individual human being has several factors or determinants at the same time and is simultaneously a member of several groups. Each determinant has several individual human beings, and each human being has several determinants. Broadly speaking, if a large number of individuals have a large number of determinants in common, it is a coincidence and not necessarily a correlation.

Prejudice is pre-judgment. It is never rational, is most often unreasoned, and sometimes irrational. Reason plays a very small part in the life of the individual or of humanity as a whole. Few individuals are deliberately irrational. Most people for the most part live the life of unreason. They continue to think and act as they were conditioned in their childhood, before their powers of reason became operative. It is the duty of all who can, to replace the unreasoned and the irrational by the rational, notwithstanding its uphill character.

Subjective prejudice often expresses itself in objective discrimination, which is a denial of equality irrespective of individual merits. Individual and accidental actions are generalised and attributed to all the members of a group unrelated to the action. Thus arise group prejudices and discriminations.

In replacing irrational inequality with rational equality, it is necessary to suit the solution to the problem.

Harijans

These principles may be applied to the problem of "Harijans" in India. "Harijans" means the "people of God", the name given by Mahatma Gandhi to the *Panchamas* or *Antyajas* or Untouchables among the Hindus. They are also called the Scheduled Castes in the Government of India Act of 1935, and the new Constitution of India.

Though Untouchability has existed for over a thousand years and today the Untouchables comprise about fifty millions in India, there is yet no generally agreed or scientific definition of Untouchability. Nor is anything definite known about its origin and development and survival. It is not necessary here to attempt a review, as it were, of the various and divergent theories advanced by several writers of varying degrees of scholarship and authority.

When the Census Commissioner of India was asked to enumerate the Untouchables as a separate category in the Census, of 1911, he had perforce to improvise a working definition of Untouchability. He suggested ten criteria or determinants. One of them was causing pollution by (a) touch or (b) approach within a certain distance. But, according to Dr. B. R. Ambedkar, the Provincial Census Commissioners were not unanimous about it, but were unanimous about three others, namely, the Untouchables did not receive the *Mantra* from the Brahmin, they were not served by good Brahmin priests and they had their own priests. (7)

The fact that Untouchables are not served by Brahmin priests but by their own becomes a discrimination if the Untouchables desired such service but were denied it. If they desired it, the rational remedy was to ensure that they had it. Brahmin priests might be persuaded to do so. Or, they may be obligated to do so, on the analogy of, say, public conveyances. But Dr. Ambedkar, who is himself an Untouchable and a champion of the Untouchables, does not seem to wish that Brahmin priests should be persuaded or coerced to give their service to the Untouchables. It is, therefore, a distinction without being a discrimination calling for its elimination.

In so far the Untouchables constitute a group in that they are not served by Brahmin priests, they do not form a group for any other factor or determinant. They are not one group but a number of groups. According to the Schedule of the Government of India Act, which Dr. Ambedkar considered was both exhaustive and authentic, there were as many as four hundred and twenty nine Scheduled Castes! What criteria or determinants distinguished them is not clear. But it would seem that the Untouchables, as defined above, do not constitute a group by race, language, vocation, inter-marriage, etc. They do not have a race, language or vocation in common. These factors cut across Harijans and non-Harijans all over the world. The appropriate action will not be special to Harijans.

Poverty is not a determinant which is common to all Harijans and which distinguishes them from non-Harijans. However poverty is defined, the individuals who have it in common are to be found in all other groups based on race, religion, vocation, etc., all over the world. The poverty group does not coincide with the Harijan group. The remedy for poverty has to be applied to all the poor, whether Harijans or non-Harijans.

Ignorance and illiteracy are not the determinants of Harijans; they will be found among Harijans and non-Harijans all over the world. The remedy for them will apply equally to all who are ignorant and illiterate, and not merely to Harijans. Common educational facilities for all is the appropriate solution.

Again, dirt and squalor are not factors common to Harijans, all Harijans, and only Harijans. The dirt and squalor group cuts across the Harijans and non-Harijan groups all over the world. Not all Harijans are scavengers of night-soil. Scavenging is a human need and service all over the world. Some current methods of scavenging are undoubtedly disagreeable. The rational solution is to eliminate them by the more agreeable methods of under-ground drainage, septic-tanks and pit-privys, etc. Indeed, it seems a terrible disgrace that anybody in these days should have to start his career, at a tender school-age, as a collector of night-soil and end up his long life in the same job. It is reasonable to dislike the *bhangi's* job, but is irrational to dislike the *bhangi* himself; it is rational solution to adopt modern sanitation, and it is irrational prejudice to shun the *bhangi*.

Segregation, residential or other, is not special to the Harijans in India. It is to be found among some non-Harijans in some other parts of the world, as, for instance, the Jews and the Negroes and Indians in South Africa, etc. Segregation is an irrational prejudice and unfair

---

7. Ambedkar. *The Untouchables*. pp. 73–4.

discrimination wherever it occurs. It should be eliminated as a general proposition all over the world wherever it occurs and by the same means, namely, rational education and legal prohibition.

Beef-eating is not a determinant of Harijans; all Harijans do not eat beef and many non-Harijans all over the world eat beef. Beef-eating divides humanity into two groups; those who eat it and those who do not, but not into Harijans and non-Harijans. Science does not seem to have given a decisive or final answer to the question: to eat or not to eat beef, or even meat of any kind. It is, therefore, irrational to discriminate for or against it.

Dr. Ambedkar distinguished between pollution as observed by some non-Hindus and untochability as observed by some Hindus. The former was individual and temporary, while the latter was social and permanent. He observed that isolation as practised by non-Hindu groups elsewhere was prescribed as a safeguard against defilement. But it was for specific and temporary reasons, like the isolation of a person suffering from an infectious disease. When the specific and temporary reason ceased to operate, the isolation also ceased. Even in India a Brahmin who touched an Untouchable and became polluted, thereby, got rid of the pollution by undergoing certain purificatory ceremonies.
But the Untouchables

> are born impure; they are impure while they live; they die the death of the impure, and they give birth to children who are born with the stigma of Untouchability affixed to them. It is a case of permanent, hereditary stain which nothing can cleanse.(8)

Whatever be the validity of Dr. Ambedkar's own theory of the rationale of the origin and development of Untouchability, he and many others with him including Mahatma Gandhi, were and are convinced that Untouchability as defined above is an utterly irrational prejudice resulting in most unfair discriminations.

In so far as Untouchability is prejudice and discrimination based on the biological factor of birth, it is not special to the Untouchables in India. Castes and classes based on birth are more general. Prejudice and discrimination cut across Harijans and non-Harijans all over the world. The most conspicuous of them is race prejudice and discrimination, as, for instance, against the Negroes, the Asistics, the Jews, etc., among some gruops in certain parts of the world. The rational remedy for prejudice and discrimination which are based on the accident of birth is the same, whether it be called Untouchability or race. Enlightened law and public opinion should do the utmost to eliminate such prejudice and discrimination. The most effective and lasting remedy is the universal spread of the latest scientific knowledge and, and more particularly, of the Social Sciences, like Anthropology and Sociology.

Prejudice and discrimination are irrational whether they are favourable or unfavaourable to a group or individual. They are a departure from equality which is rational. Discrimination in favour of an individual or a group is *ipso facto* discrimination against other individuals or groups. In so far as Untouchability is an irrational prejudice it should be eliminated. But it cannot be achieved by conferring irrational privileges on the Untouchables. The present policy, favoured by Governments and some people, of recognising the Untouchables as a distinct community and making special arrangements for their benefit in politics, administration, education and social services, is not calculated to abolish Untouchability, but to perpetuate it. Some people who hitherto disliked being Untouch-

8. Ambedkar. *The Untouchables*. p. 21.

ables and sought assimilation with other groups, have now become keen on remaining Untouchables because of the policy, followed by the State and some influential non-official bodies, of giving them special and privileged treatment. Hitherto some Untouchables changed to Christianity on the ground that they hoped thereby to emancipate themselves from Untouchability, as Christianity did not recognise Untouchability as a principle. But now there is a trend in the opposite direction. The converts are reverting to their former status of Untouchables because of the special privileges acorded to the Untouchables by the present Government. And Christian missionaries, anxious to check this trend, have urged that Untouchable converts to Christianity and their descendents were still Untouchables and should be given the same privileges as Untouchables! Untouchability has become an asset rather than a curse.

The more rational policy is to ignore Untouchability in all matters, and primarily in state and official and public affiairs. The uneducated should be educated, without reference to their being Harijans or non-Harijans. Under a system of universal compulsory education, every individual, irrespective of his membership of other groups based on race, religion, sex, birth, language, etc., will receive education. The uneducated Untouchables will also receive education, but not because they belong to the group of Harijans but because they belong to the group of the uneducated. All educational institutions and hostels should be general to all, and none special to Harijans. Poverty should be the sole criterion for scholarships and freeships, but not membership of a group based on Untouchability or race or religion or language. Economic problems need economic solutions; educational problems need educational solutions; and social problems need social solutions. The reservation of seats in the legislatures, in the administrative jobs, in educational institutions, etc., for Harijans as Harijans will confirm and perpetuate Untouchability and not eliminate it. Reservation should go if Untouchability is to go.

Conclusion

The only rational policy is to take the individual, and each of his attitudes and actions as the unit and not generalise.
As Sir Gilbert Murray observed,
> All generalisations about whole nations or groups of nations are superficial and inaccurate, even when made by scientific students without personal bias. And most of these actually current are made by prejudiced and utterly unscientific partisans. . . . . I am always puzzled by people who ask me "Do you like Indians ?", or it may be Americans, or Frenchmen, and can only answer, as I would about my own countrymen, that I like some and do not like others."(9)

He might as well have added that in the same individual he liked some things and disliked some others according to their nature. It is possible for an Indian to like some Englishmen like the late Mr. C.F. Andrews and dislike some Englishmen like Mr. Winston Churchill. Even in Mr. Churchill, he may dislike his imperialism and at the same time admire his oratory and his services as war-time Prime Minister when England

9. Murray, Sir Gilbert and Tagore, Rabindranath, *East and West* International Institute of Intellectual Cooperation, League of Nations, 1935.

stood alone. It is irrational group prejudice to like or dislike Indians as a group; it is equally irrational to admire or hate an Indian as an individual. It is possible to admire and revere the late Mahatma Gandhi for his principles of truth and non-violence but disapprove his views on Khaddar or birth-control. Even an individual is a multiple personality, with some rational, some irrational and a great many unreasoned attitudes and behaviours.

SUBLIMATION OF GROUP FEELINGS

P. G. SHAH

Study of Group Prejudices, Essential

The symposium on "Group Prejudices" organised at the present period in our history is singularly opportunate. The freedom for India has been achieved in tragic circumstances requiring the partition of the country into artificial divisions, based on group prejudices of a religious character resulting in hardship to millions of innocent human beings, upsetting their daily life in every way and embarrassing the finances of the Government to an extent unprecedented in history. In a country where poverty, ignorance, dirt and squalor create initial difficulties, where the ancient ideals of peace, fraternity and harmony have been replaced by the modern conflict between capital and labour, between the *sowcar* and the farmer, and where personal aggrandisement and selfishness on the one side and idleness and ignorance on the other have accentuated all our troubles and where new prejudices on grounds of linguistic separatism are coming up, it is essential that studies of group feelings should be conducted in the spirit of sympathy and understanding.

2. It would be idle complacency to ignore the existence of these problems and to assume that the surging waves of patriotism and loyalty to the new Constitution of our country will overcome all difficulties. It would not be enough to issue instructions to the Census Authorities against the exhibition of castes, creeds or ethnic qualities in the census returns as long as the solid facts of social or occupational, religious or linguistic groups, stare us in the face throughout rural tracts of India. They have to be studied and steps taken at every stage in the education of every child in the country to remove from its mind, the grounds and reasons for these prejudices, and to assure that the psychological and physical factors that lead to isolation and suspicion, to superiority or inferiority complexes, melt away. These prejudices are like superstitions that die hard, like the belief in witchcraft and the evil eye, which led to the murder and punishment of numerous innocent persons. It is commonplace to ridicule belief in* witchcraft or in astrology but it is surprising how many of even the so-called civilised people believe in these superstitious practices. The group prejudice is described as having its "chief feature to consist of the tendency of most people to personify evil, to ascribe evil to groups or categories of persons rather than to impersonal forces or to single erring individuals".** The problems of these prejudices are universal and if they are studied independently by impartial persons and remedies are worked out also in India, on the lines of the pioneer work carried out in U.S.A., the results will be astounding.

* W. Seabrook. Witchcraft and Its Power in the World today, 1941.

** G. W. Allport. Controlling Group Prejudices. "Annals of the American Academy of Political and Social Sciences" March 1946.

Group Prejudices in India and U.S.A.

3. The following comparative lists of problems of this type as noticed in American and their counterparts as observed in India are indicative of the fundamentally psychological character of group prejudices, which are evidently based on certain common features of ethnic human behaviour throughout the world :—

Problems in U.S.A.

1. Prejudice and discrimination against racial, ethnic and religious minorities, e.g., the problem of the Negro, the Jew, the Japanese American.

2. Regional differences of the South and the Pacific Coast.

3. Frustrations and grievances regarding (a) Employment (b) Housing conditions (c) Inadequate community services for recreation etc.

4. The problems of inequity of distribution of appointments led to the formation of a Fair Employment Practice Committee which working in conjunction with the Federal Public Services Commission had led to greater contentment among the employees in Industry, Private employment and Government.

5. The necessity of advancing national unity demands the formation of organisations for the promotion of better race relations for improvement of status of minorities.

Problems in India.

1(a). Discrimination by the Hindu community against Harijans, Aboriginal and backward tribes.

(b). Prejudices between the Hindus and Muslims leading to the separation of Pakistan.

2. Regional differences between North India and South India and various linguistic Provinces of India.

3. Frustrations and grievances arising out of the conditions of (a) Industrial labour and housing (b) Defective and insufficient health services (c) Prevalence of ignorance, poverty and disease.

4. The uneven distribution of opportunities for literary and technical education has led to uneven distribution of various groups in the superior services and other occupations. The fears of uneven distribution should be allayed by the "Fair Employment Practice" Committees in India, safeguarding the claims of the minorities without affecting the efficiency of service.

5. National unity is a greater necessity in a vast country like India. The unity programmes for better relations between the various groups and minorities and for their mutual understanding are necessary.

The Basic Similarity of the Problem

The problems of human relations are more or less common throughout the world and India does not represent either an exceptional or an isolated phenomena even though the method of approach and the availability of resources are different. Human nature is fundamentally the same yet racial and ethnic qualities make for these differences, so also ecological and economical considerations, as also social structure of individual groups. These all have to be* studied with reference to psychological background in a spirit of sympathy and service.

Suggested Approach

4. Learned discourses on the Unity of the World, Brotherhood of Man and Fatherhood of God, and plans of great organisations like World Government, League of Nations or United Nations Organisation have been all useful in their own way but they cannot help if we in India merely passively hope for the natural evolution of goodwill and happiness in the world. The demon of group prejudices cannot be overcome and a real democratic order of world happiness cannot be achieved without a study of the origin of each of these prejudices, and without active work for their removal. In the present study, the writer would press for a few essentials :—

(i) Human culture should be treated as composite from the point of view of the anthropologist and ethnologist whose conception of culture covers the whole field of the group's activities, as against the outlook of a politician or an economist or an industrialist or an engineer or a social worker in each field.

(ii) The physical and biological basis of race provides no grounds for assuming superiority in personality and culture. Though blood-group tests and anthropometric measurements provide differences, they are not of a fundamental type to discriminate between one human group and another. As Dahlberg, an authority on race biology, the author of *Race, Reason and Rubbish* puts it " Race is 'reason' when discussed from 'a laudable zeal for discriminating men' but is 'rubbish' when the bounds are exceeded ".

(iii) Castes, tribes, clans, religious groups, practices must be recognised as hard solid facts which cannot be overlooked, even though it may be possible to legislate for the cessation of their legal entity or status or for the omission of all references to caste in census or official records. The habits, manners, and customs of these groups have to be studied with sympathy and with consideration and not in an attitude of sneakish superiority or of contempt.

(iv) Progress of humanity can only be achieved through the personal approach to the individual but approached through the groups. Just as each new born baby has to be given food and nourishment, and great care has to be taken about its physical and mental development, the moral and spiritual food has also to be provided to the adult individual member through the group or society to which it belongs. It is a hopeful sign of the times that both the League of Nations and the United Nations Organisation have begun work in the fact-finding field in various areas, localities and groups before planning for relief for the uplift of the masses.

---

* Studies in Reduction of Prejudice by American Council of Race Relations Chicago, 1948.

Neurosis of Man

5. A remarkable contribution to the study of human behaviour, human relations and group mal-adjustments has been made by * Dr. D. Burrow, the founder of the Lifwynn foundation. He considers the symptoms of individual and society as but the outer aspect of impaired processes that affect the balance of the organism's internal reactions as a whole. In this sense, the human individual is unable to adjust himself to the social conditions owing to the fundamental incapacity of his brain to act as a whole, and to a functional brain twist resident within the organism of man himself. He rightly considers that the problem of man's behaviour is not a problem of politics or economics or of morals based upon personal 'rightness' with its mutable and arbitrary evaluation. It is a problem eternal to man. The neurosis of man is a problem of man's self that man has taken upon himself. It is a problem of man's organism as a species. The time has come for man to face the unilateral system of behaviour — that man alone embodies among all animal species. The moment is at hand for us to take conscious hold of our own unconscious processes by recognising the false cerebral plane upon which they rest. This spirit of individual approach should be somewhat similar to the spirit of Vedanta Philosophy which places the soul above other factors in human psychology. It is by recognising the fundamental unity of the human soul and the universal soul and by accepting that the individual soul is but a part of the universal Soul that we can escape the horrors of group prejudices. The theory of evolution of a soul by its contacts with the family and social groups among whom it lives, connects it with the social group method followed by other psychologists like Adler, Jung and Kardiner. They differ from Freud and give greater importance to the group characteristics and to the hereditary traits than the temporary mal-adjustment of an individual. The reactions, e.g., of an ordinary Hindu to a serpent would be different from that of an American because the hereditary ideas of serpent worship followed by the past generations of the Hindus are likely to affect his psychological responses towards a serpent.

Gregariousness, an Antidote to Group Prejudices

6. A hopeful sign of the problem is that, by nature, man likes to work and live together and is prepared to make sacrifices for living in the society selected by him. Man differs from other animals in his independent personality, yet the independence is over-powered by the " herd " instinct. He is fond of company and, with gregarious instincts, likes to live in flocks or groups. There are still several primitive peoples who prefer to live in isolated huts, as they are so afraid of losing their " strength " by eating and living with others. Similarly the modern civilised man prefers to be the master of his castle and his home ; yet the growth of large cities with numerous localised centres with modern methods of large scale education in schools, colleges and universities, the growing sense of municipal and joint enterprises requiring the use of the vote with adult suffrage and frequency of elections,—all provide means for strengthening group prejudices. At the same time, group institutions like denominational schools and chari-

---

* *The Neurosis of Man, The Biology of Human Conflict, Social Basis and Consciousness* are some of the books written by Dr. Burrow on this subject.

table organisations provide material and opportunities for sublimating these group characteristics for the common good of the community or the nation as a whole. New groups are created by ties of residence, marriage, habits of food, drink and living, intellectual interests, sports, amusements, ties of language and religion. Persons who are strangers get attracted to each other as individuals, and sometimes as families and groups. Experience of jail life among political prisoners and detenus have led to new political and social groups while intellectual interests arising from study in a college or social or political work has led to marriages among members of social groups which would not have been possible otherwise. Formation of queues for essential things of life like food, sugar, kerosene or bus or clothing or medical help or residence, all bring out the human side of the various groups and provide opportunities for fraternization and for social contacts. These opportunities for common goodwill and social unity have to be sought of by the state as opportunities for service and exhibition of goodwill and sympathy of the State for the masses and their difficulties. Courtesy begets courtesy and love begets love, and so also rudeness, mistrust and hatred generate the same evil feelings, which are capable of doing more harm. The aim of a State is not merely to carry out the existing laws but to evolve conditions in which increasing opportunities prevail for happiness, goodwill and peaceful life; the fact of living together itself provides opportunities for the development of the qualities that make for progress and happiness.

Synthesis through Symbiosis

7. **Symbiosis results in synthesis** and the verdict of history is that a conqueror who wins by physical force does not escape the effects of the cultural contacts with the conquered. Witness the earlier contacts between the Dravidians and the Aryans: the pre-Aryan Dravidian India had a culture of its own and had a greater stability than that of the nomadic groups of Aryans who went on colonising as they advanced. During these culture contacts, the Dravidian caste system came to be absorbed by the Aryans and so also the Phallic form of the worship of Shiva and also the dark skinned Krishna came to be first incorporated in Hindu culture. Taking later arrivals like Christians, Muslims and Parsis, they have absorbed not a little of the culture of the older inhabitants and have assimilated their social and ethnic behaviour to a common culture pattern. The Muslims and so also the Parsi settlers in India had imbibed the cultural life of the Hindus to such an extent that the followers of the purity of the religious culture had to take the help of legislature to wean them away from the customs and the practices of their neighbours. Even then the Parsis and the Muslims of India have greater affinities with the people among whom they live than with the followers of their religions in the countries in which their religions originated hundreds of years ago. Even the Sikhs who were originally Hindus, follow most of their manners, customs and social practices. For centuries they have lived together without claiming separate existence and have progressed well under a symbiotic life till the vicissitudes of politics emboldened them to claim separate electorates, separate provinces to live on the basis of separate and individualistic culture. Similarly, but for politics, the Jains, the Lingayats and the Scheduled Castes, and the aboriginal tribes would have lived a symbiotic life and not claimed separate political existence. To prevent

them from forming fissiparous groups, it, is desirable to study their social and economic problems and to suggest remedies for the removal of the disabilities that prevent them from absorbing themselves in synthetic national life.

Bogey of Linguistic Provinces

8. A formidable danger that threatens the unity of India is the bogey of linguistic provinces. The peaceful harmony of the United India has been disturbed by the separation of Pakistan consisting of only 45 millions of Muslims. The remaining 30 millions of Muslims living in the Indian Union are prospering without a murmur of discontent, just as several crores of Muslims live in the secular States of China and in Indonesia. The bugbear of linguistic provinces has been raised under the same kind of political agitation which led to the holocaust of the partition of the country, to the misfortunes of displaced persons, and to the serious problems of their rehabilitation which followed in their wake. Isolation on grounds of linguistic culture is bound to lead to additional financial burdens and new rehabilitation problems especially in the region of borderlands. The undue bitterness that was raised on account of religious differences is being created in the name of linguistic affinities. The ethnic and cultural differences that separate sub-groups of any linguistic group are being ignored on the assumption that a common language would remove them. An impartial research into the causes that led to the origin of the linguistic provinces idea would lead to the discovery of the remedies for removing the causes. Apart from questions of power and personal ambitions of a few, there are no disabilities suffered by any linguistic group that cannot be attended to or safeguards provided for prevention of their recurrence. What these disabilities are and what are the possible solutions are really matters of scientific research and not of political propaganda. If, for example, the Karnatak speaking population of the Bombay Province or the Telugu speaking population of the Madras Province or the Bengali speaking population of Bihar or Orissa or Assam have any real grievances, they can and should be attended to after proper research, study and deliberation. The moment a cry is raised about the sufferings of the people on the borderland of two great linguistic provinces, say between Kanara and Maharashtra or between Orissa and Bihar, or between Bihar and Bengal or between Bengal and Assam or between Maharashtra and Gujarat or between Tamil land and Telugu land areas, the existing group prejudices are fanned into fire and all synthetic harmony obtained by years of symbiosis disappears into thin air.

9. The following provisions in the new Constitution of the Indian Republic regarding the cultural and educational rights and the Directive Principles of State policy, raise hopes that group prejudices of the linguistic type will not be allowed to endanger the national unity of the country :—

"30(1). All minorities whether based on religion or language shall have the right to establish and administer educational institutions of their choice.

"38. The State shall strive to promote the welfare of the people by securing and protecting as effectively as it may, a social order in which justice, social, economic, and political, shall inform all the institutions of the national life.

"39 The State shall, in particular, direct its policy towards securing—

(i) that the citizens, men and women equally, have the right to an adequate means of livelihood;

(ii) that the ownership and control of the material resources of the community are so distributed as best to subserve the common good;

(iii) that the operation of the economic system does not result in the concentration of wealth and means of production to the common detriment;

(iv) that there is equal pay for equal work for both men and women;

(v) that the strength and health of workers, men and women, and the tender age of children, are not abused and that citizens are not forced by economic necessity to enter avocations unsuited to their age or strength;

(vi) that childhood and youth are protected against exploitation and against moral and material abandonment."

Social Service, not Self Interest

10. In a State based on the ideals of social service, there should be little room for group jealousies and bitterness. The groups should be competing with each other not in matters of self-aggrandisement and selfishness but in offering greatest social service to the greatest number. In a country where the average duration of life is as short as 27 years, where infant mortality is as high as 163 per 1000 births and where the general death rate is about the highest 22 per 1000 among the civilised countries of the world, where the average annual income is small, where production per acre of crop is so meagre, and where ignorance, disease and poverty face the country on all sides and where the burning problems of the day demand constant social service, no excuse should be left for petty quarrels in the name of either religion or language or power politics or party shibboleths and jealousies. A practical thinker like Lord Beveridge presses in his Third Report that "the poorer a country is, the greater is the urgency of using rightly its material resources, putting bread and health for all before comforts for any." The amelioration of conditions of work for labour, both for remuneration and housing, is an urgent necessity but it should be accompanied by increased production. This cannot be secured unless society makes up its mind to "work in the service of mankind, not for personal gain, but under the driving power of social conscience." A society which gives itself up to the dominance of the business motive cannot succeed in modern conditions of life. If humanity is not to be torn by warfare and dissensions and if the profit motive is to be subordinate and if the philanthropic motive and sense of brotherhood are to prevent the harm that groups and societies (called by names of castes, tribes, groups or nations) are capable of, they must all believe in the common purpose and common good and be ready to be tied by bonds to serve that national purpose. This national outlook is essential in a poor country like India with its immense problems, vast material and human resources, all of which have to be arranged for the progress of the nation as a whole and not for a group or a province.

Spiritual Background

11. The problem of securing national unity for removal of group prejudices and petty jealousies—which have supported religious and linguistic separatism or isolationist movements either for capital or labour or provided grounds for conflicts of various kinds—should be

comparatively easy in India where the spiritual background of the masses has responded so splendidly to the call of Mahatma Gandhi. The spirit of self-sacrifice based on spiritual values has for centuries been available for all good causes in India; and it is up to the leaders of public opinion to give a correct lead to overcome petty local jealousies and prejudices. Man is everywhere trying to realise his divine nature and rise above the mundane values of human affairs; he ought to be taught to realise the fundamental unity of all human souls—all children of the same motherland and of the same god and to place the good of the society and humanity above that of his self. The ideal of service to the motherland above self should unify all wavering groups who in their ignorance and selfishness value their prejudices so high.

INDIVIDUAL AND GROUP PREJUDICES AND UNITY

TARACHAND ROY

Indian Life, Diversity

'When one lands in Bombay," writes Prof. James Bissett Pratt [*] "the East bursts upon one like the rise of an Oriental sun....which, as every one knows, comes up like thunder in these parts. One feels that he has never seen color before. The streets are alive with it on turban, coat, skirt, loose-flowing trousers, loin-cloth, sari, and bronze and chocolate skin: while jewellery of every description hangs from nose, ear, and encircles neck, arms, fingers, ankles, and toes. A never-ending stream of every caste and religion passes by one with the silence of patient, naked feet. Those with the caste marks so carefully painted on their foreheads are Hindus, while the men with the strange head-gear are Parsees, and most of the bearded men are Mohammedans. Then there are a few Jains too, and an occasional Sikh. The scene is bewildering and it grows the more complex as one's familiarity with it increases. But more bewildering than the costume, color and caste of this multitude are the religions which they embody." Yes, the scene is bewildering if one rivets his eyes on the outside only and does not probe deeper and penetrate into the inside, no matter howsoever long one is engaged in a superficial study of the problem of variegated Indian life and thought which in its deeps is pervaded by an inscrutable power which knits the different parts together into a harmonious whole.

Obstacles to Unity, Superiority Complex

There is no doubt, however, that sometimes sinister forces crop up, both from inside and outside, which try to wreck this unity, and we have always to be not only on the alert but also find ways and means to nip them in the bud or counter their influence. There are several factors which ever and anon threaten the peaceful trend of Indian life and must therefore be radically eliminated.

First of all, there is the so-called superiority complex which eats into the vitals of our national life. We have individuals who consider themselves superior to others either because they possess a higher rank or belong to a higher caste and are thereby quite oblivious of the consequences that accrue from their supercilious behaviour and inconsiderate actions. They should not forget that they poison the atmosphere in which they themselves live and thus spell ruin not only to others but also to themselves. When they espouse the cause of their own racial, intellectual or cultural pre-eminence, they naturally create a gulf between the other people of their nation and themselves, and it is not easy to bridge over this gulf afterwards. This leads to the formation of groups which do not see eye to eye with one another.

[*] "India and its Faiths." London.

As regards the race theory, it is just possible that the genes of one's ancestors go a great way to determine one's high intellectual qualities and laudable temperamental characteristics, but they are not always the *sole* determinants of importance. And there lies the rub. One should never take to sweeping generalizations in any individual case, and still less, of course, when groups are taken into consideration. One should further not underrate the difficulties in clearing up the complexities and intricacies in the interactions of biological and non-biological processes. It is hence advisable not to lay undue stress on genetic equipment or biological inheritance, racial superiority or inferiority. Such stubborn pertinacity has often been a stimulant to perilous conflicts not seldom ending in the annihilation of both the parties concerned.

With respect to intellectual superiority, I am of the opinion that it does not, if divorced from high moral values, deserve an iota of veneration. Intellectual acumen coupled with moral turpitude has in the long run always hurled individuals and nations from the sunny heights of glory into the gloomy abysses of perdition. In no way better are those multi-millionaires who go about behaving like mere beasts of burden or incarnations of vainglorious sumptuousness. You can see through them at the very first glance. They exercise a very disastrous influence over the progressive energies of a nation. They are the focal points of different sorts of antagonisms. Instead of obviating difficulties they create new labyrinths everywhere and thus honeycomb their country with fresh obstacles and points of embarassment. We should give a wide berth to them and steer clear of all their alluring baits and tempting tricks. We should flock to those who are selfless, humble and unprejudiced, and who are full of the manifold experiences of life and conversant with the teachings of the history of the world. Their towering personality stands high above group bickerings. They know what dangers lie ahead when the security of individuals and the cohesion of groups are at stake. They strain every nerve to avert such calamities and cement the bonds of friendship between the one and the many, between individuals and between groups.

Land of Staggering Contrasts

There is no gainsaying the fact that India is a land of contrasts, a land of metaphysical grandeur and stern realities, of immense wealth concentrated in the hands of a few, an infinitesimal part of the nation, and of widespread poverty weighing heavy on unhappy and miserable millions, a land inhabited by men of multifarious interests, duties and ideals, and in spite of this very seldom social and political upheavals are reported from that country, but such is the case only after the achievement of its liberty. India is now wedded to the political creed of democracy, and she can enjoy undisturbed peace, inhabited as she is by the adherents of different parties and faiths, only if she sticks to its principles. All human beings can claim inalienable rights to life and liberty. The small country of Switzerland with its four different languages and other diversity of circumstances is an excellent object-lesson to us in India. Also America is a country worthy of note in this connection. In both these countries the existence of so many different communities, each of which wanted to be free and happy in its own way, compelled them not to withhold from others what they themselves desired so very eagerly, i.e. the right to be free and different from one another, different in language, colour, ideas, occupation and political or religious creeds, and this right to be free and different led to the birth of democracy, not only for individuals but also for groups and communities. "This development of liberty," says Everett Ross Clinchy*, "has taken the course of free enterprise in business, free study, free speech, and free press in sciences and arts; free schools in education; freedom of worship and freedom for social action in religion. Gradually it came to be recognized that groups whose numbers were small should receive the same rights and the same dignity claimed by groups whose bodies were large and powerful. This is an amazing change, for before the democratic revolution small, or 'minority', groups were considered inferior, and were not expected to receive parity of political or economic or social opportunity."

Solution through Democratic Technique

We should see to it that also in India democracy becomes a vital force in everyday affairs. We must gather from the theory of democracy all those principles which are best suited for the actualities of our political and social life and apply them practically to our present problems and given situations. It is of paramount importance to organize all those who are convinced of the worth of democracy into active groups which should establish a democracy of cultures in the future Republic of India, which should bring about a re-orientation of all and make them "fit for team-work in waging peace instead of waging war". We should not think, of course, that all social, political and religious tensions between different persons and communities will entirely vanish, but our repeated efforts to understand each other will surely deal a death-blow to a great number of prejudices which has so long proved to be highly detrimental to our common interests. We have always to bear in mind that the ignorance of the character and culture of other communities will always be a source of great harm. We should hence try our best to acquaint ourselves with the beliefs and practices of other groups. It does not matter if we are not in a position to share their views, but we shall at least not hold them in light esteem or cast slurs on their character and beliefs. We should not lose sight of the fact that we live in a world of hard competition in which a clash of interests is unavoidable, but we can do all that lies in our power to ensure fair play on a civilized plane.

It is idle to expect that we shall one day arrive at identity of religious convictions and thus indulge in no controversies or discussions whatsoever, but we can get to know the beliefs of others better and learn to cherish great respect for them and pull on very amicably with one another notwithstanding our differences. Unity can be achieved not by denying these dissimilarities but by comprehending them. A correct knowledge of the views of others makes for tolerance, and every sane and reasonable person gladly recognizes the validity of the standpoint of another " without forfeiting thereby the truth of his own native insights ", but it is a great pity, indeed, that the number of such persons is not large, so " cribbed, cabined and confined " we are within the four walls of our own conviction. We shall be able to do justice to the religious views of others if we only try to look beyond our own narrow horizon or see what lies on the other side of the mountain that

* "The Right to be Different," Harvard University Press.

bars our gaze at this moment. It is imperative upon us in India to materialize religious unity since it is one of the gravest problems in the life-process of a nation. The situation has in this respect no doubt considerably improved in India in the course of the last two years, and we can still ameliorate it if we intensify personal "informal commerce between religious persons of radically different traditions", to use the words of Willard L. Sperry*. "We are increasingly aware,", continues he, "that we need the correction of an antithetical half-truth to save our own half-truth from dying of inbreeding. But this awareness exists as yet mainly in individuals and small groups, who will have to pioneer across party lines in advance of the laggard societies they represent. Our religious freedom, which was first a right, now takes on the sterner aspect of a religious duty, not merely for the sake of the unity and integrity of our own life, but on behalf of the divided people of the wider world." It is not different in India. We are convinced of the great influence of unity in every sphere of human activity. We know that unity is something dynamic. According to the opinion of ancient philosophers unity has its place among the transcendentals, occupying the same rank as the good, the true and the beautiful.

The worst enemies of unity are prejudices, old as well as new. Most of us are born into an atmosphere, which is saturated with prejudices, religious, social and political. It is very hard for us to get away from them or shake them off, since they have entered into the inmost recesses of our mind. We have literally inhaled them, and they have become in the course of time part and parcel of our breath. Just for this very reason it devolves upon us to get rid of them as soon as possible. Every second of our life throws down the gauntlet to us with the the words: "Will you pick it up or not?" How long had we been meeting out, in the name of religion, the most inhuman and humiliating treatment to the Harijans before the law put a stop to it? We prided ourselves on our knowledge of the oneness of the human and the universal soul (Atman and Brahman) and did not hang our heads in shame when we committed such abominable deeds. The whole of our caste system clamours for a radical and thorough revision and must be overhauled in the light of changed circumstances and new situations. We have to march abreast of the times, otherwise we shall be guilty of the dereliction of duty.

"Local Relations Societies"

We can ban all the tensions that we have spoken of by means of systematic work. We must make serious effort to give practical shape to our objectives. In every town and in every village "Local Relations Societies" should be formed to solve the urgent problems of the people of those places. Let these Relations Societies be of two kinds: (1) official and (2) private. The former should be responsible to the city or village official authorities, and the latter to the committees that have been ushered into existence by the private societies themselves. They should enquire into the food and housing problems and make practical suggestions after very strict and thorough investigations. Secondly, a special Education Council should be appointed to study the school problems of cities and villages. Thirdly, Civic Reform Societies should report on the population question and marriage problems. Fourthly, Good-Will Societies should chalk out a very comprehensive programme

* "Our Present Disunity," Harvard University Press.

to pave the way for a close and fruitful contact between different groups and communities. Schemes should be worked out to fashion new and strong ties between the different people in towns and villages. Social, cultural and political isolationism should be combated everywhere, and anti-social elements should be won over by unremitting work among and for them. Fifthly, competent Agricultural Commissions should be sent to investigate the vital problems of peasants and devise means to help them in their difficulties in the best possible way.

It will be erroneous to think that our path to success will be strewn with roses. We shall have to carve it out with great difficulties—suffering privations and bearing hardships. Nevertheless, there are good reasons to take an optimistic view about the achievement of our aims. We should not forget that mankind has been amenable to amity and concord and is ever inspired by a desire for the betterment of its lot. Let us then clap our shoulder to the wheel and do not allow our fellow-beings to be dragged deeper into the mire. On the contrary, let us plod our way to the heights where the sun shines more brightly and the atmosphere is free from the choking vapours of desperation.

Section II
Religions and Prejudices

HINDUISM, A RETROSPECT AND A REVIEW

R. C. MAJUMDAR

Hinduism, Sphinx among Religions

If any one were to ask me, what is Hinduism, I would not find it easy to answer. It is used as the name of a religion which is professed by 300 million of people in India and has a continued existence for more than four thousand years. Yet it is difficult to give a simple exposition of its doctrines such as would convey its nature to an outsider.

Its Evolution

The reason for this lies in its historical evolution. Leaving aside the Indus Valley Civilisation, whose origin and antiquity are still matters of dispute, the Vedas are acknowledged to be the parent source of Hinduism. But the Vedas, though regarded as *Sruti* or divine revelations, really denote a vast literature of heterogeneous character. The earliest text, the Rigveda, is a collection of prayers and hymns addressed to gods, and the later works contain, among other things, rules and regulations about sacrifice, mystic speculations, sometimes of an abstruse character, many myths and legends, and anecdotes of historical or semi-historical character. They possess great importance as historical documents, for they convey a picture of the life led by the Aryans at the remotest time of which we possess any record. But as fountain-source of a religious system it is difficult to appraise their value. It is not easy to deduce from these texts of varied nature a coherent system of beliefs and practices such as usually forms the basis of a religion. The question is further complicated by the inclusion of sundry matters which have little or nothing to do with religion as we understand this term, but, being a part of divine revelations, enjoy a sanctity and privileged position in the minds of the faithful. Besides, the present Hinduism differs from Vedic religion to such an extent that if a Vedic *rishi* or seer would come to India to-day, he would hardly find any trace anywhere of the religion practised by him. The gods whom he regarded as all powerful have ceased to be worshipped; the new gods taking their place were either altogether unknown or occupied a very minor position in his days; the images of gods, the big temples housing them, and the elaborate mode of worship are all strange innovations; and, above all, the idea of devotion (*bhakti*) to one great god like Siva or Vishnu, even to the extent of complete self-surrender, as the sure and only means to salvation, would be perfectly unintelligible to him.

These and other essential features which transformed the old Vedic religion into Hinduism, form the subject matter of new classes of texts called the Puranas. But the neo-Hinduism derives its inspiration not only from these texts but also from the Smritis, whose authenticity ranks only next to the Srutis or Vedic literature, as well as philosophical works, and other texts of a more definitely religious character. Here, again, the vast extent and diverse types of literature, to which Hinduism owes allegiance, make it difficult to represent the essential features of Hinduism in a simple and intelligible form.

A further complication arises from the fact that these texts do not deal with religious tenets alone but also with various other aspects of life. Even though these were at first of subsidiary nature, they gradually acquired an importance by their inclusion in sacred texts, and ultimately a sort of religious sanctity was attached to them.

Its Features and Anomalies

This process of evolution explains some of the characteristic features of Hinduism. In the first place, its scope was extended so as to cover almost the whole activity of man. A Smriti text, for example, deals with political, economic and social life in minute details, and though often treated from an objective point of view, the facts or principles laid down in these texts came to be regarded as moral or religious injunctions and essential parts of Hinduism. Thus religion embraced almost everything concerning the life of a man, and Hinduism may be best defined as the sumtotal of the life and thought of a Hindu (i.e. inhabitant of ancient India) as envisaged in sacred literature.

The second typical feature of Hinduism was the predominance of the Brahmin class. This is not the proper place to discuss the question whether Brahmins by birth alone could interpret the scriptures, or those who did so came to be regarded as Brahmins. But there is no doubt that the very multiplicity of sacred texts and their complex and conflicting nature necessitated a class of such interpreters and vested them with great power and responsibility. They undoubtedly performed this task with great ability and kept the huge machinery moving. But soon they outlived their utility. Instead of moving with the time as a progressive force, they became conservative and rigid and hence retrograde in character. Power corrupts, and absolute power corrupts absolutely. This is not true in politics alone.

Another typical feature was the contradiction between theory and practice. Perhaps no other religion has elevated the conception of the equality of man to such a high philosophic level as the Vedantic theory that individual souls are mere illusory manifestations of one eternal soul. Yet in practical life no other religion in the world has been more guilty of maintaining invidious distinctions between man and man even of the same religious persuasion.

Again, the most fundamental conception of Hinduism is the high place accorded to soul, as distinguished from the ephemeral body. The nature of the soul and its liberation forms the chief concern of our religious philosophy which almost ignores the body and relegates it to a minor position. Yet in actual practice the physical purity of the body looms large and forms the keystone of our religious architecture. The injunctions about the physical chastity of woman form the best illustration of this.

It was not easy to reconcile the rigid theory of four castes with the actual state of things in society. Hence the most curious and absurd explanations were offered to account for the existence of mixed castes. It illustrates how a normal social phenomenon is invested with religious sanctity and then stands in the way of a frank recognition of social development and obstructs its free progress.

But the same causes which produced these defects and anomalies also gave a fluid and flexible character to Hinduism. It could incorporate new views and doctrines without being troubled by any ideas of inconsistency or incompatibility with the old ones. Thus Vaishnavism was gradually incorporated into Vedic culture though there were wide divergences and even fundamental differences between the two. Siva, the wild god of primitive tribes, and the form of Linga worship, once regarded with undisguised contempt, gradually occupied a prominent place in Hinduism. Even the great Buddha, once described as a demon, came to be regarded as an *avatara* or incarnation of Vishnu, and Buddhism was well on the way of becoming a sect of Hinduism like Saivism and Vaishnavism. Similarly many primitive beliefs and non-Aryan religious practices found a safe refuge in Hinduism.

Hinduism, a View of Life, not a Faith

Thus, strange as it may seem, it is not easy to define Hinduism, or explain precisely what it is or stands for. It has no single prophet like Christ or Muhammad as the source of its inspiration, nor is there a single treatise like the Bible or the Quran to which it can look for guidance and authority. Our sacred texts are many and varied in character, and so are the gods or saints whom we worship and revere. It is difficult to draw up what may be called 'articles of faith' to which one must subscribe in order to become or remain a Hindu. Sects like Saivas and Vaishnavas, which have not unoften proved antagonistic, have prospered under the fostering care of Hinduism which has kept its doors wide open for embracing new faiths and religious practices.

All this may be due to the process of its growth described above, or catholicity of outlook, and perhaps both causes were at work. But however we may look at it, the fact remains that the complex system which is known as Hinduism is, at its best, more a view of life and an attitude of mind than a specific belief or faith. This particular trait seems to distinguish it from all other religions and forms at once its strength and weakness.

To this peculiar characteristic Hinduism owes that freedom of thought in matters both secular and religious which we miss in most other religions. Hinduism never laid down that salvation was the monopoly of any particular religious faith or practice, or that God was to be thought of or worshipped only in a particular form. As a matter of fact, a Hindu might very well doubt or even deny the existence of God, or hold any belief about the origin of the earth and its relation to the Sun, Moon and stars, without incurring odium, far less any penalty, with which he would be visited in Christendom in the Middle Ages.

Freedom of Thought but Restriction of Action

But while the mind of a Hindu was absolutely free, his hands were heavily tied. He could think as he liked, but almost every act of his life was prescribed by authority to an extent unknown in any other religion. He had no freedom to marry whom he chose; to eat or drink whatever, whenever, or with whosoever he liked; to take to any particular vocation or profession that suited him. His whole life was a sort of rigid routine laid down without any reference to his personal habits and tastes, and from birth to death he had to move in a narrow groove from which he could deviate only at great peril. Thus Hinduism took away with one hand what it gave with the other. For real freedom of thought is hardly compatible with the rigid uniformity of action sanctioned by religion. Unquestioned and implicit obedience to such a code of conduct renders a man unwilling, and gradually incapable, to exercise free judgment, and as an inevitable consequence he becomes impervious to reason and argument. Of course, better minds revolt, and either win or perish in fight, as testified to by the history of dissident sects. But average man succumbs to the steady process of regimentation to which he is subjected from birth to death. Free thinking being an impediment to an easy and smooth way of living, he unconsciously becomes a part of the machine. Life becomes easy and peaceful, but it ceases to become the life of a rational being. Good government is no substitute for self-government, and an imposition of even the best moral and social order in the name of divine authority, followed by irrational acceptance, degrades the human spirit by destroying the powers of judgment and sense of moral and social values.

It may appear somewhat curious that Hinduism should combine the utmost freedom of thought with the most severe restrictions of action. But perhaps one was, at least to some extent, the necessary corollary of the other. A society or community, in order to be a homogeneous unit, must have some common bond. In religious sects or communities, this is usually furnished by the commonness of faith and belief. But as this was not a very prominent characteristic of Hinduism, a rigid uniformity of action took its place. In other words, the test or distinctive badge of Hinduism came to be, not so much the religious view that one held but his social life and practices. This is true even to-day. An orthodox Hindu may, with impunity, hold most extraordinary views about man and God and the relation between the two, but would not dare keep his daughter unmarried beyond the age of 12, or marry her on a day not regarded auspicious for the purpose, and with a boy, otherwise suitable, but not conforming to the conditions prescribed by the Smritis more than a thousand years ago.

When India first imbibed the western ideas, the Hindu youth openly uttered all sorts of blasphemy about his god and religion, and the society did not mind. But the moment he took beef, made a voyage to England, or married a widow or a girl quite suited to his tastes but not belonging to his caste, he would cease to be a Hindu. Hinduism never cared for what one thought, but bothered very much for what one did; for nothing but this uniformity of action in daily life served as the common bond to keep alive, as a separate entity, the fraternity called Hinduism.

Thus came into being what may be best described as a theocratic society, on the analogy of the term theocratic state i.e. a state in which the temporal and spiritual power is vested in the same individual or in which the state is governed on principles sanctioned by religious authority, such as the Caliphate or Muslim State of which we hear so much to-day. The idea of such a state has justly been denounced in modern days. But the evils in a theocratic state do not differ in kind, but only in degree, from those in a theocratic society. It would be ridiculous indeed to suggest that religion, through revealed texts or their traditional interpreters, should dictate the form of government that we should set up in our country, the way in which we should exercise our civil and political right, or the economic system and foreign policy which we should adopt. But a little reflection will show that the control of religion over society is sometimes equally ridiculous. If it is preposterous for religious authority to dictate how I should vote at a General Election, is it less so when it decides for me how I should marry, and what and with whom I shall eat or drink? It will perhaps be argued that marriage is a sacrament, and the food being the nourishment for the body which sustains and shapes the mind and spirit, they come within the purview of religion. But similar arguments have been used in respect of political, legal, and economic institutions, and that is why the laws, political principles and economic doctrines were incorporated in the Smritis. The fact has to be recognised that marriage and food are primarily questions of sociology and hygiene; these sciences have made striking progress in recent times, and should be studied independently as a means to human welfare, and not treated as a mere appendage to religion. In other words, we should regulate marriage, food, and such other things in the light of accumulated knowledge and experience, and approach the problem only from the point of view of social welfare and development of health. This is all the more necessary as the laws of marriage or food are bound to vary with time and circumstances, as well as individual tastes and requirements. The old Hindus evidently realized this and hence we find radical and revolutionary changes taking place in both. Is there any Hindu to-day who would not shudder at the very idea of levirate and beef-eating which were at one time ordinary practices of everyday life? To hold the present customs regarding marriage and food as sacrosanct, and therefore not amenable to any change, is as ridiculous or irrational as to revive those old practices on the same ground.

Need to Secularize Hindu Society

In India both law and government, including public finance and industry, were once regulated to a large extent by the Smritis, but gradually they have shed this religious character. It has now been publicly declared, amid universal applause, that India shall be a secular state. That is indeed a right step in the direction of progress. But the process would not be complete, if we do not proceed further and make the society also a secular one. It does not mean that there should not be social rules and regulations and every individual should be at liberty to do whatever he likes, any more than a secular state would abolish all laws and give perfect license to every individual to go in his own way. It means that men should be at liberty to frame social laws and regulations with a view to the welfare and progress of the society alone, without being subjected to any undue influence of past revelations or hopes of future reward in heaven. In other words, Hinduism should be confined to the sphere that properly belongs to religion and must not be allowed to encroach upon state or society which falls beyond its purview.

What, then, it may be asked, will remain of Hinduism? The answer is simple. It will serve its main object if it helps the individual in his quest for salvation. But it can do much more. We shall regard the spiritual ideas and experiences inherited from our forefathers as a rich and precious heritage, and maintain and develop that catholic spirit and liberal attitude of mind which has been the greatest contribution of Hinduism to the civilisation of the world. Hinduism teaches us that the *dharma* it envisages is not a mere collection of creeds to be imposed by force, or a garb to be put on only on ceremonial occasions. It is a mode or attitude of mind that should permeate our whole life, give colour to our thoughts and visions, and influence all our actions. It ought to shape our conception of what is good or bad, and of the ultimate end at which we shall aim. The spiritual ideas of Hinduism should thus form the background of our policy and supply directives to those forces which guide us in different walks of life.

Need of Rational Thought

The spiritual ideas of Hinduism may thus shape our ideas of state, society, and international relations in a way very different from what prevails in the modern world. We may have a clearer view and perhaps more correct grasp of what constitutes the real values in life, and the true welfare of state and society. This may be illustrated by a concrete example. The Hindu view of life is based on a harmonious pursuit of the four chief conceivable objects in life viz., *dharma* (religion), *artha* (wealth), *kama* (enjoyment of senses) and *moksha* (salvation). In other words it insists on a balance of spiritual and temporal pursuits as the best means of attaining happiness. Neither striving for material wealth, nor asceticism or a spirit of renunciation should be eschewed altogether or carried to the extremes, the neglect or the excess of either being detrimental to real happiness. It also teaches us the universal brotherhood of man, or rather its essential unity, as all individual beings are regarded as parts of the one eternal soul. If these principles guide us in our political and social legislation and international relations, we may avoid the pitfalls which have led the countries of the west into a desperate situation by putting the whole emphasis on national greatness and interpreting it in terms of its material wealth and power. We may base our policy on the conviction that greatness does not depend upon material wealth alone, realising all the while that wealth and power are not to be looked upon as ignoble ends in themselves. Humanity has lost the balance of life and is rushing headlong towards destruction. India may offer a new way of looking at national and international questions. But these are details which must be worked out in a rational spirit of inquiry after we have got rid of the incubus of religion that strangles our free thoughts and movements in every walk of life.

Above all, it is only by divesting Hindu religion of its accessories in other spheres of life that we may emphasise its essential features and avoid the usual error of mistaking the husk for the grain. People have come to believe that by following the rules about food, purification, untouchability, etc. they fulfil all the obligations that religion imposes upon them. As Swami Vivekananda once exclaimed, in anquish of heart, the Hindu religion is now confined to the kitchen. How far external forms and ceremonials can override morality and religion is remarkably illustrated by a female character in a Bengali novel of Sarat Chandra. She publicly took pride in the fact that although she lived with a paramour of lower caste for twenty years, she never allowed him to enter her kitchen! This is the inevitable tragedy of mixing up religion with social laws. To use a parable, Hinduism was like a precious jewel enclosed in a casket. This was handed down from generation to generation and zealously guarded. In course of time the jewel was lost, but nobody took notice of it and continued to guard the empty casket with the utmost zeal. Hinduism has lost the costly jewel and its outward observances and ceremonials are merely the empty casket. It is high time that we should throw it off and institute a search for the jewel itself. We should not also commit the mistake of putting it again in a casket and conceal it from public view.

RELIGIOUS PREJUDICES AS A CLOG ON NATIONAL UNITY

P. C. DIWANJI.

Origins of Religious Prejudices

It is undeniable fact that the population of this land is sub-divided into numerous groups and sub-groups, each having its own religious beliefs, ways of approach to the deity and modes of life. Individuals from amongst them having the same intellectual level or cultural training are capable of some concerted actions in matters of common concern. Nevertheless, the gulfs that divide them on the emotional plane are found on occasions to be unbridgeable, when those are occasions on which sentimental urges have a free scope. It is easily understandable why it is so. Every child receives from its parents some degree of religious and moral training upto the age of adolescence when the dormant faculty of independent thinking begins to function. This training consists of compelling obedience to certain precepts based on certain religious beliefs, ways of approach and modes of life impressed on their minds without explaining the reasons why they should not be deviated from. These naturally create certain inhibitions in the young hearts, the seat of emotions. These are confirmed, totally or partially, when a youth begins to move about freely amongst the members of other groups or sub-groups, according as they are deeply or superficially impressed on his or her heart in its earlier age. To the extent to which they are confirmed, they become the fountain-source of inherent likes and dislikes, resulting in the inspiration of love towards some and hatred towards others, which are the causes of the senses of oneness and separateness.

These prejudices or pre-conceived notions are not however the determining factors in all the matters of common concern on the physical plane. A general survey of the history of the wars, which have taken place in the civilised portions of the globe, shows that whereas on the one hand believers in the same deity and votaries of the same culture had not been able to combine together against a common foe from the religious standpoint and has fought bitterly amongst themselves on certain occasions, believers in different deities and votaries of antagonistic cultures had made common cause against a foe believed to be common from the secular point of view. The most glaring instance of the former is that of some of the Rajput rulers having assisted the Moghuls in subduing other Rajput rulers and that of the latter is that of Hindus, Musalmans, Parsis, and Christians having combined together to demand Home Rule from their British rulers, although most of them had not ceased to have faith in their religion by birth and had been adhering to their respective cultures so far as they could do so in the midst of the changed environments. And we know to our cost that even residence in the same country is no guarantee of loyalty to a common cause when other passions are aroused by interested parties. Mr. Jinnah, who was once a Congress President and an ideal fighter against the alien rulers, did not shrink from raising a revolt against it and aiding the same rulers in resisting the demand made by it forcefully, when he felt that under the national government formed by the combined Congress executive there would be no room for communal representation and separate electorates. And take the case of the Congress Hindus. We see before our very eyes mutual accusations and open ruptures springing up amongst them in several provinces ever since the transfer of power by the British on dividing the country into two Dominions. The persistant cry of the Andhras, Kanarese, Maharastrians, and a section of the Sikhs for the formation of separate linguistic provinces also points to the sad truth that the same countrymen and co-religionists, who co-operated with the leaders in wresting power from the hands of another nation, would not selflessly support them when they begin to wield it.

Greed, Source of Evil

The reason for the defection of the Moslem Leaguers from the congress fold was the confident expectation fostered by the conduct of British administrators, that if they remained adamant they would succeed in their object of getting separate slices of the country for themselves or at least in getting satisfied their jealous instinct of preventing the transfer of power into the hands of the Congress as the representative of the nation as a whole. That for the revolt of the groups of Congress Hindus and Sikhs is that they cannot bear to see their comrades in office secure in their saddles till an election takes place under the new constitution, riding their hobby horses recklessly and enjoying the loaves and fishes of office. The Hindus of divergent linguistic regions are the source of constant trouble to the Congress High Command because they are jealous of those of the other regions in the same states because the latter being in the majority have secured a larger number of influential positions in the body politic and some of them, being confident of their positions, openly favour the residents of their own regions in various ways at the expense of the states, and leave them to chew the cud as they did in the days of the domination of the British.

Is there any reasonable ground for hoping that all this envy, greed and hatred would be eradicated from the hearts of the disgruntled and the boisterous if some formulas based on a policy of appeasement are evolved and implemented ? Is there any guarantee that fresh groups on other lines would not crop up to make the minds of the men then in power uneasy ? The answer to the first question is in the affirmative but that to the second in the negative because when you approach the dissidents from any movement in a spirit of conciliation and they have a sincere desire to do good to the nation as a whole, it is highly possible that they may come round to work together for the national welfare in a spirit of service. But if their hearts are swayed by narrow selfish ambitions, the particular individuals may be appeased, as were the Moderates or Liberals, when the British threw open a few posts of members of the executive councils and ministers during the interim and the diarchical regimes. Such restoration of peace was, however, of short duration, for within five years of the establishment of diarchy a fresh group of the Home Rule Leaguers was formed and began to agitate for Home Rule, which meant independence in internal affairs. Similarly the Socialists and the rebel Congressmen began to show their teeth within two years of the attainment of independence.

Moral Uplift Needed

The proper remedy for the establishment of an era of lasting internal peace and harmony is to eradicate the Spirit of evil itself from the body politic as far as it is humanly possible to do so. I anticipate many from amongst my readers springing up from their seats and thinking aloud that this is but an old platitude as the inaugurators of all the higher religious systems known as Hinduism, Jainism, Buddhism, Confucianism, Taoism, Shintoism, Judaism, Zaroastrianism, Christianity and Mahomedanism had held out the same promise when they began to get supporters but their devout followers, not seeing its fulfilment, gave currency to varying interpretations which have been the cause of the rise of numerous sects and sub-sects within each of them. It must be painfully acknowledged that this objection is well-founded. Let alone the distant past. The movements started by the Saints Kabir and Nanak, when they saw Musalmans fighting with the Hindus, Jains and Buddhists and also amongst themselves, have been started to create a feeling of fraternity between the different sections of the population in Northern India. on the basis of the dogmas that God was one only, that prophets of different regions speaking different languages have given different names to Him in order that those to whom they were imparting the knowledge which had come to them through revelation as a matter of grace from Him may grasp the meaning of what they had said and that the different modes of worship recommended by them were but the different paths leading to the same destination, out of which one can choose any that suits one's temperament and environments. Instead of leading to the extinction of divergence in creeds it led to the addition of one more, namely that of Sikhism, to the already existing ones. The attempt of the Emperor Akbar to establish an eclectic religion, called Deen-e-Ilahi, the dogmas whereof had been decided upon as the result of considerable and impartial research studies, and to put an end to the independent authorities of the various religious heads, by putting himself up as the spiritual head of the new religion, was proved to be infructuous in his very life-time. I also anticipate a warning from some quarters that the problem which Akbar was required to tackle, was much simpler than it is at present, for whereas the number of Christians then in India was infinitely small, there were not the Sikh and Anglo-Indian communities to think of and the discoveries of modern science, whose application to the problems of life, both public and private, which has served as a powerful agent for compelling the acceptance of the European culture of the secular type based on riches as the best that had yet been evolved by man, had not yet been made.

Social Reconstruction on Vedic Lines

Although these are facts which must be taken into consideration while suggesting a remedy, they are not the only ones which go to determine the possibility or otherwise of the remedy which I am going to suggest being successful in the present conditions. The others are (1) that the democratic principle that whenever there is a difference of opinion on a particular point, the opinion of the majority of the population should prevail ; (2) that, although, from the point of view of extent of territory, India has suffered by the creation of two dominions, both have gained the liberty and the scope to establish a new order of society according to the genius of its citizens and its past traditions, and that being so, the followers of the indigenous religions of India, who have inherited a rich legacy of traditions from their ancestors extending over a period of not less than 4,000 years, have an opportunity to prove to the world once more as their ancestors had done several times before this land was overrun by the fanatical hordes of the folllowers of Mahomedanism, that the principle on which their social order had been originally founded are of so universal a nature that they can serve as the foundation for erecting any superstructure suited to the conditions prevailing in any age in order to bring order out of the chaos which may have resulted from the clash of different class of civilizations. It is an undeniable fact of the history of civilization as opposed to barbarism that, whereas numerous other civilisations like the Sumarian, Egyptian, Assyrian, Persian, Greek, and Roman succumbed before the onslaughts of the adherents of a more powerful one, the ancient Indian has survived to this day in spite of its having been attacked from within by the Jains and Buddhists and from without by the Persians, Greeks, Sakas, and other trans-border tribes from the north-west and the Portuguese, Dutch, French, and British from the western sea board. The foreign elements that had been mixed with the indegenous till the seventh century A.D. were absorbed in the latter and made to forget their foreign affiliations but those that entered this land since then, either to seek shelter or to rule over the land or to carry on trade or to start industries, have kept up their individualities and the Musalmans from amongst them have even succeeded in getting the country divided between them and the remaining inhabitants. Still the problem is not solved even so far as they are concerned because their number is too large to be accommodated within the limits of the portions placed at the disposal of their leaders. Although this circumstance gives rise to clashes occasionally because those of them who reside there wish to establish there an exclusively religious society on the Islamic model, the presence of several millions of their co-religionists in India will give an opportunity to the authorities there to demonstrate to the world that the Indian social order is so broad-based as to enable several religious communities to live together peacefully under a government dominated over by the catholic members of one of them.

How can they do that is, therefore, the problem before them. The way which I have to suggest for doing so is to organise a new social order from amongst the citizens without regard to their religions by birth on the broad ancient Indian lines which were adopted by the sages of the early Vedic age when the quarrel between the Brahmans, the protagonists of spiritual culture, and the Kshatriyas, the protagonists of material culture, was finally settled. Those lines were that, there should be a division of functions between the members of the four classes into which the then society was divided, in view of their inherent characteristics and adaptability as proved so long by the pursuit of certain occupations. Thus it was that when the institution of kingship was first founded, the supreme authority in the state fell into the hands of the Kshatriyas but there also fell on them the responsibility to protect the inhabitants of the forests and villages as well as of the towns and to be guided by the advice of the priests and the people, the Brahmins and the Vaisyas. The task of keeping the torch of knowledge burning brightly by paying devoted attention to it in a spirit of self-secrifice, indifference to the objects of sense-perception, capacity to bear hardships, fortitude and straightforwardness, fell to the lot of the former. Being the repositories of learning they were occasionally called upon to assist the rulers and the people to guide them and to officiate at the sacrifices and the diarchical regimes. Such restoration of peace was, however, undertaken by them. The people of average intelligence were left to pursue the callings of growing crops, tending cattle and eagaging in trade, commerce and industry. They looked upto the Brahmins for guidance and to the Kshatriyas for protection. These three alone were the intelligent classes. They were mutually dependent not only in the matter of their functions but also in that of the wealth, the medium of exchange. The Brahmins depended for their means of livelihood on the sacrificial fees, reward and pious gifts received from the members of the two other classes. The Kshatriyas were dependent on the taxes which the law authorised them to recover from those who were engaged in agriculture, cattle breeding, commerce, trade and industry. The Brahmins and Vaisyas were dependent upon the Kshatriyas for ensuring freedom from molestation while engaged in their peaceful occupations while the Kshatriyas and Vaisyas were dependent upon the Brahmins for guidance in matters both spiritual and temporal, especially the former. All three had an equal access to the literary treasures but while the latter devoted their lives solely to replenish them from time to time, the two former practically severed their connection with them from the time they became engaged in their occupations except to the extent to which they were of practical use to them in their worldly pursuits. The non-intelligent class of the Sudras had to remain satisfied with earning their livelihood by serving under the members of the three intelligent classes, and acquiring such learning and wisdom as they could acquire by observation and precept from the others.

The earliest mention of these classes in literature is to be found in the Purusa-hymn of the 10th. Mandala of the Rgveda. That is a Mandala which according to the researches of the oriental scholars falls in the group of six Mandalas composed in the Later Vedic Age. But since there and in the Bhagavadgita these classes are represented as having been created by the Lord of Creation, it is reasonable to infer that they had come into vogue from such an earlier age preceding that of the composition of the hymn, that the specific name of the sage who was principally responsible for the recognition of that classification had been forgotten and his spiritual designation given to him by his contemporaries, because of his having evolved order out of chaos, was only remembered. That these were dynamic, interchangeable classes, not static, mutually exclusive castes, and that the principle of division was the inherent characteristic and the pursuit of specific callings determined by personal fitness and individual choice, is again clear from the Bhagavadgita. It has been established by research scholars of international reputation that it formed part of the original Bharata Epic and has, owing to the sanctity attached to it ever since its composition, been preserved in its nascent purity, and that, although variations in the readings of some of its verses and some additional stanzas and half-stanzas have been found in the Kashmir rescension, they therefore discovered a score of years ago that there is absolutely no difference between the two rescensions so far as the stanzas in the 4th and 18th chapters thereof pertaining to the point under consideration here are concerned.

Evils Rooted in Western Social Structure

I can realise the difficulty likely to be felt by those brought up in purely western surroundings in accepting a division of the Indian population under the contemplated new social order even though based on the said moral and spiritual principles. To them my answer is that the principle of "liberty, equality and fraternity" which the French Revolution has made popular is alright as an idea, that it has been accepted in our Constitution by enacting the provisions in part III thereof bearing the heading "Fundamental Rights" but that the same Constitution also contains part XVIII bearing the heading "Emergency Provisions" which enable the President to suspend the operation of the former in times of emergencies. Just as the latter are provisions therein enabling limitations to be imposed on political rights, there is Item No. 5 in the Concurrent List in Schedule VII to the Constitution enabling the Union and State Legislatures to pass legislative measures embodying social as well as economic plans for the establishment of a new social order suited to the modern conditions. And the Government of India has already appointed a Planning Commission. In the economic sphere there are already the Upper, Upper-Middle, Lower-Middle and Poor Classes based on the western model. That model has come into existence even in the western countries as the result of industrialisation based on scientific discoveries the earliest of which do not date earlier than the middle of the 18th century. It is acknowledged that this economic-social order is the cause of class clashes inside each nation and of wars between nations and groups of nations. Karl Max was the first to think over the problem of reducing the possibility of such catastrophies and to suggest a new social order based on a recognition of the facts that capitalists were powerless to manufacture goods without the active co-operation of the labourers and that though individually they were not in a bargaining position, collectively they were. It was as the result of the popularisation of this doctrine of Marxism that the Russians revolted against the Czar and, after wresting power from his hands, founded the Communist Union of Soviet Republics, during the continuance of the first world war. At the end of that war, the Germans banished their Kaiser and founded a Fascist Republic, which soon proved itself to be a republic founded with the object of establishing the suzerainty of the German nation over all other civilised nations of Europe, Africa, and probably Asia also, on the strength of its military and naval forces organized by the use of its superior scientific skill. A similar Fascist regime was started by Mussolini in Italy and both combined to defy the old Imperialistic European powers. The latter, not finding their combination powerful enough to meet their challenge, sought the aid of the U.S.A. When they got it, Japan started its conquest of Asia. The combined might of western and Russian powers succeeded in winning the Second World War but ever since the day of the armistice in France, the British and the Americans on the one hand and the Russians on the other are mustering their strength to prepare for a Third World War for the final decision of the question whether the people of the world as a whole would like to be governed according to the Soviet System or the western system of democracy. Thus there is every possibility of a major war breaking out at any moment and if it does, every thinking man agrees that it will result in the destruction of men and property on a far larger scale than the last one did. All this has taken place within the course of this first half of the 20th century and so the eyes of all thinking men not involved in politics are turning towards India in the hope that it, having now been placed in a position to work out its own destiny according to its own genius, will do that in such a way as to serve as an example for the war-weary nations of the western hemisphere to copy.

Westernism or Vedism

Now therefore is the time when the knowledge, foresight, statesmanship, and courage of the men at the helm of affairs in India will be put to the severest test. They have to make their choice for the basis of their policy between the moral and spiritual principles enunciated and acted upon by their patriarch who was so unegoistic as to allow his name to be merged in the Almighty along with his soul, and any one of the two offshoots of the politico-economic principles propounded by Karl Marx, that narrow visioned pupil of the German philosopher Hegel.

Religion of a particular institutional type may not be looked upto for guidance in this secular state but philosophy cannot and should not be ignored. The above principles of Indian origin are the principles of the Karma-yoga philosophy as expounded in the Gita and summarised in its last chapter. If it is intended that the Indians should be happy and prosperous as well as contented and be the guides of the bewildered nations of the world on the path of progress towards man's ultimate destiny, the proper line of action is clearly in that direction. It is not at all necessary to adopt the nomenclature which has become associated with the name "Hindu" and the system of castes since the advent of the Greeks in the 2nd. century B. C. It is enough if the principles are accepted as a guide and attempted to be acted upon as far as may be possible in the present circumstances prevailing in this country and the world at large. It seems from the announcement of our worthy President at the Haradwar Gurukul on the 5th. March that "Bharat now demands the services of selfless and competent men and women as ministers, legislators, administrators, public workers and technicians," that he and his Ministers are fully aware of the high ideal above alluded to and are only waiting for the right psychological moment to take adequate steps to realise it. Would that such a moment may soon arrive and that bearing in mind the adage that example is better than precept, as they did this year in the matter of a voluntary cut in their salaries, they may prove by their voluntary action that they have full faith in that ideal and try to realise it with courage and fortitude.

It would not be presumptuous to add a word of caution. Legislation on the right lines will be necessary but moral and spiritual uplift can be secured and hypocracy can be banned more effectively by the spread of education on the right lines as well through reliable non-official agencies as through the Universities re-modelled on the simple ancient Indian lines with due regard of course to the needs of the present age, as had been done by the late Poet Rabindra Nath Tagore at the Vishvabharati.

ISLAMIC LAW AND CUSTOM

A. A. A. FYZEE

Islamic Law, Character and Principles

Islamic Law has co-existed with other systems of jurisprudence for fourteen centuries in a dozen lands and among diverse peoples. While retaining its peculiar characteristics, it has fully mingled with different juristic standards and distinct ethical norms. In essence it is a religious law, a law based upon the sanction of the Almighty Himself, working through human conscience. "Jurisprudence" says a well known definition, attributed to Imam Abu Hanifa, "is the soul's *consciousness* (or cognition) of its rights and obligations".

The law of Islam and its concepts were first introduced into India by the early Arab traders, who settled on the Western and Southern Coast of India even before Muhammad b. Qasim's invasion of Sindh. Later when the Muslim conquerors came and established their rule, Muhammadan Law became the law of the land; and still later, with the advent of the British, the question arose whether it should be retained or abolished. And they wisely decided to follow the policy of the Mughal rulers of India and allowed both Hindus and Muslims to retain their own peculiar systems of law.

The object of this paper is to examine some of the fundamental juristic notions of Islam and compare them with those of Hinduism, to consider some of the important customs, to discover the causes of tension and disagreement and to find a way, if possible, to synthesize the divergent elements in order to create a unified culture and national consciousness. We shall begin by trying to understand the fundamental principles of Islamic Jurisprudence.

Islamic Law is based upon the dogma that it is God-made; in this respect it is at one with Hindu Jurisprudence. The Shariat (sacred law) is, according to the jurists, based upon four corner-stones:

I. *Koran*, the word of God,
II. *Hadith*, the word of the Prophet,
III. *Ijma*, concensus of opinion among the learned,
IV. *Qiyas*, analogical deductions of the classical jurists.

It is therefore analogous to the Dharma which is founded upon the *Sruti* (that which is heard) and the *Smriti* (that which is written). The first may be likened to the Revelation, as it is found in the *Koran*; the second embraces the work of illuminated rishis throughout the ages. Thus in both the systems, God is the ultimate focal point; but human endeavour is given its proper importance. In terms of modern jurisprudence, it may be said that God is a legal fiction used by the jurists to create the ethical and moral sanctions for obedience to the law. Both in the Dharma and the Shariat, the ethical considerations are supreme and of primary importance.

In countries which are predominantly Muslim, we find three classes of cases. The Muhammadan Law in its original purity is hardly applied anywhere, except perhaps in Saudi Arabia. The vast majority of Muslim countries have a mixture of modern law and the ancient jurisprudence. Illustrations of this may be found in India, Pakistan, Palestine, Syria, Lebanon, Persia and Indonesia. And lastly, there is one case where a predominant Muslim country has completely secularized the law, and adopted the Swiss Civil Code and the Italian Criminal Code for all its nationals, and this is found in Turkey.

In India, we have two different processes which modify the sacred law; first, legislation, like the Wakf Acts and secondly, the influence of custom, although since the Shariat Act, custom has lost its importance in most Muslim communities. If the desired end is unification, it must still be borne in mind, that however small a minority is, it would be unwise to employ a steam-roller process to iron down all differences and produce a homogeneous pattern. The process of unification must be based not on force or coercion, but on the persuasive logic of national awakening and the development of social ideas.

Let us now take specific instances to illustrate our point.

Marriage and Divorce

In the laws of marriage and divorce, there is a fundamental difference. Hindu law treats marriage as a religious sacrament; Muslim law, as a civil contract. Now, in spite of this cleavage, social workers have realized that an unbreakable marriage is in some instances a terrible burden, while, it is also felt acutely, that a *nikah* capable of dissolution by mere words, pronounced at any time and even without cause, may result in great hardship. Hence irrespective of the law, society itself creates moral standards which insist on the sacredness of the marital tie among Muslims, and on a just scheme of divorce for Hindus, and millions of people of both communities follow the same social standards, and the so-called evil effects of law are to a large extent nullified.

The laws of marriage in India give rise to a number of problems. An acute one is that of inter-communal marriage. The vast majority of people, while not entirely opposed to such marriages, are still of the opinion that in the present conditions of the country, it is better to avoid them. Secondly, there are a few persons who are entirely against such unions and consider them as unlawful connexions and as such favour the extreme view that the children of such unions should be deemed to be illegitimate. And lastly, there are a few enthusiasts who are ardent advocates of such marriages, believing that it is only by such means that internal harmony and friendship can grow on a nation-wide scale.

Whatever view one may adopt, it is impossible to deny that there is no satisfactory law of civil marriage in India. If a Hindu wishes to marry a Muslim, such a union is prohibited by the laws of both the communities, and recourse is therefore had to the special marriage Act of 1872. Under this Act, both parties have to renounce their religion before marrying. This is a mockery of the law. For, the people merely renounce their respective religions in order to legalize their marriage; they do not in reality give up their religious convictions. Now, if we could enact a proper law of civil marriage, unaffected by religion, that would constitute a considerable advance. In addition to the case mentioned, if a Muslim marries a Christian or a Jew, certain complications arise and no satisfactory answer can be given to some of the legal problems.

The best solution appears to be that a permissive code of marriage and divorce should be enacted, whereby any person could by a simple declaration declare himself to be governed by that code, without renouncing his religion. After all, even the most religious would probably concede that living in sin is a lesser crime than renouncing one's religion, and hence after a few years of trial, this permissive code of marriage and divorce would have a chance of becoming a part of the regular law of the land.

Laws of Inheritance

Let us now briefly consider the laws of Inheritance. In this branch of the law, Muslim law divides the heirs into three classes. Class I consists of those persons to whom a specific share is allotted by the Koran, and they are mostly females. Class II consists of male agnates, who represent the tribal heirs according to ancient Arabian custom. Class III consists of females and cognates, both male and female, who were given a share of the inheritance for the first time by the Koranic reform.

It will thus be seen that on the whole women are treated more generously in Islam in this branch of the Law than in Hinduism. For in Hindu law, the widow, the daughter and the sister get comparatively smaller rights, whereas in Islam, they get specific shares of the inheritance. For example, a Hindu being a member of a joint family dies and leaves a widow surviving him. She is entitled ordinarily only to maintenance whereas in Muslim law she is entitled to a two-anna or four-anna share, depending on whether she has children or not. She obtains one-eighth of the husband's property if there are children, and one-fourth if there are none.

Although the treatment of the widow in Islam is slightly better, modern systems of law in Europe give her far greater rights; and she may obtain, not only one-half of the estate absolutely, but may also retain for her life an interest in the whole of the estate in some cases. Thus the spirit of modernism impels the Hindu or Muslim widow to ask for greater rights and it is commonly to be observed in India that careful and far-sighted husbands make proper provision for their widows during their life time, by gift, trust or instance. This shows that society is constantly moving ahead and legislation can only make headway when things become unbearable. In other words, law is conservative, and ought to be so, for unless certain ideas are crystallised by society, there would be dangers in precipitate legislation based upon attitudes of mind which may lead to results not contemplated even by those who advocate the reforms.

The proper remedy in all these cases is again Permissive laws. If a satisfactory code of Inheritance is placed upon the Statute Book, giving every citizen of India the chance to follow it if he so desires, but not otherwise, a new opportunity will arise and people will gradually take advantage of it. If a man wishes to be governed by a simple and modern system of inheritance as is laid down in the Succession Act, for instance, it should not be necessary for him to renounce his religion. This is the position now; and it is a position which is hardly to be found in any of the Western countries.

Customary Law

Customary Law is an important branch of law in India. Full effect is given to custom in the Hindu system, where it is stated that an ancient and well-founded custom may have the effect of abrogating the written text of the law. Such a doctrine is not to be found in Islam; Muhammadan law, in the main, gives greater importance to the law itself, and yet we find that custom has eaten into the core of the law in all countries where Islam exists, and has produced interesting social results.

In India, we are now governed by the Shariat Act, 1937, which has to a large extent abrogated custom in the case of Muslims, but prior to that several instances of customary law were to be found in India, where both Muslims and Hindus were governed by similar customs.

It is difficult to say what is happening now, but in the Punjab the *riwaj-i-am* to a large extent supersedes personal law. In the Malabar, the matriarchal system of Marumukattayam law governed both Hindus and Muslims. Similar instances can be quoted from Indonesia, Egypt, Syria and other countries where a considerable Muslim population exists. The effect of custom upon the Islamic system is also very ably discussed by a modern jurist, Dr. S. Mahmassani, in his *Philosophy of Jurisprudence in Islam* (an Arabic work, published in Beirut, 1946), where he shows that the Islamic Law has shown its adaptability to the existing social and economic conditions.

Wherever custom applies, it tends to follow the dictates of the economic urges of society. In Bombay, for instance, the Khojas were governed by the customary laws of inheritance whereby the daughters were deprived of their share of the inheritance as laid down by the Koran. But the Khojas are themselves a prominent business community, converted to Islam from Hinduism and a considerable proportion among them were not at all happy at the prospect of fragmentation of property and division of business assets and good will, which would necessarily result from the strict application of the laws of Shariat. Thus there are two trends of public opinion; some raise the 'Back to the Koran' cry, and others are content with the conditions that prevail, as this causes the least amount of re-adjustment.

Need to Adapt Law to New Conditions

In India the condition of the people exhibits such wide diversity that a general rule is difficult to formulate. What may be practical in the case of a Punjabi peasant may not suit the business community of a city like Bombay; and again the literate and professional classes, highly imbued with the desire to follow Muslim Law and to give rights to their women, may not see eye to eye with rich landlords like the Taluqdars of the United Provinces. It appears, however, that social and economic factors are changing so rapidly that law will increasingly pay attention to them rather than to the dictates of ancient religion, which, hallowed and sanctified as they are throughout the ages, no longer represent a proper measure of justice and fairness in the context of modern life.

The greatest need of the day is peace and good will; and a determination on the part of all to be worthy citizens of a great and ancient country. The law in the main must follow public opinion; but the judges must remain free to criticize the actions not only of men of all stations in life, but also of the Government in power. Thus law affects public opinion; and public opinion moulds the law. In this mutual process it is highly desirable that certain rules be remembered; *first*, that where there are different religious systems of law, a steam-roller process of ironing out differences by the will of the majority is an unwise course; *secondly*, that the process of unification will only flourish by the development of a common social life and a common struggle for economic improvement; and *thirdly*, that due attention must now be paid to the enactment of permissive codes of Marriage, Divorce and Inheritance, which may be applied to all persons by their own free choice and not by the process of compulsion.

RELATION OF CHRISTIANITY WITH OTHER RELIGIONS
Specially (a) Hinduism, (b) Islam, (c) Others

S. K. GEORGE

Hinduism, its Assimilative Genius

"Hinduism has swallowed every religion it has come across. It would fain swallow Christianity too; but Christianity refuses to go down and sticks in its throat". So said an ardent advocate of exclusive, orthodox Christianity. This unfriendly aspersion draws pointed attention to what is an essential feature of Hinduism or, more correctly, the *Sanatana Dharma* of India—for Hinduism is a term of foreign coinage and is not really expressive of the genius of a religion that claims no single founder and enforces no single creed or cult upon its votaries. That genius is one of genuine synthesis, of active assimilation, of the diverse elements that have gone into the making of Indian Dharma. And the spirit of militancy implied in that remark, of pitting one religion against another, as if Truth establishes its sway by its partial realizations demolishing or swallowing, instead of fulfilling and completing, each other, is untrue also to the spirit of the Founder of Christianity. "Except a grain of wheat fall into the earth and die, it abideth by itself alone; but if it die, it beareth much fruit", said he, showing what manner of fulfilment he expected his message to have. Christianity may indeed have to go down the throat of Hinduism and get digested within, so that it may be thoroughly assimilated into the life-blood of Hindu Dharma, in order to produce the fruits of the spirit that its Master intended it to produce in all mankind.

India's Suspicion of Christianity

Christianity has so far been viewed in India as a foreign religion, brought in the wake of foreign conquest and exploitation by the dominant races of the Christian West. This is in spite of the fact, not as widely known as it ought to be, of there having been a community of Christians on the South-West coast of India almost from the beginning of the Christian era, and flourishing there under Hindu rulers. But the Syrian Christians of Kerala were not a proselytizing church, and were content to exist alongside of their Hindu neighbours, forming almost a caste within Hindu society, and steadily prospering materially, if not spiritually. It was only with the advent of the missionaries, first the Roman Catholics and then the varied brands of the Protestant West, that Christianity became a militant religion in India, making inroads on Hinduism and bidding for the soul of India. Its association with the marauding bands from the West and later with the imperial power that established its political sway over the land gave it a questionable prestige and a distinct bad odour. This last was not wholly dispelled even by the great and devoted services it rendered to the country in pioneering educational activities, in providing much-needed and highly-appreciated medical aid and more notably in seeking and saving the lowliest and the lost in the land. It gathered its converts mainly from the so-called submerged sixth of India and its signal successes in uplifting these stirred the conscience of India with regard to the great crime of untouchability. The Christian church has strengthened itself in India mainly by large accessions from these neglected children of Hinduism; and it was inevitable that such converts should look to their Western saviours for guidance in all things. Even the smaller number of converts from the upper castes were very much under the dominance of their Western teachers in their thinking and even their ways of life. That was why Indian Christians as a body, with a few shining exceptions, were apathetic and even hostile towards the national upsurge in India. But the Christian community has taken less time than other minorities to fall in line with the rest of India and has given the lead to other minor communities in unreservedly trusting the majority and in not obstructing the growth of healthy democratic traditions in a free India. This is not merely due to worldly wisdom, but as much to the sanction the religion itself gives to the demands for freedom and social justice.

Yet Christianity in an Independent India, with a renascent Hinduism, faces an unprecedented crisis. India is awake after the sleep of centuries and her religions will no longer be on the defensive against the onslaugnts of other militant faiths. The submerged millions are being integrated into Indian society and the blight of untouchability has been removed. The Harijan need no longer look for social uplift in folds other than Hinduism. The ancient culture of India which found its flowering in Vedanta is not only reasserting its appeal to all thinking minds in the country but is carrying its light to countries in the West and kindling seeking souls there. Above all in Mahatma Gandhi, with his roots deep down in Indian soil and culture, but giving a practical demonstration of the workability of the ethics of Jesus, which forms the kernel of Christianity, India has thrown a stupendous challenge to that religion which it dare not pass by unheeded. Indian Christianity if it is at all alive to the situation, at all sensitive to the signs of the times, has to rethink itself, reorient itself to the new India, rediscover its basic substance and interpret that in terms acceptable to the Indian mind and genius.

But though unprecedented for Christianity in India, the religion itself has met and weathered such crises in its long history, especially in its early days. It faced such a situation when it was confronted for the first time with the philosophy of ancient Greece, in the second century of its era. Daring thinkers there were in those days, particularly in the church of Alexandria, who were bold enough to appropriate the culture of Greece and to claim its greatest protagonists, Socrates and Plato, as "Christians before Christ". But that strain in Christian thought did not predominate and gave way to the legalism and the sacerdotalism of the church of Rome. In the teachings of the Vedanta and in the person of Gandhiji Indian Christianity meets a greater challenge alike to its spirituality and its ethics. Will it produce thinkers like Clement of Alexandria and Origen, who will do far more for Indian Christianity in the 20th century than what these thinkers attempted to do for the church in 2nd century Alexandria?

Hinduism, Supreme Religion of Spirituality

The fact is that there is little of spirituality that Christianity has, or needs, to teach to religion in India. India has a long record of spiritual quest and realization. The pathways of the spirit, the disciplines or *sadhanas* for self-realization, have been mapped and marked out by the *yogis* and *rishis* of India with a thoroughness and elaboration unequalled in any other religion. Christianity may indeed have much to learn from this search and realization. What it needs is to find its own place among the systems or *margas* recognised by a religion that is far more truly catholic than any form of Christianity. Christianity, as it has been developed in most of the churches that practise it, is essentially a *Bhakti Marga*, with Jesus Christ as its *Istadevata*. That is a conception and a status that Hinduism will readily grant. Of course, Christianity has its own distinctive emphasis, which it has maintained with a clarity that is often lost in the welter of margas and rituals that go to make up Hinduism. And that is its emphasis on the ethics of Jesus, on his revelation of God as Love, and its ringing demand that he who professes to love God must necessarily love and serve his fellowman. "If a man say, I love God, and hateth his brother, he is a liar: for he that loveth not his brother whom he hath seen cannot love God whom he hath not seen", says a New Testament writer, rightly expounding the moral demand of Jesus.

Christianity, Supreme Religion of Righteousness

And there is in Christianity an element that it has inherited from its own Semitic ancestry in the religion of the Hebrews. This is its demand for social righteousness. Though heavily overlaid in orthodox, organised Christianity by its accumulated vested interests, it is something that makes essential Christianity a revolutionary force wherever it is earnestly practised. This is summed up in those profound utterances of Christ, so glibly repeated and so often taken for granted by Christians, the *Beatitudes* of the Sermon on the Mount, which a modern student of religions has rightly called *The Code of Christ*.* What Gandhi, the Hindu, has preeminently demonstrated is the practicability of this code or way of life, which may after all be the only way out for a world which has seen revolutions play themselves out and cancel each other, the violence of Communism provoking the counter-violence of Fascism, bringing the world to the brink of catastrophe. Indian Christianity, if it is alive to the implications of the message of its Master and to the challenge of this great non-Christian, living the Christian life, but outside the pale of its churches, will rise and meet this challenge and integrate itself with Indian religion at its best, in an effort to realize its own ideal of the Kingdom of God on earth, or to achieve *Sarvodaya* to give it its equivalent in the present Indian setting and context.

Christianity and Islam

With Islam Christianity has much more in common than with Hinduism. Monotheistic and non-idolatrous, Islam sprang from the same roots as Christianity. Both revere the same Hebrew prophets; and Islam holds Jesus, the son of Mary, in reverence less only to that it gives to its own Prophet. In fact, Islam arose, and still stands, as a rebuke to the tritheism and sacerdotalism developed in certain sects of Christianity. It has the same concept of God as the Creator, Ruler and Judge of all mankind; only Christianity goes deeper and fuller into these

---

* Gerald Heard : *The Code of Christ: An Interpretation of the Beatitudes* Cassell & Co.

fundamental concepts and sees in God not only an Almighty, though merciful, Judge, but also a loving Father, who so loved the world that His unique son and revealer was willing to die in his work of seeking and saving lost humanity. In its doctrines of incarnation and redemptive vicarious suffering, and of the mystical union of believers with God in Christ, Christianity establishes its links with many aspects of Hinduism. If ever there was a religion called upon to play the part of a bridge-builder between Hinduism and Islam, it was Christianity in India. If that work of reconciliation has not been attempted and achieved it is as much due to the failure of Indian Christianity to understand its opportunities and rise equal to its tasks as to the loss of nerve and initiative of a decadent Hinduism. A Hinduism largely dormant during two centuries of political subjection could not carry on and complete the process of assimilating this virile religion that had been initiated by some daring religious geniuses in North India during the fourteenth and fifteenth centuries. And Christianity in India has been too much concerned with adding to its numbers and strengthening itself as a community against other religious communities to attempt any work of religious reconciliation. But the challenge and duty still remain. There are still forty millions of Muslims in India who have yet to be integrated into Indian society, so that they may resist the temptation to separatism which the militant character of their religion and the lure of Pan-Islamism outside present to them. A renascent Hinduism and a vitalized Christianity truly Indian ought to rise equal to this great opportunity and challenge to reconcile Islam to India, to assimilate the elements of strength and truth in it and to accord to that dynamic religion a place in the scheme of Indian thought and life.

Christianity and Zoroastrianism

The religion of Zarathustra too has many elements in common with Christianity. Zarathustra stands undoubtedly in the line of the great prophets of mankind, the bringers of Light to the darkness of the world. He can rightly be regarded as a forerunner of Christ, quite as much as any of the Hebrew prophets accepted in that role by Christianity. Its dualism, the conflict between Light and Darkness, and the final triumph of the Good is very closely akin to the dominant strain in Christian thought, and Zarathustra's *Philosophy of the Good Life* * finds its fulfilment in Christ's ideal of the Kingdom of God. A revival of this ancient faith among its Indian votaries is devoutly to be wished for and a genuine Christianity will do all it can to stimulate it, on the principle that the flourishing of any religion does not depend on the languishing of others, but on the devotees of all religions practising what is best in every one of them.

Christianity, Buddhism and Jainism

In Buddhism and its sister faith of Jainism, Christianity has a faith very close to its own religion of love. Jesus the Christ would undoubtedly have recognised in Gautama the Buddha a kindred spirit, perhaps an elder brother. The systems of Cosmology and Soteriology

---

* This is the title of Bishop Gore's very sympathetic study of Zoroastrianism; Everyman's Library: No. 924.

developed in these Indian religions of redemption are vaster than those of the later Semitic faith. But the spirit that informs them is remarkably akin to that of him who went about doing good out of compassion for the multitude and who calls to all mankind: "Come unto me, all ye that labour and are heavy-laden, and I will give you rest. Take my yoke upon you, and learn of me; for I am meek and lowly in heart: and ye shall find rest unto your souls. For my yoke is easy, and my burden is light". "Your Christ appears to me to be a great Bodhisattva", said a Chinese Buddhist monk to a Christian scholar. That appraisal, truly characteristic of Buddhist attitude towards Christ, is a hand held out in fellowship and good-will towards a kindred faith. Will Christianity hold back dissatisfied at the response to what it holds to be unique about its Founder? Is it not more in keeping with his spirit to accept the hand of fellowship and walk in company with these people, who certainly are "not far from the Kingdom", in a common quest after Truth and the Good Life?

A "Fellowship of Friends of Truth"

What religions to-day are called upon at this time, when the world has become one, when adherents of different faiths jostle each other in offices and universities, in market places and running trains, is to an adventure of faith, a full sharing of the deepest and best within them, without a thought of any religion battening itself on the spoils from others, in a joint endeavour to achieve a just and peaceful world-order, which seems to be the very condition of human survival at all on this planet which has considerably shrunk in its dimensions in relation to the human mind. This coming together is not to be on a basis of indifference to what is distinctive in the different faiths. Nor is it to be in the interests of an artificial mixture of all religions, a working out of the Lowest Common Measure of all faiths, which may not offend any one, but will satisfy no one but the speculative theorist. The Fellowship of Faiths that is here advocated is, in the words of Prof. S. Radhakrishnan, "no easy indulgence of error and weakness or lazy indifference to the issues involved. It is not the intellectual's taste for moderation or the highbrow's dislike of dogma. It is not the politician's love for compromise or being all things to all men; nor is it simply a negative freedom from antipathies. It is an understanding insight, full trust in the basic Reality which feeds all faiths and its power to lead us to the Truth. It believes in the deeper religion of the Spirit, which will be adequate for all people, vital enough to strike deep roots, powerful to unify each individual in himself and bind us all together by the realization of our common condition and our common goal".

An adventure on this deeper and dynamic level of inter-religious fellowship is being attempted in a new movement under Christian auspices in India—a *Fellowship of Friends of Truth*.* Walking through the fields of Noakhali, East Bengal, with Gandhiji, one day in January 1947, Mr. Horace Alexander, the well-known English Quaker friend of India, put it to him thus: "It seems to me that what the world, especially India, needs above all to-day is some religious fellowship which can be and will be joined by adherents of all the chief religions. I am not now thinking of a 'syncretistic' movement, like Theosophy, which deliberately tries to take the best from each faith and joins them

---

* See a pamphlet on this by Horace Alexander, obtainable from the Friends' Settlement, Rasulia, Hoshangabad, C.P.

together. I am thinking of a union of hearts, a fellowship in which men of each faith, Hindu, Buddhist, Parsi, Jew, Muslim, Christian, all find themselves at one, because they are seeking together to practise the truth of God in the world. And I have wondered whether the Society of Friends, the 'Quakers' so called, could help to provide such a meeting ground. Of course, if you could show me that in fact some other group, such as the Brahmo Samaj or the Ramakrishna Mission, is better fitted to provide such a fellowship, then I ought to consider joining such a group. What do you say ?". Gandhiji did not answer without first giving some time for thought. Then he said: "No, of the societies that I know, I do not think any other would be better or even so good. I think the Quakers are the best. But only on one condition: Are they prepared to recognise that it is as natural for a Hindu to grow into a Friend as it is for a Christian to grow into one ?" To this Horace Alexander replied: "Some would agree to that condition and some would not. I for one am one of those who would readily accept that position, not only for Hindus but for Muslims and others".

It is on the basis of this full acceptance of the naturalness of people of all faiths growing into a unity of spirit in the bond of peace, that a few Quakers in India, as members of a historic Christian community, have given the lead in such a fellowship of faiths. To me it seems to contain the germ of a genuine fellowship of religions which is needed in India and in all the world, which will organise the forces of good fostered by all the religions of the world for the overthrow of entrenched evil both in the individual heart and in society. To me, as an Indian Christian, this seems to be the beginning of Christianity's answer to the challenge of Gandhiji.* It may be that in meeting it Christianity will have to allow itself to be swallowed by the religion of India, to die in order to find a larger and fuller life in Indian Dharma. But that would be in the spirit of its Master, in the spirit expressed in that truly Christian hymn, as applied not merely to the individual but to institutional Christianity as well:

> O Love that will not let me go,
>   I rest my weary soul in Thee;
> I give Thee back the life I owe,
> That in Thine ocean depths its flow
>   May richer, fuller be.

* See *Gandhi's Challenge to Christianity* by S.K. George: Navajivan Publishing House, Ahmedabad.

CHRISTIANITY IN INDIA

REV. PRINCIPAL KELLOCK

Christianity and Ancient India

Christianity's connection with India is ancient. There is a legend, recorded in a book written in the 3rd century A. D., that the Gospel was brought to India by Thomas, one of Christ's twelve disciples, in 50 A. D. The Syrian Church in Travancore cherishes this tradition which declares that St. Thomas was its founder. It is said that he came to North India when King Gudnaphar reigned there, that afterwards he went South to Travancore, and that some time later he proceeded to the East Coast where he met with a martyr's death.

We are on the ground of solid historic fact when we state that a Christian Church existed in the South-West of India in the 4th century. Edessa in Mesopotamia had become a centre of Christianity in the 1st century and from it the Christian message was carried to Persia. It is thought by historians that the Syrian Christian Church in India arose either out of the missionary activities of the Persian Church, perhaps in the 2nd century; or that it arose in the 4th century when a persecution of Christians by a Sassanid Emperor of Persia caused a group of Christians with their bishop and clergy to flee from Mesopotamia and take refuge on the West coast of India. For 1000 years this Syrian Christian Church in India maintained its self-contained existence, acknowledging spiritual allegiance to the "Katholikos" in Mesopotamia.

Christianity and Medieval India

In the 13th and 14th centuries Roman Catholic missions worked in India, but the converts were few and no permanent body of Christians was established.

In 1498 Vasco de Gama discovered the Cape route to India and the Far East, and a new epoch of world history began. Portugal became a power in the Eastern hemisphere. The object of Portuguese policy was mainly economic. It aimed to get hold of the overseas trade, to divert it from the Arabs and from the mercantile cities of Italy, and bring it to Lisbon. The Portuguese therefore occupied strategic places on the trade routes. Their first headquarters in India was Cochin but in 1530 they made Goa the chief seat of their rule in India. They were content for the most part to be mistress of the seas and did not attempt to acquire wide territories.

The King of Portugal was closely connected with the Roman Catholic Church and regarded it as his duty to assist by all political, economic and social means the propagation of the Christian faith. Missionaries came to India under his auspices. Trinitarians and Jesuits were soon at work. Franciscans set up centres at Goa, Salsette and Bassein and towards the end of the 18th century were said to be ministering to about 40,000 Christians. Dominicans were at work at Bassein, Diu, Cochin and Bengal. A mission called the Order of St.

John of God had houses at several centres, their object being chiefly the care of the sick. The Theatines were at Bijapur, Golconda and Goa. At Goa the Augustinians had a school for the sons of Brahmins. The Oratorians and the Carmelites had houses in several places. The French Capuchins started work at Pondicherry in the second half of the 17th century.

The most vigorous and widespread of these Roman Catholic missionary bodies was the Jesuits. Francis Xavier who belonged to that Order came to India in 1542. He came as envoy of the King of Portugal and Apostolic Nuncio of the Pope. He regarded his mission as being to the whole of the Portuguese sphere of influence in the East. He died in 1552 while trying to get entrance into China. The following words of Latourette indicate the nature of his activities: "A devoted friend, intensely interested in individuals, seeking by love, gayety and a timely word to lead men into the Christian faith or into a deeper Christian life, Xavier also had an imagination which covered vast areas and peoples. He endeavoured to raise the level of Christian living of the Portuguese adventurers and their nominally Christian mixed-blooded offspring. He strove, through his Society, to bring the Christian gospel to the many lands and peoples opened to the west by Portuguese discoveries and commerce. He recruited members for the Society, sought new missionaries from Europe, and made provision for the training of natives of the East for the service of the Church." (The History of the Expansion of Christianity: Vol. III. p. 253).

Another famous Jesuit missionary was Robert de Nobili who came to Madura in 1605. He tried to naturalize Christianity in India and to win the higher castes. He lived in a hut in the Brahmin quarter, described himself as an ascetic and a Roman Rajah, studied Sanskrit and adopted Indian methods and customs to the fullest extent to which he thought he could go without compromising essential Christian principles. He recognised caste in not allowing low caste Christians into the same Church as that used by the higher caste Christians. He let Brahmin converts continue to wear their caste mark. His methods were strongly criticised, but the Pope, with some reservations, gave judgment in his favour in 1623. De Nobili, it is to be noted, also took an interest in the Pariahs. There was a Christian community of about 100,000 in the year 1700 in the area where Nobili and his mission had been working, the great majority of them being Sudras and Pariahs. It may be noted that this area was outside the sphere of influence of the Portuguese.

By the close of the 16th century nearly all the people in the neighbourhood of Goa were professing Christians. A good deal of coercion seems to have been applied by the State. Even while Xavier was alive a royal decree prohibited the practice of Hinduism in Portuguese territory and ordered the destruction of idols. Brahmins were required to attend the Sunday discourses of the missionaries. Public festivities were held to celebrate baptisms. Protection against reprisals was promised to those who sought admission to the Christian community. In 1567 the Portuguese Viceroy decreed that temples and mosques should be destroyed and that orphans under 14 should be baptized. When the ruler of Travancore denounced his Portuguese alliance and persecuted Christians, a fleet was sent against him and he was compelled to renew the alliance and to allow Jesuits to preach in his domains.

On the other hand it is to be noted that these coercive measures were the work of the State, although the Church of that time was closely identified with it. But the first Provincial Council of the Church in Goa, held in 1567, declared that no one was to be constrained to be a Christian by force or intimidation, that Christians were not to make Hindus break caste by eating with them and that children were not to be baptized without the consent of their parents or slaves without the consent of their masters.

While it is true that the Portuguese State aided the work of the missionaries in providing a base of operations in the State territories and in positively helping the work of conversion, on the other hand the association with the State was a hindrance to the work of the missionaries in many ways. The Portuguese did cruel and barbaric things that brought disgrace on the Christian cause. The ideas of caste made it inevitable that becoming a Christian seemed like becoming Portuguese. Another difficulty was the inefficiency and low morals of the Church organization that resulted from the hold of the State over it. The Pope had given the Portuguese King authority over the Church and its agents. He was to provide missionaries and clergy for his territories between the Cape of Good Hope and Japan, and had the right to appoint the bishops. But frequently complaints were heard that churches were without clergy and dioceses without bishops and that many of the clergy were leading disgraceful lives. The jealousy that arose between the Portuguese and the Spanish clergy was demoralizing. In one way or another, however, through pure spiritual motives, through self-interest, through coercion of different degrees, through the offspring of the union of Portuguese with women of lower castes, and through natural increase, Roman Catholic Christians in India numbered about two to two and a half million in 1700. One hundred years later the number is said to have declined to between 475,000 and 1,200,000.

This decline may be accounted for by the following difficulties that overtook the Roman Catholic Missions in the 17th and 18th centuries:— (1) The Portuguese power decayed. She lost many of her strongholds and much of her commerce. The mission felt the effects in lack of recruits, straitened finances and diminution of political support. (2) The Portuguese were driven out chiefly by the Dutch and the British which were Protestant powers and not inclined to look with favour on the Roman Catholics. For example, after the Dutch captured Cochin in 1633 all Roman Catholic missionaries were ordered to quit, and at the beginning of the 18th century Portuguese clergy were expelled from Bombay for a time. (3) There was conflict between the Portuguese authorities and the Pope who wanted to strengthen the Roman Catholic missionary effort in India and saw that this could not be done through a decaying power like Portugal. The Portuguese obstinately held on to the right of patronage which had been granted to them in the heyday of their power. Missionaries who were not Portuguese and who came to Goa were often hampered because they did not have the permission of the Portuguese King. Portugal still wanted to control the Church in regions where her political power was of the flimsiest, and moreover she could not provide adequately in funds and clergy for these places. Long and enfeebling controversies issued out of this situation. (4) There was bitter dissension over the methods followed by Jesuits such as de Nobili for adjusting Christianity to Indian ideas and customs. (5) The political disturbances in the latter part of the 17th and the first half of the 18th century caused disorganization and loss among the Christians. The Marathas captured Bassein and Bandra in 1737-1740. Hyder Ali and Tipu Sultan wrought havoc in the second half of the 18th century. During these events churches were destroyed, many Christians were enslaved, many migrated and many went over to Hinduism or to Islam. (6) Finally there was the loss caused by the expulsion of the Jesuits from Portuguese and French possessions in 1759 and the suppression of the Society by Rome in 1773.

The Moghul Empire and the Portuguese regime began in India about the same time. Akbar, trying to work out a new religion to unify his subjects, induced the Jesuits to send three representatives to Delhi in 1579. They dreamed of converting Akbar and through him the whole Moghul Empire to Christianity. At Akbar's request a second mission followed in 1590, and a third in 1594. He allowed his subjects to accept the Christian faith. A church was built at Lahore. The Jesuits had missionaries or adherents at Agra, Lahore, Delhi, Kabul, Peshawar, Srinagar and Garhwal. But the number of baptisms was never large and later rulers put restrictions on the Jesuits' efforts. The mission gradually waned and finally ended with the expulsion of the Order by the Portuguese in the second half of the 18th century.

The coming of the Portuguese to India deeply affected the Syrian Christian Church which had existed in the South-West since the 4th century. At the Synod of Diamper held in 1599 the Portuguese made the Christians in Malabar who belonged to the Syrian Church renounce all connection with the Katholikos in Mesopotamia and accept the Roman Catholic form of Christianity and the Pope's authority. But when the Portuguese power decayed, a large part of the Church returned to its Syrian allegiance. Thereafter the Syrian Church in India was divided into (1) a *Uniat* section which was united with Rome though keeping Syriac as its liturgical language instead of Latin and retaining its distinctive ecclesiastical customs such as the marriage of the clergy; and (2) a Jacobite section which acknowledged the Patriarch of Antioch as its spiritual Head—called "Jacobite" after Jacob Baradai, a monk belonging to a monastery near Edessa who defended Monophysitism at Constantinople in 540. (See Macnicol: The Living Religions of the Indian People: p. 272). From the Jacobite section in recent years has issued a Reformed body called the Mar Thoma Christians. They seem to have been brought to separate themselves from the older body as a result of the inspiration obtained from the Anglican C.M.S. mission that has been working in their neighbourhood.

The period 1500 to 1800 may be called the time of the effort of Latin Christianity to win India for Christ. The first missionaries seem to have been dependent largely on interpreters but soon study of the Indian languages was encouraged. In 1575 language schools were started. Roman Catholic literature was appearing in at least seven of the Indian languages in the 17th century. The English Jesuit, Thomas Stevens, at the end of the 16th century wrote in Marathi a Christian *purana* which met with much appreciation. The Roman Catholics made efforts to create an indigenous clergy, though it was not until the 20th century that the policy was whole-heartedly adopted.

Between 1500 and 1800 there were Armenian Christians in India. They were immigrants and did not attempt to expand their numbers. Under the Moghuls they had communities at Delhi, Lahore and Agra. In 1805 there were said to be seven Armenian churches, having 14 priests and one bishop. Also there were 2 Greek churches with 4 priests.

It may be noted that between 1500 and 1800 the number of accessions to Islam in India was much greater than the number of accessions to Christianity.

In the early years of the 18th century at Tranquebar a movement was started that laid the foundation of some of the most flourishing of the Protestant Christian communities of the 19th and 20th centuries. Tranquebar took first place amongst the Danish trading posts in India, and in 1706 King Frederick IV of Denmark decided that missionaries should be sent to the non-Christians who were within touch of the Danish trading and colonial activities. He secured two Germans, Ziegenbalg and Plutschau, to start the work and from their efforts, reinforced and extended by missionaries from Denmark, Germany, England and America, a Christian community was built up which, about the end of the 18th century, numbered about 20,000—mainly Sudras, Pariahs and the mixed stock called *Portuguese*. As in the case of the Roman Catholic missions in this region, some concessions were made to caste prejudices.

With their fairly large Indian communities and their large number of clergy, a striking spread of Roman Christianity took place in India in the 19th century. The staffs of the Orders already working in India were reinforced, the reinstated Jesuit Order again sent out many workers, and organizations that had not hitherto taken part in India sent out missionaries—the Silesians, the Oblates of Mary Immaculate, the Holy Cross Fathers, the Society of Foreign Missions of Milan, the Benedictines, and the German Society of the Divine Saviour. Most of these missionaries were fully occupied in looking after the Christian flocks, but some devoted themselves to winning non-Christians. A considerable proportion of the converts were the result of mass-movements. Relief given in time of famines frequently resulted in large accessions of this nature. Caste tended to be tolerated by the Roman Catholic authorities, being regarded as a civil or social affair rather than a religious matter. In propagating the faith extensive use was made of Indian catechists. Use was made of dramatic forms to present the Gospel message. Christian literature was widely spread. Schools and colleges and theological seminaries were opened. Philanthropic institutions of various kinds were established—hospitals, widows' homes, orphanages, homes for boys and for girls, leper asylums. As converts were often cut off from their old means of employment, institutions were started to enable them to earn a living such as industrial schools, cottage industries, agricultural enterprises, land banks and other co-operative institutions. Organisations of the characteristic Roman Catholic types for lay people and for persons desirous of renouncing the world and living a religious life were set up.

In 1911 the number of Roman Catholics in India was said by the Church to be 2,223,546; and there were 966 European priests, 1142 Indian priests, 440 lay brothers, and 2778 lay sisters.

The Protestant figures in 1914 were stated as follows:—1,000,000 baptized members, 5465 foreign missionaries, and a native staff 4 or 5 times as great as the foreign staff.

In 1886, after a great deal of friction between Portugal and Rome, a hierarchy was created for India. Seven Archbishops provinces were set up, namely Goa, Bombay, Agra, Calcutta, Madras, Verapoly and Pondicherry. This took the larger part of India away from Portuguese jurisdiction. Friction however continued and a fresh settlement was made in 1928.

Christianity and Modern India

The East India Company, which in the beginning had been quite tolerant of the idea of missionary enterprise, had become unfavourable to missionaries and opposed to any effort to spread Christianity in India. In the 1790's and the early 1800's it refused to give missionaries passages in its ships and prohibited them from preaching in its territories. However at the time of the renewal of the Company's charter in 1813 and 1833 most of the restrictions on the missionaries were withdrawn.

Towards the close of the 18th century and early in the 19th century, Chaplains came to India who were much interested in spreading the Christian faith among the non-Christians—e.g. David Brown, Claudius Buchanan, T. T. Thomason and Henry Martyn. They did much to start and encourage the modern phase of Protestant missions in India.

With the arrival of William Carey in India in 1793 a new era for the Protestant missions began. He worked as superintendent of an indigo factory for six years, during which time he studied Bengali and Sanskrit, translated most of the Bible into Bengali, and also exercised his interest in Indian vegetation by making a study of Indian plants. The East India Company was adamant against letting him open up mission work within its territories but he was permitted to do so by the Danish Government at Serampore within whose small territory that town was situated. There he was joined by Ward, an experienced printer, and by Marshman, a self-educated school-master. This famous trio for about 30 years carried on a very notable set of activities. By 1832 they had printed portions or all of the Christian scriptures in 44 languages or dialects. Grammars and dictionaries were published. The *Ramayana* was translated and a large part of it printed. Mission stations were opened up, schools started and a College to train Indians to reach their fellow-countrymen with the Christian message was established. The curriculum of the College was the Bible and Christian theology and the philosophies and religions of India. Carey also collected plants and started the Agri-horticultural Society of India with the object of improving the soil and the grains, and he corresponded with savants all over the world.

From 1813 an Anglican Ecclesiastical Establishment of a Bishop and 3 Archdeacons was set up, and permission was given for missionaries to live and work in the Company's territories. In consequence many new missionary societies started operating in India. This was prompted and facilitated by the freedom of travel that came about at the end of the Napoleonic wars, by the foothold offered through the extension of British rule over additional territories, and by the rise of interest in missionary effort in Britain, Continental Europe and U.S.A.

In 1833 the Bishoprics of Bombay and Madras were established and the Bishop of Calcutta was made Metropolitan (equivalent to Archbishop). The two great Anglican bodies, the Church Missionary Society and the Society for the Propagation of the Gospel, extended their work. There were considerable accessions to Christianity, mostly from the low-caste and out-caste strata of the population. They were partly attracted by the protection and security and the chance of escape from oppression through education and material improvement which connection with the Church brought to them. The American Board of Commissioners for Foreign Missions started work in Bombay in the second decade of the 19th century, and later extended to Ahmednagar and then to Madura.

A very important new phase opened when Alexander Duff in 1830 started the school which evolved into the Scottish Church College, Calcutta. His object was to give a modern liberal education in the English language with instruction in Christian truth as the central thing. He thought that this would be efficacious both in overthrowing error and in safeguarding from atheism and agnosticism those who came under the influence of Western scientific thought. There was occasional opposition, especially when there were conversions, but the high quality of the institution always brought the students back. The converts were few but some of them were of high-caste and became very influential Christian leaders. This College and the 40 or so others that have been established on similar lines in India have been very effective in permeating the country with Christian ideas. Raja Ram Mohun Roy, one of the great makers of modern India, who had been much impressed by the Christian teaching though he did not become a Christian, heartily supported Duff's efforts and the introduction of the Western system of education into India. The popularity of this *English* education grew as it was realized that it opened up opportunity of employment and advancement under the British *raj*.

John Wilson of the Scottish Mission started similar English educational work in Bombay in 1832 and out of it evolved the Wilson College. He attracted many to Christianity. He put more stress on education in the Indian languages than Duff did but was with him in the advocacy of English for higher education. He was a great student of Indian literature, and a pioneer in the collection of Sanskrit manuscripts and in the deciphering of rock inscriptions. He had a wide circle of friends among Hindus, Muslims, Parsees, Jews, Abyssinians and Negroes as well as Christians.

The Madras Christian College developed out of a school that was started by the Church of Scotland Mission in 1837. Under William Miller it became a union institution, supported by Anglicans and Wesleyans as well as by the Church of Scotland, and it did much to make Christian thought a force among the educated classes of South India.

The Scotsman, Stephen Hislop, went to Nagpur in 1844, made converts among the Tamils, Marathas and Telegus, and founded the College now known by his name. He was distinguished as a scientist and pioneered the study of the geology of Central India. Space forbids us to mention in detail the many other great Colleges that came into existence in the course of the century—such as St. John's College, Agra, founded by the C. M. S.; the Forman Christian College at Lahore (American Presbyterian); the Isabella Thoburn College of Lucknow (Methodist Episcopal); St. Stephen's College, Delhi (S.P.G.) where C. F. Andrews, who so won the affection of India and who was the close friend of Gandhi and Tagore, began his career.

Between 1813 and 1858 there came to take part in the missionary enterprise Baptists, Wesleyans, Plymouth Brethren, Irish Presbyterians, American Presbyterians, American Lutherans, Methodist Episcopals, representatives of the Dutch Reformed Church, the Swiss Basel Mission, the German Gossner Mission, etc. Gujarat and Kathiawar, Orissa, Assam, the Himalayan foothills, the Punjab, the Karnatak and Central

India were brought into contact with Christianity through their efforts. There was less confusion than might have been expected through this multiplicity of bodies. The sense of engagement in a common cause tended to prevent duplication or over-lapping and the idea of "comity" developed.

The Sepoy Mutiny of 1857 did not seriously affect the Christian communities. About 38 missionaries and chaplains and members of their families were killed and also some 20 Indian catechists, teachers and their wives and children. Government adopted a more friendly attitude to the propagation of Christianity after the Mutiny, though it was never given the same degree of support as the Spanish and Portuguese gave in their colonial possessions in the 16th, 17th and 18th centuries.

In the second half of the 19th century we find Christian missions established on the border of Afghanistan, in Kashmir, on the passes into Tibet and among the Santals and in many other places. More than a score of organizations whose names were new to India sent workers to participate in the enterprise, many belonging to U.S.A. and some to Canada, Australia and New Zealand. It would take too long to list them all. We may however mention the Salvation Army which started in India in 1882. The story of the arrival of its first contingent in Bombay under the leadership of the ex-I.C.S. man, Booth-Tucker, makes interesting and amusing reading. The Government of the day were scared at anything calling itself an "army" coming to evangelize India and did all they could to prevent them, and Booth-Tucker adopted very sensational methods to overcome the opposition. He was successful and the "Army" remained to develop a great work of service for the under-privileged.

The Indian Sunday School Union to encourage and promote Sunday Schools in India started in 1876. The Christian Endeavour Movement, which seeks to strengthen and deepen the Christian life among the young people, began in India in the 1880's. The Young Men's Christian Association began in India in 1890, and the Young Women's Christian Association a little later. Other societies that fit into the general picture of Christianity in India as auxiliary bodies to the more directly Church and missionary organizations are the British and Foreign Bible Society (and since 1944 the Bible Society of India and Ceylon which has taken over most of the control that the London Society formerly exercised) which has done so much for the translation and distribution of the Scriptures; the Christian Literature Society and the several Tract and Book Societies whose work it is to produce, publish and distribute books of all kinds from learned treatises to children's stories and religious tracts.

We must not finish this account of the movement to spread Christianity in India without mentioning the indegenous bodies that are engaged in the task. There is the famous Pandita Ramabai's Mukti Mission whose headquarters is in India and which is a thoroughly indegenous body though it depends partly on assistance from abroad. There is the National Missionary Society which was founded in 1905 and which carries on extensive missionary work in several parts of India and whose personnel, support and control are all Indian. There are a few other indegenous missionary societies such as the Mar Thoma Syrian Christian Evangelistic Society.

We have now given a brief sketch of the way in which Christianity came to India. For 450 years Christian missionaries have been coming to India, bringing with them the Bible, their humanitarian services and the story of Jesus. Explorers and traders have opened up paths for them, and they have been both helped and hindered by the wielders of political power. Their message has found a response sufficiently deep and sufficiently wide to cause the Christian Church to take root in India.

Indian Christians To-day

Probably the most striking features about the people in India who call themselves Christians are (1) the way in which God is worshipped and (2) the way in which educational, medical and social and economic services are associated with the enterprise to which they are related. Under Christian auspices over 300 high schools and about 40 colleges are being conducted. In training institutions young men (and in many cases their wives also) are being prepared for their future work as pastors, teachers and leaders of the Christian communities. In most cases their work will be in the villages and efforts are being made to fit them to make their church the centre of socially progressive activities and to make them leaders in the work of rural uplift.

Efforts and experiments to improve material conditions have been a common feature of the Christian programme. Some of these have been wide in their scope and ambitious in their aim, like the great Christian Agricultural Institute at Allahabad, with its University course in the science of agriculture, its model farm, its research projects, its home economics classes, etc.; others have been in the nature of humble but useful efforts to help the villagers to carry on home industries such as bee-keeping, fowl-raising, sericulture, toy-making, mat-weaving, etc.

Influenced by the example of Jesus and faced with the appalling amount of preventible disease and the high infant mortality that exists in India, Christians have been foremost in establishing hospitals and dispensaries, sanatoria for T. B. partients, Leper Homes, etc., and in training doctors, nurses, dispensers and midwives.

Indian Christians and National Reconstruction

In consonance with the general plan of this volume let us, in conclusion, consider the fundamental attitudes of the Christian with a view to discovering whether or not they are likely to give rise to fissiparous tendencies. In attempting to do this it is necessary to remember that religious faith, sincerely experienced and held, articulates itself in terms of truth or assertions about reality; expresses itself in numberless personal effects; and projects its influence in far-reaching ways into the social sphere.

Amid many varieties of expression, emphasis and detail all Christians believe that "God was in Christ reconciling the world unto himself." On this basis a conception of the nature of spiritual reality is built up, and flowing from it a world-view or general apprehension of the nature of the universe in which man finds himself. It is the function of Christian theology to prove that this interpretation of reality is true. There are other interpretations of reality—e.g. the Vedantist, the Buddhist, that of Islam, of Jainism, of Zoroastrianism, of Marxism and scientific materialism. Considered as systems claiming to be the true interpretation of reality, these different world-views are, in parts of their assertions at least, in fundamental opposition. To that extent they may be called fissiparous. We must, however, all be loyal to the truth as we see it and experience it. It is the truth that we really want, and it is only by the truth that we can satisfactorily live. The remedy for the fissiparous tendencies inherent in the intellectual formulations of the different world-views is not to be found in shutting our eyes to the differences and pretending that they are all the same. That is no more justifiable than it would be to say that a number of scientific hypotheses are all equally true and to abandon any further search for truth with regard to the matter. Nor is the remedy to be sought by seeking to impose any one view by methods other than discussion and persuasion of mind. The remedy lies in the sincerity that deals honestly with truth, and in the wide tolerance that respects and seeks sympathetically to understand the sincere convictions of others. In a secular State where human personality is respected and in an enlightened social system where religious belief is recognized to be a legitimate matter of personal choice there need be no fear of anything harmfully divisive in the activities of different religious groups.

Turning now to the effect which the Christian faith has on the personal lives of individuals, perhaps the most generally true thing that one could say is that this faith tends to make a beginning in individual lives of the "fruits of the Spirit". This is the common feature to which the Christian experience gives rise under all the different forms of Christian worship and organization and creed. The fruits of the Spirit are love, joy, peace, good temper, kindliness, generosity, fidelity, gentleness, self-control. We are not, of course, claiming that these qualities are found in everyone who is designated by the name Christian, but only that the genuinely experienced influence of Christ results in the shaping of human character after the pattern of these qualities. There is nothing fissiparous about these qualities. They are, on the contrary, unifying, harmonising and befriending qualities.

The fruits of the Spirit appear in many different places and manifest themselves amidst many different credal systems. This fact indicates an underlying unity in which we may rejoice, however difficult it may be to reconcile it with water-tight theological dogmas. The Governor-General of India, Mr. C. Rajagopalachari, in a message on the occasion of the centenary celebrations of the Malabar Christian College, mentioned the "intimate identity of aims between St. Paul and Mahatma Gandhi," and added: "The thirteenth chapter of the First Epistle to the Corinthians is not different from Mahatmaji's autobiography." It is as Van Dyke says in his poem :—

> Who seeks for heaven, alone to save his soul,
>   May keep the path but will not reach the goal ;
> While he who walks in love may wander far,
>   But God will bring him where the blessed are

or as Whittier in his hymn says :—

> O Lord and Master of us all,
>   Whate'er our name or sign,
> We own Thy sway, we hear Thy call,
>   We test our lives by Thine.
>
> We faintly hear ; we dimly see ;
>   In differing phrase we pray ;

> But, dim or clear, we own in Thee
> The Light, the Truth, the Way.

As regards the effects of Christianity in the sphere of man's social life, we are here concerned with the question whether the Christian faith, maintaining itself in a land of many religions, will be fissiparous, divisive or un-cooperative. Three statements may be made on the matter and in connection with the first two it may be said without fear of contradiction that the tendency of Christianity is to unify, strengthen and uphold the general social life of the nation. (1) Christianity teaches its adherent to be a good citizen and a good neighbour. Jesus said: "Render unto Caesar the things which be Caesar's, and unto God the things which be God's,"—which may be interpreted: Conform to the system of law and order of the State to which you belong, but be better than the system in the way that conscience requires. Jesus also said: "Whatever you would like men to do to you, do just the same to them; that is the meaning of the Law and the prophets." It is difficult to conceive of a better formulation of the principle of good neighbourliness than that. And it is significant that Jesus regarded this formula of the good neighbour as the essential meaning of the sacred scriptures. Pandit Lakshmi Kant Maitra, in a speech in the Constituent Assembly on 6th December, 1948, when fundamental rights conferring freedom of conscience and freedom to profess, practise and propagate religion were being discussed, recognized the tendency of Christianity to produce good citizens and good neighbours when he said that the Christians were the most inoffensive community in the whole country. They were, he declared, spending over two crores of rupees every year on maintaining educational institutions and other institutions for the uplift of the people. And he went on to say that if they had spent this money on proselytisation, then, instead of numbering only seven millions to-day, they would have numbered seventy millions. (2) The conception of the Kingdom of God, which was the central idea in the mind of Jesus, directs human thought, emotion and enterprise towards the attainment of a just and fraternal social order, which would be a true community of mankind because based on righteous and universally valid principles of human brotherhood. Christianity in its social influence tends to have a fundamentally unifying effect because of a number of social principles that flow from the teaching of Jesus. The chief of these are the worth of human life and the sacredness of human personality; the solidarity of the human family (with its foundations in the Fatherhood of God and the Brotherhood of Man, and its imperatives of loving God with all your being and loving your neighbour as yourself); and the principle that the privileged must be concerned for the under-privileged and the strong stand up for the weak. By imbuing individuals with these principles Christ brings them to participate in his own spirit, releases in them the hidden springs of aspiration, hope and love, and directs them into the ways of service for their fellow-men. In this way Christianity is a deeply and persistently active unifying element in any social system, making for the elimination of those factors which are essentially disruptive. (3) But the Kingdom of God is opposed to all that is evil; and there is much that is evil, imperfect and in need of correction in our existing political, social and economic systems. Besides the evil that infects individual desires and wills, and the moral laziness that makes us tolerate injustice and wrong, there is the social pressure of evil that lowers the moral level of society, and there is the satanic frustration of good for the attainment of selfish aims. Christianity therefore not only seeks such enlightenment of individuals through Christ as will develop within them an appreciation of the true life-values, bring about inner renewal and release the springs of faith and hope and love, but also summons the Christian mind and will to the battle against evil in society in all its forms. The Christian is conscious of the call to help to mould the things of earth in accordance with the pattern of the Kingdom of God; and he is conscious of this call more or less keenly according to the reality and depth of his vision of the Kingdom of God. It is only on this level that Christianity could with any justice be accused of being fissiparous. It cannot be content with things as they are, because, things as they are, are in too many ways out of harmony with that perfect righteousness, justice and love which is the Kingdom of God as set forth by Jesus. The Christian's ultimate allegiance is to God as He is revealed in Christ. The Christian must obey God rather than men and cannot conform to anything that is against that conscience which the enlightenment of Christ has created in him.

While therefore Society and the State cannot for the Christian be the ultimate authorities, he believes that Society and the State are part of God's plan for the good of mankind and he is always ready to give them fullest co-operation and allegiance compatible with his allegiance to God in Christ. If he has to be fissiparous with regard to existing social or political affairs, it will only be with a view to opposing what his conscience tells him is evil and with a view to attaining a better, a more just, a more truly fraternal Society and State.

In the providence of God Christianity has during the past 400 years taken root widely and deeply in India. It is now generally acknowledged that the Indian Christian Church, besides being Christian, is also truly Indian, and that it forms a valuable element in the total life of the nation. Christians in India go forward into the new era that began in August 1947, rejoicing in the respect and tolerance accorded to them and to the members of all the different faiths by the Indian Secular State. They go forward in co-operation with good men of all persuasions, eager to help to build the new India that shall be, a great and a glorious nation, and determined in this high common task to give in fullest measure their own peculiar contribution.

INDIA'S UNION

YOGI SHRI SHUDDHANANDA BHARATIAR

Absence of National Harmony

We have now an Indian Union in a divided India. But India's Union has not yet been fully achieved and forces of disruption and disunion are often conspiring against our national harmony and solidarity. This is chiefly due to the upsurgence of 'I and mine' egoism, and ignorance of the basic inner Spirit which holds together all souls even like the thread holding the beads in a rosary—Sutre mani ganaiva. Sparrows live together, fly together and are happy; bees swarm in a honey-comb and murmer to man the secret of social unity. The steller bodies march in peaceful harmony towards the dawn. But man has not yet learnt to live in a happy concord with the brother man—and why?

For man often forgets that he is a member of the human aggregate; his egoism arrogates itself against the psychic consciousness which is always for unity, and which sees the ONE in the multiplicity of embodied souls.

Narrow-Minded Individualism

This egoism has taken the shape of narrow-minded individualism. It often forgets that the earth, we live in, is a small home in the infinite space, an atom spinning amidst the vast myriads of stars and planets. A supreme Power which we call GOD pervades all the space and effects through Nature the evolution of beings from the inert dust to the intelligent man. Plant, worm, insect, bird, beast and man are all one family of living beings breathing the same air, walking on the same earth, enjoying the gifts of one vast heaven that canopies above the limitless universe. God gave man the unity of consciousness to live in tune with men, his other-selves. God gave man the capacity of cosmic consciousness which sees and feels the unique one in the multiplicity of beings. But man has not cared to develop these virtues latent in his heart. He sees everything through the divided twilight-mind and thinks in the terms of I-alone and Mine-alone. This I and Mine maya is the root of divisions and the fruit is what we see around us, hatred which makes man dangerous to man. Until man merges his separative egoism into the universalised consciousness, and until man touches the one Spirit which pervades all, this forbidden fruit shall not cease to tempt him and posison his life. Saviours have come and gone; reformers and armchair philosophers have spoken volumes; but the world is what it was for, man is still ignorant of what he is and what he ought to be and how. Raise your Self by your own Self, lower not your Self—Uddharet Atmnah Atmanam; Atmna Avasadayet—says the Gita. Yourself is soaked in the nectar of bliss; be conscious and be free and happy, says the Vedic Rishi. But who goes to the deeper Self when the selfish hunger and thirst for selfish pleasure dominate the mind? This hydra-headed selfishness and self-seeking infect every field of life, individual, domestic, urban, provincial, national, international, social, economic, political, and religious. The caste, creed, colour and race prejudices are offsprings of this gigantic selfishness in man. The white hates the black for the former would have the world and its joys for its self. One religionist hates another; why? For he thinks God and heaven and virtue are his monopoly. One province hates another and WHY? Because one refuses to acknowledge the cultural beauty of the other and is always shrewd in exploiting the resources of the other provinces for its selfish aggrandisement. One language hates another for it refuses to know and acknowledge the beauty in the other. Now let us apply these general principles to INDIA and try to evolve a solution for its social and political perversities.

"I am Man"

During my political career, I was closely shadowed by the hounds of Intelligence. They assumed various forms to come in personal contact with me and watch my open and secret movements. I was once conducting a Gurukul just to raise up an army of heroes for the nation after the example of Guru Govind. The District Magistrate sent me his C.I.D. and the latter wanted full details of my life, my native place, parentage, caste, creed etc., etc. 'I am a free man" said I; "God is may Father, Nature my Mother, the Sky-bound is my country; India is my home; humanity is my kith and kin and CONSCIENCE my religion". The C.I.D. reported to the magistrate, " This revolutionary hides his identity for a dangerous purpose."The magistrate called me. He was a Musulman, the very man that condemned great patriots like Chidambaram Pillai. I appeared before him. He demanded my caste: " I know you are a Brahmin; but I want you to lay it down in black and white for the purpose of law ", said he. I took my pen and wrote, " I am Man homed in India, a friend of humanity; I dislike all notions of black and white, caste and creed ". The magistrate looked rather surprised and said, " Is it amiss to call me a Musulman?" " You are MAN, Sir, before you call yourself a Musulman" was my quick retort. A long discussion developed from this incident; after long threatening me for my impertinent universality, the magistrate, at the instance of the collector, wrote against my name " Evidently a Brahmin, but a universalist ".

Hinduism, Religion of Human Unity

The world is torn into bits of mutual hatred by unnecessary divisions raised by mere mental conceptions of this ism and that ism. Nature gave us one world and one humanity. All great prophets from Krishna to Gandhi taught us the gospel of spiritual socialism and communal unity. But the separative egoism in man has built thick-walled isms around this prophet and that prophet and has baffled the vision of those great souls. For instance the Vedas are the scriptures of India. The Vedic Rishis did not create any caste or religion around their names and forms. They did their spiritual service to humanity most impersonally. "God is one and unique; to attain Him is the highest goal of man; that God pervades all space and is present in every heart. Realising the One Truth, Consciousness, and Bliss in the heart, the seer sees That in all everywhere, and is never perturbed by the multiplicity of things in nature." Here the inspired seers have laid down a broad universal basis for the social harmony of mankind. They never spoke about Hinduism, Brahminism or non-Brahminism. They taught us the universal Dharma; their voice was the voice of the Conscience which is the greatest law-giver of the world. The most ancient universal Law of living—Sanatana Dharma—allows the freedom of conscience and the free evolution of every soul towards its divine consummation.

Its Subsequent Degeneration

But interested clanish mentalities have so much divided this nation that the ideal seems almost impossible to be attained. The Guna Karma Vibhagas—functional gradations of the society—have become water-tight compartments of sectarianism so that we see more than two thousand camps in India in the name of religions, castes, Acharya Pitas, maths, and creeds. Gurudom is the source of divisions. Each Guru has a thick walled sect, secration laws, and fanatic disciples who declare their Guru as the Almighty God or Avatara and cry down other Masters. They cry out "heaven for us and hell for others." God is eclipsed behind these self-sufficient personalities. For instance there are more than a hundred personalities representing Shri Krishna and a hundred more representing the omnipotent Divine. All of them claim superiority over others, build egoistic walls around their names and forms and thus divide the land and the society into psychological opposites. There are cases in which the Acharya of one sect prevented his devotees from supporting the election of candidates who belonged to other sects. There are beings who close their eyes and ears and run away when they hear or see disciples of another sect. One is pleased to call his God Shiva and would not tolerate another to call the same God Narayana. One would worship Krishna and would not care for a Ramabhakta. Another man would like only a particular trade-mark on the front of his neighbours. U mark hates the Y mark, the perpendicular line hates the horizontal. One will not interdine with another not to speak of intermarriage. One will bathe if he chances to touch the man of another sect.

Modern Reformers

Reformers like Dayananda, Ram Mohan, Ramkrishna, Ramalinga and Gandhiji came to clear the ignorant mist between men and unify the nation. The result was, one was poisoned and another shot dead. Dayananda and Mahatmaji, the two gems of Gujarat, are two peerless forces of unity and human solidarity. They have done their best to remove all social disabilities. There is none to our knowledge who has touched the mass-mind so deeply as Mahatmaji.

But he has made just a beginning. His moral force has given a mass awakening and has liberated India from the foreign yoke. Another force, a Spiritual Force, must manifest to unite the human entity in the self-conscious Truth. East or West, Black or White, North or South, all can live together as one family. This possibility was stressed by the Vedic Rishis. All can live like birds nestling in a garden, says the seer voice. This attempt was culturally made by the Poet Tagore. But the spiritual achievement of the great ideal of unity rests with a Yogi like Shri Aurobindo. Shri Aurobindo has revolutionised the psychology of existence by bringing together, people of different types and creeds to live in one communion. By birth all are equal; by accident they belong to this or that religion, sect, creed, caste, Math, Guru etc. Recently there was a great saint in South India who stood for a universal communion of humanity free from the notions of caste, creed, and clime. His name was RAMALINGAM. He was a contemporary of Ramakrishna. He has sung more than ten thousand songs with the spiritual passion for the unity of mankind in the Divine consciousness. "Deign to hear me, O people of all corners of the earth", he proclaimed, " God is ONE and unique. His Grace rules the world. All are one in Him. Realise this fundamental unity and live a new life of spiritual communion free from the old notions of caste, creed, feud, race and religion."

Pre-Requisites of Human Unity

There must be a mutual recognition of merits and a free exchange of spiritual ideas and an intermingling of cultures. The wide spiritual intuitions of the Vedic Rishis, the universal compassion of Buddha, the non-violence of Mahavira, the patience of Christ, the equal mindedness of Kabira and Nanaka, the love of Chaitanya, the Divine fervour of St. Vagisadna Maniccavachaka, the heart of Sukha, the brain of Vyasa, the devotion of Ramkrishna, the voice of Dayananda, the do-or-die spirit of Mahatma Gandhiji, and the victorious adventure of Shivaji must go together to build up a new united race here and perpetuate the ancient spiritual ideals in a transformed modern life. The individual must universalise his heart, mind and life. That sort of training must begin in schools. Indians must be Indians, must be the members of the universal communion wherever they are born and whatever may be their birth and pedigree. There shall not be a separate caste or community like Brahmin or Harijan. The citizens of India must have the liberty of breathing the air wherever they like. A Musulman is a Musulman in the Masjid, a Christian is a Christian in the Church, a Hindu is a Hindu in the temple but all are Indians and all have an equal right to take their proper place in the Indian Commonwealth. The group prejudices can be overcome only by group living. Here are some of the possible means of removing all the mental and vital obstacles to the broad unity of Indians in FREE INDIA.

1. A free intermingling of provinces and sects by means of cultural co-operation, intermarriage, and industrial enterprises.

2. Sound education: the ancient Rishi Culture and the modern scientific culture must unite in the new system of education. The text books must be so prepared that they promote unity of consciousness, humanities and higher aspirations in the mind of the students. The school is the miniature country and the student the pattern of the coming nation. So the New India of communal and cultural harmony must be worked out in the class room and the professor must be the able architect of the nation's hero.

3. There must be one lingua franca for India—say Hindustani and one international language—say English. The mother tongue or the regional language must be given its deserving place. One province must have regard for the language and culture of the other and often an All India Cultural Union must be gathered for the exchange of thoughts and the promotion of literature and science. In this Union, all the important languages of India must be duly represented and the best works in each language must be merited and prizes awarded for them. Such works must be translated into Hindustani and English so that the world can understand them. For instance, there are hundreds of works in the Tamil literature worthy of translation in the world language. If the Cultural Union undertakes the work, the misunderstanding between the South and the North can be easily removed. There are hundreds of high souled saints here and their life and teaching would be very useful to humanity. The saints of one region must be recognized by the people of the other region without the provincial or the linguistic egoism. There must be a conference of the Acharyas of differ-

ent sects and they must put their heads together to create spiritual unity and harmony in the nation. One Guru must not raise thickwalled sectarianism around his heaven and curse hell for others. The Gurus must recognise the uniqueness of God, the unity of souls and the universality of the individual. A common Book of Prayers and Meditations must be compiled with selections from all the inspired scriptures. This book must serve as the Bible of the nation and it must be widely circulated and broadcast on the Radios.

4. The root cause of provincialism is the pride of one province which refuses to recognise the merit of the language and literature and culture of the other. This can be removed by a free interchange of knowledge and culture and by constant lectures by savants on the beauty of the several Indian languages.

There is also economic concern. Each province must be made self-sufficient; no province must be allowed to exploit the resources and the markets of the other province. The province must be given pre-eminence in commerce and industry. It can export its surplus and import things that cannot be procured within its area. The industry and trade of each province must be in its own hands so that it can give work and goods to its citizens. Experts from other provinces and countries can be invited to instruct its youths and train them for modern industries. If this is done, a Bengali will not be jealous of a Marwari.

5. A standard can be set up in dress too. Birds of the same feather often fly together. A dhoti, a shirt, and a Gandhi cap will do for India and a Chadder if necessary. This can be the civilian dress. Officials can put on their conventional dress.

6. An All India University must be raised in a suitable centre in which students from all the provinces can study special technical subjects and make research. This must develop like the Sorbonne in Paris.

These are some of the suggestions for the removal of group prejudices and for the unity and solidarity of the nation. More than all these things there is the Congress platform which is open to all irrespective of caste, creed or province. The present Constitutional Assembly has passed laws and regulations for the real union of the Indian Union and if Indians are loyal to the laws of the Indian Union, their unity is assured and all the stumbling blocks shall be removed by and by. Every Indian must feel his neighbour as a brother Indian and give him brotherly help. This is the secret of unity and progress—UNITY OF CONSCIOUSNESS.

Section III

Social Prejudices

INDIAN UNITY: A RETROSPECT AND A PROSPECT

G. S. GHURYE

Study of Past, Guide to Create Future

'Not the "history of the future" (as the old writers used to define prophecy), but that of the past which is epitomised in the present, is necessary for work and for action—which would not be real action if it were not illumined by the light of truth. And from this necessity is born also this new meditation that we have gone through, and that we invite others to go through, of the history of India'.1

India's Past Culture, its History

Long before Chandragupta Maurya or his more famous grandson Asoka brought under one political dominion almost the whole of what was known as India before the 15th August 1947, Taxila situated almost at its Northwestern threshhold had come to occupy the position of a University for students and intellectuals all over the land, a position which in later history came to be occupied by Benares (Kasi Varanasi) till almost the beginning of the 16th country. Thereafter till today there has been no similar place serving as the centre of intellectual life for the whole country.

When Asoka desired to make the message of Buddha, as he himself understood it, known to the people of India he could have it inscribed on rocks and stone-pillars in one script almost throughtout the whole length and breadth of geographical or British India. At least in the India east of the river Ravi the script of the writing was one and the same with very slight modifications. And the differences that are observed here and there are mostly such as might have been or rather must have been the result of the indifference of local masons towards correct writing. It is a fact proven for a long time and capable of positive proof to any doubting soul that all the contemporary scripts of our India, excepting the script in which Urdu is written, are derivable from that Brahmi script which Asoka found ready as a moccom heritage and which he used for conveying his Master's message to his people. While the single parent was intelligible all over India its manifold progeny today is not so. Thus in respect of our script we have strayed away from unity into diversity.

The language to be used for conveying the message was specified by the Master himself. The disciple had not to think about it. Buddha desired that his teaching should be made known to the people through their language and not through Sanskrit, the language of the elite. Experts inform us that the language of Asoka's inscription is basically the then official language of Magadha (Bihar) with minor provincial or regional variations. The variations are either so small or so insignificant that a native of the region round about Delhi of those times going to Mysore and that part of the country and suddenly coming upon the

---

1 We apologise to Benedetto Croce, the Italian philosopher who is convinced that all philosophy is but history, for substituting the word 'India' for the three words 'the nineteenth century' in the above quotation from his HISTORY OF EUROPE IN THE 19th CENTURY.

Asokan inscriptions there could without much difficulty read and understand them. There was thus in the time of Asoka the overall unity in the shape of language intelligible from one corner of our India to the other. Today there are at least twelve different languages which are mutually seperate over the same area. Most of them have highly developed literatures of their own. The speakers of these separate languages can hardly understand the medium of one another. Today when people from different parts of our India come together and decide to converse on some topic of intellectual interest, if they do not know a workman-like use of the English language they find themselves terribly handicapped. Most of them are nonplussed and wonder whether their country or culture is a unity or a bundle of separate units. In the matter of language, of the medium of expression, which is perhaps the most obvious mark of emotional community of a people and a culture, but for English our India would have been in the same position as in that of script, the medium of writing the expression.

From a hoary past, so ancient as almost to be mythical, royal families of the people of Northern India, have married into similar families from all parts of India. In their marital behaviour the royal families demonstrated their unity from Gandhara (the North-West Frontior Province) and Sauvira (Northern Sindh) to Kamarupa (Assam) on the one hand and Vidarbha (Berar) and Dravidadesa (Madura) on the other. The traditional homogeneity of the royal households was so far believed in, that Megasthenes, the Greek ambassador at the court of Chandragupta Maurya was sure that the daughter of Herakles, Krishna, was the ancestress of the then ruling family of the Dravidian Madura. And the city itself was so named after the Northern and Aryan Mathura. A Hindu grammarian of about the same time was convinced that the Pandyas of Southern India were the descendants of the famous Pandavas of the *Mahabharata*. The so-called native princes of British India, partly because they were not so catholic in their outlook as their hoary ancestors and partly because the paramount power looked with disfavour on such alliances, only off and on followed the old custom of marrying into royal families anywhere in the land. Whatever visible index of royal homogeneity was provided by this marital practice was already badly cut into by the emergence and establishment of non-Hindu Islamic royalty in its midst. And all that badly shattered practice will very shortly pass into the limbo of time and space. The so-called native princes who are at present in the process of absorption will eventually vanish off the scene. There can be no question of royal marriages serving as a visible index of the oneness of Indian royalty all over our India, which will be a democratic state interested in the actions of ordinary men and women, leaders in the political, social and intellectual field.

Since how early the fundamental traits of the culture complex represented by the Vedic and Brahmanic lore appear in the cultural make-up of Eastern and Southern India we do not know. We know that the author of the *Ramayana* was certain that the culture which Ravana or Ceylon represented was fundamentally the same as that cultivated by Rama and his immediate ancestors on the far north at Ayodhya. Yet the culture of the folks occupying the intervening area was not more like that of the Northern peoples. The poets of the *Mahabharata* are aware of differences in regard to certain marital institutions between the culture cultivated by the Kurus of the sacred region of Kuruksetra and that of some other folks. These latter were not confined to the South but were found also in the North-West and even the West. The fact that the heroes of the Epic, the Pandavas, too had some peculiar customs regarding marriage and that their friends and relatives, the Yadavas of Mathura and Saurashtra favoured a special type of marriage not very much in evidence in the Madhyadesa leads one to the conculsion that these poculiarities of the marital institutions noticed in the North-West, the West and the South were looked upon as only provincial varieties of a single culture-complex. It is in keeping with this inference that one finds the poets of the *Mahabharata* treating of the whole of the subcontinent of India as one cultural unit in their descriptions of the various pilgrimages which either the heroes of the Epic or some of the well-known sage made for different purposes. The sacrificial horse, too, of the great Asvamedha sacrifice roamed over more or less the same territories. Ever afterwards when a monarch is represented as desirous of a conquest of the world, 'digvijaya', he is described as having traversed the length and breadth of India. Thus *Kalidasa*, who stands to Hindu culture as Shakespeare to British or Goethe to German, lavishing his poetic skill and pouring his sentiment over either the 'digvijaya', the world conquering exploit, or the 'swayamvara' success, victory in the field of choice marriage, of a prince of the Raghu lineage, the family of his choice, brings in most of the regions and peoples already looked upon as belonging to a homogeneous unit by the early poets of the *Mahabharata*. The celebration of the horse-secrifice seems to have continued to be the ambition of every great monarch, whether of the Madhyadesa, of the Deccan, of Kanci or of the region further south till about the 11th century A. D. All this indicated a consciousness both of the royalty and the elite that from one end of India to the other the people were the inheritors of a more or less homogeneous culture, who had a right to, or had to be brought under, one political jurisdiction. For after all, the distinction and difference between the North and the South was bridged over by the hallowed connections of worthies commanding common respect. If Parasurama was a scion of a Brahmin family, which filled the office of the Purohita, the officiating priest, of the great Haiyaha dynasty of the Narmada valley, he was but a descendant through the daughter's line of the Ksatriya family of Kanyakubja (Kanouj), one of whose members was the far-famed Vishwamitra of iron will. The same Parasurama by his exploits and consequent remorse came to be associated in legend with the whole coastal strip from Broach, Bhrgukaccha, to at least Cochin, if not Cape Comorin, and has been traditionally looked upon as the patron-ancestor by the people of that region. Similarly Agastya, the Vedic Seer, who is famed in mythology as one who humbled the Vindhya mountain and is cherished as the husband of the Vidarbha beauty Lopamudra, again of Vedic associations, is passionately looked upon as their patron-saint by the Tamil people, who ascribe to him much that is good and useful in their culture.

The fundamental and overall unity which was felt all over old India almost prophetically comes to be confined to and concretized in respect of the political India of today by the great preaching and organising activity of Sankaracharya, who disputed and wrote, preached and organised, almost the same time that the Muslim power was knocking out the Hindu faith and culture from Sindh. The religious 'maths', centres of religious preaching and authority, which Sankaracharya established left out India west of the Ravi as beyond their purview.

The great Sankaracharya firmly planted the Vedantic school of Hindu philosophy as the supreme and almost the only significant school of philosophy among the half a dozen or so of orthodox schools and three or four heterodox ones. He thus gave the Hindu society, accustomed to free, desultory, and even contradictory and contending schemes of philosophical thought for about fifteen hundred years, a unified and uniform philosophical basis for the social mind for about three centuries. And though he hailed from Malabar he carried on his preaching and writing activity through Sanskrit, the language of the elite, which for its clarity and trenchance stands unsurpassed. His is the poineer and the first argumentative treatise on philosophy embodying the result of philosophical speculations which started with the Upanisadic teachers. It gave the final *coupe-de-grace* to two systems of thought on Life and Beyond, which were embodied in similar argumentative treatises earlier: one was that of Buddhist thinkers and the other was the much older scheme of life against which both the Upanisadic teachers as well as Buddha had protested but which, not more than a century before Sankaracharya, was vigorously presented in an argumentative treatise of great polemic success among the contemporary teachers by Kumarila Bhatta. It was the philosophy of sacrificial ritual and activity, which was evidently not suited to the changing conditions of mundane existence.

It is a curious coincidence not yet taken full cognisance of by Indologists that very soon after the rise of Sankaracharya creative Sanskrit literature ceases to flourish. Thereafter Sanskrit remains principally as the medium of intellectual life. Literature on philosophy, on law and jurisprudence, on poetics and on music continued to be embodied in good Sanskrit. The local dialects or languages had already begun to be utilized by preachers to convey their religious message to their local brethren. The Tamil Vaisnava and Saiva saints appear to have been the first to use their local Tamil medium to sing the praises of God before their Tamil brethren. A long succession of them had done so for about five or six centuries when the famous Vaisnava reformer Ramanuja in the 11th century A. D., desiring to put before the then intellectual world of India the system of philosophical thought organised by him on the basis of the teachings of the Vaisnava saints of Tamil India, chose the medium of Sanskrit for his great treatise *Sribhasya*, though he was himself a Tamil and a disciple of a Tamil saint-preacher. Till then the Unqualified Monism of Sankaracharya was considered to be the only valid Vedanta philosophy. Ramanujacharya scored such success and secured so many followers that his system of Qualified Monism soon came to be considered as a more or less equally valid aspect of Vedanta philosophy.

The fruits of the ferment of thought, speculative, critical and synthetic, which the intellectual elite of India conveyed through the medium of Sanskrit, were visible in the manifest overall unity or homogeneity of the country and its culture which presented itself to even critical foreign observers and students of the time. Alberuni, the Islamic sojourner, observer and critical student of the India that was already conquered by his Islamic royal patron as well as of that which yet remained to be brought under Islamic suzerainty in the 11th century A.D. has not almost a word to say regarding the diversity of peoples, languages and cultures of the land much less their differences and animosities, if any. The whole country and the people, despite many political divisions and contending royalties, manifested a unified and homogeneous front to a foreign observer, excepting for its caste-system.

Students of history, readers of traveller's accounts or other discriminating students cannot say as much of the India from about the 14th century A. D. upto the end of the British dominion on the 15th August 1947. Nor can the contemporary observers, whether its citizens or strangers, can, wih truth unviolated, predicate the same of even the free political India of today. Overall unity and homogeneity of the peoples and cultures of politically free India is yet to be achieved and is a task for the future, for the accomplishment of which sound foundations are to be laid today.

In this India of Hindu culture, which with all its countrywide variations presented an overall unity, with its single religious system accomodating varieties of religious experience and practice within its fold, with its single language of intellectual culture and its common centres of learning and pilgrimage, was implanted firmly about the middle of the 13th century, a new religio-social culture, the culture of Islamic rulers. Curiously enough just a little before this event, when the great Ghori conqueror was pounding the gallant Rajputs, one prince among them who distinguished himself even in his defeat was glorified in bardic poetry, which was couched in the local language, the prototype of modern Hindi. It is significant that no court poet enshrined his eulogy in classical Sanskrit, though about the same time the Kashmirian Kalhana was resuscitating the glories of the forgotten kings of Kashmira in Sanskrit poetry through his *River of Kings' Rajatarangini*. About 1275 Jnaneswaram, the Marathi saint-poet and philosopher, expounded the old Bhagavadgita for the first time through the local dialect of Marathi and once for all fixed Marathi language. This vernacularisation of religion and philosophy went forward progressively to the great edification of the mass of people. As it benefited without the slightest doubt a very large section of the population it must be hailed as a healthy development. Yet it furnishes evidence that cracks in the homogeneous looking frontage of culture had begun to appear. It concretises in the cultural province what was happening in the politico-military field, viz. lack of sympathetic understanding and effective co-operation among the diversity of regions and peoples.

It is a matter of common knowledge that the various local dialects which began to produce literature from about the 6th century in the South and about the 12th in the North went on developing with rapidity during the period of the Muslim rule of India. The Muslim occupation and rule itself added one more language, as it brought in an additional religio-social system, different from the languages which were getting established. Whereas the Urdu language was the result of culture contact and represented at least in its form and structure the influence of both Persian and non-Indian language, and Sanskrit, the Indian language, the Muslim culture in its elite form was a purely Islamic religio-social system, utterly different from the elite Hindu culture. The local languages in the course of the few centuries that have elapsed have, many of them at least, built up highly developed literatures of their own. These are not confined to religious poetry and disquisitions but cover almost all items in both emotional and intellectual fields. Each of these languages, therefore, represents to its speakers the working content of their culture. This complex is still preponderatingly an interpretation of the old unified Sanskritic culture with a fair leaven from the content of modern English culture and only a very slight addition of a dynamic nature from the cultural stock of one or two sister-languages. What political consequences this development would have led to, if the period of foreign domination had not coincided, we do not know. We actually find at the end of two foreign dominations, spread over a period of about six and a half centuries, that the speakers of these different languages, though looking upon the separate treasure as their specific culture, only consider it as a variety of the Hindu culture, that was and that is developing. Politically they think of all of them together as one nation in whose destiny their own separate destinies are inherent.

The Muslim rule of India, its introduction of the religio-social system of Islam and its creation, the Urdu language, have resulted in an altogether different development. The Urdu language with its non-Indian script had even before the end of the British rule over our country come to be looked upon as the mother-tongue of the Muslim inhabitants of the land. Since the partition of the country and the creation of the free state of Pakistan it has now officially been stamped as the national language of the erstwhile Muslim inhabitants of the country. The creation of the free state of Pakistan, which has formally declared itself to be a Muslim State, out of a portion of the country, which had remained one indivisible whole for at least twenty-two hundred years, though from time to time it was politically parcelled out among three or four ruling houses, did not make the other part of it, the free state of India, a more or less homogeneous cultural unit as the whole of India was till the establishment of Muslim power in the country. There has remained in political India as her citizens a fair number of the followers of the religio-social system of Islam. Their language or mother-tongue, by implication, recent history, and I believe even by pronouncement, is Urdu, whether they are the citizens of a Tamil-speaking province or of a Bihari-speaking one.

There are other non-Hindu groups, received first by the Hindu kings and then grown in numbers, either by dubious conversion or by growth or by both. Not only are they not significant in numbers but also are they not such compact religio-social systems as that of the Muslims.

Fissiparous Tendencies in Free India

Free political India is thus a new set-up, within which there are far greater potentialities of fissiparous tendencies than in the geographical India of the 10th or the 11th century A.D. The task of the immediate future is to lay sound foundations for the integration of the linguistically differentiated units as well as of the other units of compact culture. That linguistic realities will concretise themselves in the form of linguistically determined political units within the great Fedration or Union appears almost certain. To guard against the legitimate and healthy realisation of linguistic separateness, militating against the overall homogeneity of political India, there must be comparable central organisation for intellectual and cultural life, just as there are the political organs of the Indian Parliament and the Government of India. On the political and administrative side we can trust to our political leadership to devise appropriate techniques to see that the various groups above referred to feel at home as one political unit, leaving enough scope to manage their own affairs without interference and yet being subject to such wise supervision and even guidance as may keep the centre strong and respected. To achieve the objective of overall community of feeling and of intellectual and cultural homogeneity it is necessary to create the modern counterparts of Taxila and Kasi with appropriate modifications to suit the new set-up. In short, we must have an Indian

University directly under the Government of India financed by it, situated at a suitably central place, whose climate is on the whole conducive to intellectual work for the best part of the year.

European Parallel

Before we sketch the scheme of such a centre of unification let us try to appreciate our country's position and its task by contemplation of the condition of Europe with which its linguistic and politico-ethnic history has notable similarities.

In Europe to-day there are more than twenty-five separate political states with about forty languages spoken by their inhabitants. These languages though separate entities can be and are derived from not more than four different families. More than thirty of these belong to one family of languages known as the Indo-European, to which also the largest number of our Indian languages of to-day belong. Within the Indo-European family of the European languages further closer relations indicating a unity of some of them in the not very distant past can be recognised. Thus there are principally five branches of languages, which are (1) the Celtic, (2) the Teutonic, (3) the Romance, (4) the Greek and (5) the Slavonic. The contemporary European languages are written in half a dozen different scripts which are finally derivable from either Greek or Latin alphabet. Of the five principal Indo-European branches of languages the Celtic is represented by only one or two and the Greek by only one. The Teutonic and the Slavonic each has more than five or six descendants today, though the former till the 3rd century and the latter till the sixth century A.D. was one undifferentiated language. To the Romance group belong four or five European languages of today. They are all derived from Latin. They appear to have been the earliest to produce some literature, which very curiously both as regards its genre as well as its dating parallels Indian literature. *Chanson de Roland* in French is considered to be the earliest considerable work in any modern European language. And it was a sort of heroic chronicle, not very unlike our *Prthvirajarasan*. It was produced during the 12th century, thus almost synchronising with the above work of Canda Bardai. The greatest early work in any European language, however, was Dante's *Divina Comedia* written in about 1305 A. D. It not only fixed the Italian medium but was a religious work of the greatest significance. Here in India as we have noted the saint-poet Jnanesvara wrote his famous commentary on the Bhagavadgita in Marathi about the year 1275.

It is well to remember that Europe, which has today a population which is larger by about 10 to 15 per cent than that of our political India, was till recently a cultural unity more or less. Over all from about the 3rd century A. D. had spread Christianity, which formed one unifying factor throughout later history. From about the 1st century B. C. to about the 9th century A. D. over a very large portion of Western Europe first Roman and then Frankish rule had produced and maintained a political as well as a cultural unity. And it was after the death of Charlemagne that modern European languages and states made their definitive appearance on the unified horizon. Throughout this period the language in Western Europe of not only administrative routine and intellectual life but also of the well-to-do people was Latin. Latin continued to be the language of the intellectual elite till about the beginning of the 18th century. It was also about this time that the great Slavonic state of Russia first got oriented to the Western European standards. Thereafter the Modern European languages swept the board of European life. The consequences of the slow yet steady and complete unfolding of the feeling of linguistic unity and nationality on this horizon are a matter of modern European history. Their poignancy for great and thoughtful Europeans can be gauged from the proposals and writings of some of them. It is well known how in 1930 the French politician-statesman M. Briand put forward a scheme of European Union intended to procure all kind of smoother living for the Europeans ostensibly under the League of Nations but practically beyond it and above its scope. H.A.L. Fisher, the great historian-satesman of Britain, writing in 1935 recorded his well-founded and deeply felt lament and trepidation in words which deserve to be quoted as they epitomise what we have attempted to state above. He says: "One by one the great attempts to impose a common system upon the energetic self-willed peoples of Europe have broken down..... Nor has any system of secular ideas been more successful in obtaining universal acceptance. ... Yet ever since the first century of our era the dream of unity has hovered over the scene and haunted the imagination of statesmen and peoples. Nor is there any question more pertinent to the future welfare of the world than how the nations of Europe, *whose differences are so many and so inveterate* * may best be combined into some stable organisation for the pursuit of their common interests and the avoidance of strife."

Solution

The geographical unity of British India, whose population was about that of Europe, can hardly be said to be greater than that of Europe. The repeated exploits of great generals in both the regions bear out the truth of this statement. Yet the early forefathers of the Hindus in spite of great odds succeeded in producing during the course of about two thousand years a cultural homogeneity over the whole land quite sufficient not only to make the huge population willing citizens of a single political state, whenever such was provided, but also to make them wish for such a one. Political history and the earlier cultural leaven helped by it during the last nine hundred years have conspired to cut badly into that unified horizon, though the former has not only provided a central administration but also has, during its latest period, given a common language for the educated elite of the whole country and a well-trained and loyal army. The design of the army as well as the pattern of the central administration require great modifications to suit the new set-up and are being assiduously attended to by the political leaders. The provision of a central language is being warmly discussed. The question being frought with difficulties created by the political history as well as by the cultural upset is one which evokes more emotional reactions than reasoned arguments in its deliberation.

To us it appears that shorn of its sentimental aspects the question of a common language ought to be viewed either from the point of view of the provincial languages and cultures or from the international one. The latter viewpoint is rather premature for us, situated as we are. Our country once made the mistake and paid heavily for it. We refer to Asoka and his international mission of peace. In his pacifist enthusiasm he forgot the task of strengthening the unity and the will to resist of his own people. Partially as a consequence of this premature enthusiasm and partially as the result of other circumstances soon after the passing away of this masterful personality our country suffered dis-

---

* Italics are ours.

memberment from which we by ourselves hardly ever recovered. The path of safety lies through the strengthening of ourselves as a buttress against possible internal dissension. Unified strength of ours by itself will push forward the cause of world peace. Therefore the more urgent and relevant consideration in the decision regarding our common and national language is the nature of the provincial languages and their relation to the common language. The cultures of the largest bulk of these provincial languages must not feel that they are subordinated to, much less superseded by, any of their sister or foreign languages. The common language must be such as will be accepted by most of these provincial cultures and languages without a feeling of mortification. A moment's thought for those, who have known the history of the formation and development of these languages and the scripts they use today, will convince them that the only language which answers this description is Sanskrit. Many of the provincial languages have been derived from it and those that are not derived have incorporated in them such a large vocabulary from Sanskrit that the latter cannot but appear in the guise of a benefactor. With such history the learning of Sanskrit ought to become fairly easy for the speakers of most of these provincial languages. The Devanagari script thus cultivated can be sooner or later used as the one script of all the provincial languages. Our Muslim brethren, having allowed their erstwhile co-religionist compatriots to form their own independent state and having themselves chosen to be the citizens of political India, will, we hope, seek inspiration from Akbar and Dara rather than from Alauddin and Aurangzeb. If they do so they would not object to learning Sanskrit as a common language of the country and its elite. Sanskrit is a highly developed language in which there is ready to hand varied terminology for not only humanistic studies but also some of the modern sciences. The effort required to make the terminology quite complete and comprehensive will be small. Thus there is this further advantage with the selection of Sanskrit as the common national language that the transition period will be short, and that the adoption of a common language will be a fait accompli very soon.

That some language will be stamped as the common national language there is not the least doubt. Our task here being concerned with the creation of a centre for intellectual unification, we have discussed the question of the common language as facilitating this process of homogeneity. As observed above for homogeneity to be established a new centre of intellectual life, which should form the focus for the crystallisation of the modern point of view and thence should introduce the binding cement of intellectual culture through the medium of the common language of the nation, is the desideratum. Such a centre in modern times can only be formed by a University. It is necessary to establish at a suitable place the Indian University financed principally by the Indian Government and partially by every one of the Provincial Governments. The language of instruction at this University shall be the common national language. The stage of instruction which this University should handle should be only the highest. It must be only the postgraduate courses that should be the concern of this University. All the Humanistic Studies and the Pure Sciences should be represented in the teaching and researching staff of the University. The M.A. and the M.Sc., degrees in Humanities and Pure Sciences of all the Provincial Universities must be made to be based on a uniform curriculum spread over two years. At the end of the second year an examination in the whole curriculum shall be conducted by the Provincial Universities for their own candidates. All candidates for these degrees shall be required to spend their junior year at the Indian University, where complete instruction shall be offered through the medium of the common language on the curriculum of the junior year of the courses for the M.A. and M.Sc. degrees. The travelling expense and one-half of the other expenses involved in residence at the Indian University of each student shall be borne by his Provincial Government, the rest shall have to be found by the student himself. The Indian University shall offer at the end of the year, after whatever test, to at least thirty per cent. of the students cash prizes, each equal in value to half the average expense of a student in residence there. The academic staff of all grades may number about 700 members. About 10,000 students may be allowed to be in residence under proper instruction. Of these about 1000 may be research students, working for their Ph.D. degree. These would have been admitted after selected from among all the Provincial Master's-degree-holders. They being absolutely the select lot of the students of the country their expenses shall be borne by the Indian Government and the Indian University and they shall have free education. Thus every year about 10,000 students, almost the pick of the educated intelligence as well as some of the would-be powerful emotion-workers of the nation, would have drunk at the fountain, where the teachers are Indian, and the language both of instruction and social intercourse is the common national language. In a generation's time the number of such engaged in the various walks of life through the different provinces would be large enough to provide an effective binding material for a homogeneous class. The intellectual output of the Ph.D. students and the large staff devoted to learning and research should, at the same time, make the common national language the most outstanding of all the Indian languages.

We hope this plan will commend itself to the leaders of our country. Before concluding we shall only mention the fact that between Britain and France a scheme somewhat like the one adumbrated here, with appropriate variation, has been mooted and perhaps already partially implemented.

THE HINDU SOCIAL ORDER

K. G. MASHRUWALLA

Caste Complex Universal

Of all the puzzling problems with which we are faced, I give the first place to the problem created by the Hindu Social Order, popularly known as the Caste System. I am conscious that the foundations of this ancient order have been considerably shaken in recent times. Some, indeed, hold that it will be extinct in about a generation more. I do not know. The Hindu Caste complex is one of the various representatives of a psychological complex, which has a very strong grip, not only upon the masses, but also, under various names and in various forms, upon the average politician and race—and sect-minded leaders of the people throughout the world. Even the most intellectual minds—including those who declare themselves to be its enemies and victims, as also those who are outside or have ceased to be within its pale,—are not free from it, and often, consciously or unconsciously they attempt or desire to give a fresh lease of life to it, perhaps in a different external dress.

Indeed, it seems very few men are or can become altogether free from it.

The complex consists in an extraordinarily strong grip of the idea that one unavoidably, and often irredeemably, belongs to one or more limited groups of mankind. It has before its eyes the existence of other groups, from which it regards and keeps itself distinct and more or less unamalgamable. Both by the force of habit and the training imparted to him, he feels a deep loyalty to that group. The loyalty is so deep that he is generally unable to shake it off, even when it is disadvantageous to him or he is intellectually convinced of the necessity of shaking it off. Naturally, when it is advantageous to him to belong to that group, it becomes a matter of pride for him to belong to it. The pride often amounts to vanity and arrogance and the position is regarded to be a privilege, which he seeks to preserve jealously and exploit profitably.

Caste, its Origin and Essence

The group complex may have been based on various factors; e.g., colour, clan, birth, original or present place of residence, religion, sect, language, occupation, marriage alliance or dispute, difference of opinion about right food or drink, some social or other custom, or any other cause whatsoever. In fact, a caste may come into existence on any ground, on which a separate association could be formed. The difference between a caste and an ordinary association generally consists in the caste becoming at some period of time or another also an association for forming marriage alliance amongst its members. Whatever may have been the original cause, which led to the formation of the group, and whether it came into existence consciously, deliberately and at a particular point of time, or unconsciously, unintentionally and at an unascertainable time, as soon as it reaches the stage when marriage alliances within the group alone get insisted upon, and those outside it disliked or punished, the group may be regarded as having taken the shape of caste. A caste may be a body within a larger group, or it may consist of several smaller groups. Thus, as a member of a larger group, a person may be a Brahman, but if he can marry only, say, with a Brahman, whose forefathers hailed from Malwa, he is a Malaviya Brahman and not just a Brahman. Similarly, a person restricted by custom to marry within a circle of families originally residing in Cutch and Kathiawar and known as Khojas, is a Khoja by caste, although by religious faith he may be a general Muslim, or an Agakhani, or even a Hindu Vaishnava.

In this way, we have in India Hindu castes, Muslim castes, Christian castes, Sikh castes, etc., as also mixed Hindu-Muslim, Hindu-Christian (and, may be, also Hindu-Muslim-Christian and Hindu-Sikh castes), not to mention Jain-Vaishnava castes. Not all castes prohibit inter-religious, or inter-provincial or inter-linguistic marriages. With such castes, religion, region or language is a personal matter, and in mixed marriages, it gets adjusted according to mutual convenience. On the other hand, there are castes which are based on no definable principle. Some accidental and temporary cause—just a dispute over a dinner—may have created it, and it persists even though no one remembers the original cause or is able to ascribe any reason for its continuance. Many castes exist only by the law of inertia.

Caste, a World Wide Phenomenon

The caste complex is present all over the world. Perhaps, it is not yet as hard set amongst newer civilizations as here. It is not unnatural that in an old civilization like that of India, its roots should be very deep. The creation of the Anglo-Indian and Anglo-Burmese castes by the British and the disdain for inter-racial, particularly inter-colour—and the dislike for inter-national or inter-church marriages in Europe and America indicate the presence of the complex amongst all races. Mohammad had to yield to it, when in spite of his attempts, he could not bring about peace between Zainab (an independent Arab) and her husband Zaid (who was a freed slave), and had, not only to consent to their divorce, but to take her as his own wife, as no independent Arab would consent to marry the divorcee of a slave.* Indeed, the "whites" are fast becoming caste-minded in the same way and with the same implications as those connoted by the term "Caste Hindus." That is, it is not merely a caste *plus* superiority complex. The complex of caste superiority seems to be an accompaniment of success in political, economic or intellectual sphere by an organized group. But it should be remembered that caste complex is not necessarily a superiority complex. It may be accompanied with an equality or an inferiority complex also. As I look upon it, it seems to me to be the fountain-head of several of our problems, such as the Harijan, the Pakistan, the Anglo-Indian, the Christian, the Sikh and communalism generally, as also of racial politics in India and abroad.

THE VARNA SYSTEM

The caste system must be distinguished from the *Varna Vyavastha* (order, system) as promulgated by the Hindu Smritis. It is a special classification of the various castes under four heads, Brahman, Kshatriya,

---

* On the authority of Pandit Sundarlal's **Hajrat Mohommad aur Islam.**

Vaishya and Shudra. It is difficult to say when this classification was promulgated and how it came to be adopted throughout India. It is also difficult to say whether it was super-imposed upon castes, or whether the caste-system came into existence at a later stage. Possibly caste arose through clan and regional causes, and Varna through ritualistic reasons. The basis of the classification was the observation of certain fairly well-expressed temperamental and actional aptitudes * of the people under the jurisdiction of the Hindu law-givers. It does not appear that the law-givers ever made any attempt to abolish castes based on distinctions other than the aptitudinal or even vocational ones. It seems to have been just a scientific or ritualistic division, not interfering with the actual social divisions of the day. On the vocational side, the classification does not seem to be more than a mere recommendation. Thus there have always been some Brahman castes in the army, agriculture, commerce and handicrafts, and even menial service. Kshatriyas have almost always been agriculturists or cattle-breeders in times of peace. On the other hand, Vaniks (Banias) who are generally classed as Vaishyas, have hardly ever personally been agriculturists and cattle-breeders.

The inference is that the *varna* institution was rather a special classification. To a certain extent, it commemorated caste or clan history, and was recommended as an ideal of social organization. But the controllers of social order never made it a compulsory one—except for ritualistic purposes—and it never superseded the caste. They attempted to tack the vocation to the caste, so that caste loyalty took the form of loyalty not only for choosing the bride but also for choosing the vocation. The vocational loyalty has been considerably—if not completely—destroyed by the " modern " civilization. Varna no longer connotes vocation, whatever else it might continue to connote. It no longer binds, even if it did once, a person to a particular profession and in that sense

* I explain the word **guna-karma** as the temperamental and " actional " aptitudes of a person. A vocation is well chosen, when it fits with one's temperamental and actional aptitudes. Whether these aptitudes are hereditary or environmental may well be regarded as yet not definitely settled. The tendency of modern scientists inclines towards regarding several things, which were all along assumed to be hereditary, as merely the result of environments. But as this is a very modern opinion, one thinking in terms of haredity might be excused. It should also be noted that " environments " include cogenital associations also. This makes the distinction between hereditary and environmental factors very negligible for practical purposes. Thus the controversy, whether the **varna** or **guna-karma** of a person should be regarded as determined by birth or environmental development seems to me of academical interest only. Further, it should be noted that the verses in the Gita, which refer to the four varnas, define the Brahmana and the Kshatriya according to their temperamental aptitudes, and the Vaishya and the Shudra according to their actional aptitudes ; and the latter again are made concrete by naming particular vocations. As the temperamental aptitude also plays a prominent part in determining a person's vocation, the **varna** classification has come to be regarded as a classification of people according to their vocations.

Personally, as I have said in the body of the article, I do not regard vocation as an essential part of the classification. I think that the classification was made rather for ritualistic purposes than for economic and social purposes. I would therefore translate gunakarma vibhaga as " divisions according to temperamental and actional aptitudes," or in short " aptitudinal divisions."

the *varna* order has ceased to exist, except for some rapidly dying ritual ceremonies.

Caste versus Varna

Not so the Caste. In turbulent times, it had been able to preserve the Hindu society from political and social extinction and had proved to be a convenient method as much for absorbing foreign or heterogeneous but peaceful elements as also for resisting the inroads of aggressive ones. Towards some it maintained a superiority complex; with some, it established equality, and over others still, it imposed and cultivated a sense of inferiority. Marriage restriction was the common element in all. Restrictions on co-dining—another important social function—was another element to help it. "Superiors" could generally give their food to others, but would not take it from them. "Equals" generally took it from those, who were prepared to receive it from them. That is, they either freely inter-dined or mutually excluded one another. "Inferiors" could receive food from others, but not give it to them. Politically powerful foreign tribes could destroy the political power of the Hindus but they could not destroy the superiority complex of those who had developed it before their arrival, or the equality complex of those, against whom the aggressor tried to put up a superior show. Sometimes protestant religious sects deliberately developed the equality complex of 'boycott-all' type. The "inferior" castes suffered at the hands of all.

The caste is still in existence. As stated above though there might be other factors also in the existence of this or that caste, the most essential factor is the restriction of the sphere of marriage, and next to it of co-dining.

In course of time, the castes have become too many. They have grown either by additions of different groups of foreigners or by subdivision *ad infinitum*. No serious attempt seems to have been ever made to amalgamate castes, though in times of difficulty brides have been received from "equal" or even "inferior" castes. No caste seems to have ever allowed entry of an outsider into it by conversion or any other process. Consequently, castes have always increased numerically. But this necessarily diminished their sphere of marriage and of social contacts resulting from marriage.

Generally, one would expect that marriage presupposed intimate previous acquaintance. But, paradoxical as it might seem, in course of time the caste designation became more important than actual acquaintance with a family for arranging marriage. Thus an Agarwal living for generations in Delhi may contract marriage with an Agarwal living for generations in Hyderabad Deccan, without ever having known a single member of the latter's family, but may not marry in the family of a Maheshwari neighbour known to him intimately. So, the caste has defeated to a considerable extent its psychological basis also, and has become a burden to all. The burden is particularly hard upon those who cannot assume a superiority complex or are endowed with an inferiority one. The result is that the system has become now an object of severe attack almost universally, and, whether it takes long or short time, its extinction seems certain.

Extant Attitudes to Caste and Varna

But in the meantime, it is inevitable that even thinking people should be divided into groups of various degrees of radicalism, reformism and conservatism. So, the present state of *varna* and caste has given rise to the following different ideologies :—

(i) those who still regard the abolition of both *varna* and caste as calamities, and wish to preserve both ;

(ii) those who welcome the abolition of caste but not of *varna*, and would revive or organise the latter in a suitable manner ;

(iii) those who regard both institutions as calamities, but not being hopeful of their extinction and labouring under a sense of frustration, desire to form " equal " castes or rival federations of castes (that is " communities ") in place of " inferior " ones ; and

(iv) those who want their total extinction in every shape or form

Conclusion

An institution will be long-lived and possessed of phoenix-like character, only if it fulfils some immediate social need and represents some fundamental human nature. And, whether it comes into existence haphazardly and empirically or in pursuance of a deliberate plan, it is never an unmixed good or an unmixed evil, and cannot be kept alive in its vigour after it has ceased to fulfil the need for which it came into being. An attempt to do so will only cause delay in its dissolution, if not also gangrene in the social organisation. On the other hand, to the extent the institution represents a fundamental trait of human nature, it cannot be annihilated by even the most radical of revolutions. It can be made only to change its outer form and dress. The Radical need not, therefore, be too hopeful, or the Conservative too apprehensive of its demolition. Man's sagacity lies in choosing for it from time to time new forms and dress, which will suit the changed conditions of life. If this is not wisely and consciously done and matters are allowed to run their own haphazard course or are given short-sighted and narrow mouldings, the resulting institutions will be like those monster fish, which, it is said, the Chinese used to breed for the pleasure of fashionable society. They showed all manner of distorted bodily shapes, inconvenient to the creatures themselves, and mere objects of curious inspection for spectators.

Marriage alliances with any degree of permanence will generally take place in limited spheres. Whether they are arranged by the parties themselves or their friends, most people will marry in familiar circles and amongst equals. Similarly, as long as a vocation supplies a social need and is socially respected and provides a living, most people will keep to it generation after generation. Indeed, the conservatism of the people is generally such that they cling to it even when the respect and the living are inadequate. I do not think that this is peculiar to India. But when these natural tendencies are made compulsory by punishing their breach with fine, excommunication etc., there is a hard set caste. It creates social, economic and political inequalities and prevents the development of the man whose talents are different from that of the group, to which he belongs, and which he is not allowed to give up.

It has created serious political problems already—such as that of Harijans and Sikhs within Hinduism, and the communal problem between people of different religions. The abolition of the caste complex is essential for loosening the grip of all these.

HINDU SOCIAL ORGANIZATION

GOKUL CHAND NARANG

Caste; Misconception of its origin

Caste system is generally considered a weak spot of Hinduism, and the wild growth of innumerable castes and sub-castes into which the present-day Hindus are divided lends strength to this view. Much of the criticism is, however, based on ignorance or sectarian bias. The prevailing view of critics is apparently based on some sort of belief as if Manu assembled all the Hindus of the world in one place and stamped some as Brahmans, some as Kshatriyas, some as Vaishyas and the rest, out of contempt or malice, as Shudras, and handed over to each group a card mentioning the duties and functions which members of each group had to discharge, viz., those stamped as Brahmans had to teach others and conduct religious ceremonies, the Kshatriyas had to protect the people and to establish charities, and the Vaishyas had to engage in trade, to breed cattle and carry on agriculture, while the others had to serve all the other three groups with devotion and without any murmur.

Caste, its Genesis

Such a supposition is absurd on the face of it. The very nature of the functions, e.g., those assigned to the Brahman group, militates against this *ad hoc* division of the nation. The more rational view is that Manu did not make an arbitrary assignment of these functions but noted down this classification *ex post facto* after an observation and examination of the functions actually being performed by different individuals of the community. In course of time these functions became hereditary. This was but natural and in no way detrimental to the social or economic welfare of the nation. Sons would naturally be inclined to follow their fathers' professions and would find it easier to acquire efficiency in them, not only by influence of heredity but also by the facilities provided by home environments and parental guidance. Nor would there be any loss of dignity in following one's hereditary occupation even if it is that of a sweeper. This went on for centuries, perhaps for milleniums with the result that these divisions became crystallised into castes, and caste, instead of being determined by profession or occupation, came to be determined by birth. Those who were not fit for any of the functions assigned to three higher divisions or were destitute of the means to follow any of their occupations remained as Shudras.

Pride of caste grew in course of time and crystallisation of these divisions grew more rigid with the lapse of centuries, and Shudraism also became hereditary as their occupations also became hereditary. Barbers and Kahars (water suppliers), cobblers, sweepers and so many others of the so-called Shudra class have been following their professions from generation to generation and their castes have become as rigid as other so-called higher castes. And the beauty of it is that each caste had a pride of its own and no one felt ashamed of his caste and till recently there was no ill-will between members of one caste and those of another on the ground of superiority of the one and the inferiority of the other. On the other hand, each respected the other. In the Punjab a barber is addressed as Raja, a potter as Prajapat, a Kahar (water carrier) as Panch, if he is a Hindu, and Bhishti if he is a Mussalman and a sweeper as Jamadar or Mehtar. A Jamadar is a military officer and Mehtar means a nobleman and is in fact the title of the Ruler of Chitral!

The classification, rigid as it has become, has never stood in the way of the Hindus in recognising merit wherever it is found irrespective of caste. Hindus of all castes have been paying their homage to saintly persons of all castes including such men as Ravidas, a cobbler, Nam Dev, a washerman, Sain, a barber, and even Sadan, a butcher by caste.

Caste, its Occupational Basis

The fact is that caste system is not an essential part of Hinduism regarded as a religion. Caste rests on one's occupation and position in society, and it exists in one form or another in all parts of the world and among all people. Colour bar which is creating so much trouble in South Africa and more or less in all countries dominated by white populations is nothing but a sort of caste system. The Pegging Act and other such provisions excluding coloured people from Whitemen's hotels and restaurants, relegating them to separate compartments in Railways and even in Tramcars are manifestations of the same prejudices as are ascribed by Non-Hindus to the caste system of the Hindus. Among the Muslims the pride of caste is no less marked among the Syeds, Moghuls and Pathans than that among the Brahmans and the Rajputs.

The fact that in its origin, caste was determined by one's occupation is not only a matter of historical proof but is also shown by the process which during comparatively recent centuries led to the growth of sub-castes. Lohars (blacksmiths) Tarkhans (carpenters), Sonars (goldsmiths), Chamars (chramkars or cobblers and leather-workers), Dhobis (washermen), Nais, (napits or barbers) and others have all grown into separate castes simply because their families have been engaged in their respective professions since times immemorial. Bajaj (Bazaz, a cloth merchant) has become a sub-caste among Khatris including Aroras and Banias and obviously because their families dealt in cloth for a sufficiently long time. Gandhi is another sub-caste among Khatris and Banias because their ancestor's dealt in *gandh* or scents. Khandpuras (dealers in sugar), Chawalas (dealers in rice) and Gorowaras (Gurwalas or dealers in Gur or jaggery) are other instances in point.

So far the religious or theological aspect of the question is concerned, caste system as such, as stated above, has nothing to do with Hinduism as a religion. All human beings, whether barbarians of Africa or Dons of Oxford, may adopt Hindu doctrines and Hindu discipline for spiritual emancipation as so many have already done in Europe and America, and their Hinduism would not be any the less genuine or complete simply because none of the stereotyped caste names may be applied to them.

The Veda has mentioned the words Brahmans, Rajanyas, Vaishyas and Shudras in a verse in the Purusha Sukta, but the verse can, with perfect justification, be interpreted as referring to the four main natural divisions of mankind, viz., the scholarly and educated class, the ruling and fighting class, the trading, industrial and agricultural classes and the unskilled labourers, all forming as it were the head, the arms, the thighs and the feet of the Body Politic or Virat. Barring this verse there is no dissertation or discourse on caste system, in any of the Vedas. On this flimsy foundation rose a whole fabric of castes and sub-castes. Blame is laid at the door of Manu for having created these invidious distinctions but the condemnation of this greatest lawgiver of the world has been much overdone, as Manu himself has laid down many provisions qualifying and mitigating the rigour of caste. He is supposed to have been very partial to Brahmans but he has counter-balanced their privileged position of sacerdotal superiority by imposing upon them many disabilities, hardships and self-denying ordinances.

A Brahman must devote his life to the study of the Vedas and to teaching others. An uneducated born Brahman, says Manu, is like a milkless cow, a deer made of leather or an elephant made of wood.[1] A Brahman is to lead a life of poverty and shun worldly honours like poison.[2] A Brahman who, omitting to study the Vedas, devotes himself to other pursuits soon becomes a Shudra along with his family.[3]

A Brahman must sacrifice all means of making money if they interfere with his studies. His chief duty is anyhow to be able to teach.[4]

If the teacher is reduced to starvation he may seek aid from the Ruler or from those people who are regular in the performance of religious duties but never from anyone else.[5]

He should live a life of truth, piety and noblest conduct. having acquired complete mastery over his arm, tongue and stomach he should teach his pupil righteously.[6]

A Brahman who does not study the Vedas and does not perform any *Tapa* and yet accepts charity, goes down like a stone boat in the water along with him who is guilty of giving charity to such a Brahman.[7]

An ignorant Brahman by birth should not take even the smallest charity from anyone, otherwise like a cow stuck fast in a bog he will sink deeper and deeper in the mud of sin.[8]

Even water should not be given to a Brahman who knows nothing of the Vadas or of religion and is a hypocrite like a mouse-catching cat and a fish-catching heron or King-fisher.[9]

These quotations would suffice to show that Manu has regard and respect only for the learned, pious, public-spirited and useful Brahmans and regards others as no better than Shudras. He has gone further and has said that whereas a Brahman can become a Shudra if he lacks in Brahmanic qualification, a Shudra can become a Brahman.[10] The same has been laid down in *Apastamb Sutras*.

1. Manu Ch. II, 157, 158, 165, 166.
2. Manu II. 162.
3. Manu II. 168.
4. Manu IV. 17
5. Manu IV. 33

6. Manu IV. 175
7. Manu IV. 190
8. Manu IV. 191
9. Manu IV. 192
10. Manu X. 65

It is thus clear that the original classification was based not on mere birth but on qualifications, occupation, character and temperament (Guna, Karma and Subhava).

This is exactly what Bhrigu told Bhardwaj Muni. "All were created by God. There is no difference between one man and another. It is by their actions that mankind were divided into different *Varnas* or classes." * And then he goes on to explain how according to their character temperaments and occupations, some became Kshatriyas, some Vaishyas and some others Shudras. There are instances available, like that of Vishwamitra, how people were elevated or degraded from one class to another.

So far as the Vedas, the most authoritative scriptures of the Hindus are concerned, I have not found any reference therein to any untouchable classes as such. Dasyus are mentioned but Dasyu simply means a thief or an enemy, but even they are not held untouchables. On the other hand the Vedas have strongly urged upon all the importance of union, co-operation and close association. † They have gone further and have directed all to have common food and drink and common worship. "Let what you drink, your share of food be common. Together with common bond I bind you, serve God gathered round Him like spokes about a chariot's nave."‡ And it is noteworthy that not a word is said about any discrimination between one class and another.

Untouchability

The practice of untouchability is a later growth, brought about mainly by the insanitary occupations of some classes like latrine sweepers and the skinners some of whom eat dead animals. As these professions became, like most professions in India, hereditary, some classes or castes sprang up with the curse of untouchability attached to them. In some cases heinous offences or serious breaches of social laws led to social boycott of certain individuals which persisted to their descendants and in course of time led to untouchability.

Thanks, however, to the present political and economic conditions as well as the efforts of various Hindu organizations like the Arya Samaj and notably those of Mahatma Gandhi, untouchability will soon be a thing of the past, unless some self-seekers among the Scheduled Castes, choose for their own ends to perpetuate it to secure seats in legislatures and other special concessions. High caste Hindus frequently dine in large numbers with large numbers of sweepers, Chamars and Mahars and in the schools, both run by Government and private Hindu organizations, no untouchable is now refused admission. Many youngmen belonging to Scheduled Castes have received the highest education not only in Indian universities but have secured diplomas of Shastri, Vidya Vachaspati and Vedalankar after passing highest examinations in Sanskrit Literature and in Hindu philosophy and Theology. Many of them, I am told, are acting as family priests to Hindu households. A **sweeper** by birth has been preaching from the pulpit of the Arya Samaj, Delhi, for years and is probably still preaching in its Sunday gatherings. A so-called untouchable has recently retired after completing his term of Principalship of a first class Hindu College at Hoshiarpore (Punjab).

* Mahabharat. Shanti Ch. 188.
† Rigveda X. 191. 2-4.
‡ Atharva III. 30.6.

Untouchability has now been abolished by law and all temples, schools, and hotels and restaurants have been thrown open to all castes. Statutory sanction has recently been given to all inter-caste marriages. Inter-marriages between different castes among the Hindus are now of daily occurrence and are recognised as lawful and valid irrespective of the *Anuloma* and *Pratiloma* distinctions. *

As many as one hundred and fiftythree out of Scheduled Castes have been elected to the various legislatures and quite a considerable number of them hold offices as Parliamentary Secretaries and as many as seven of them are members of Provincial and Central Governments. Another was Speaker of the Madras Assembly, elected unanimously, and Madras is the stronghold of orthodoxy and its Legislature contains an overwhelming majority of Hindus, many of whom are Brahmans.

Caste among Muslims

It is noteworthy that those, like Muslims, who proclaim equality of all believers have since the introduction of Constitutional Reforms in India never returned a single depressed class co-religionist of theirs to any of the Legislatures or even to a Local Body not to speak of sharing with them ministries and other high offices which are monopolised by their upper classes. They cannot deny that there are millions among them whose status is the same as that of Hindu depressed classes. These millions living mostly in rural areas are called and even described in Revenue Records as *Kamins* or low-born. They cannot acquire land and cannot claim ownership even of the sites of their huts even if they have occupied them for generations. They can claim no equality with higher castes such as Syeds, Moghuls, Pathans, Jats or Sheikhs. No inter-marriages take place between them and the higher castes. Sweepers nominally converted to Islam are not even called Muslims but form a separate class called Mussalis and their occupations are the same as of other sweepers. All these *Kamins* are at the mercy of other Mussalmans and are liable to *begar* or service without payment as refusal to oblige the village landlords makes them liable to ejectment from their humble dwellings which except the material they cannot even dispose of. The educated among them have often complained in the press about their disabilities and have appealed to their co-religionists to follow the example of Hindus in the uplift of their backward brethren.

Conclusion

Caste system is bound to lose its sting entirely in the near future and sub-castes will be no more than family surnames like those in Europe and America. It should be the duty of every sensible and patriotic Hindu to accelerate the process so that the distinction and rivalries of Brahmans and non-Brahmans which disfigure the public life and Politics of certain parts of India should soon become a thing of the past and the Hindus may become a well-knit and powerful nation and regain the position they held in Manu's time as world teachers. There will be no infringement of Shastras if the differences between castes and castes are eliminated. An immediate beginning may well be made by the merger of sub-castes.

*. A marriage between a man of higher caste to a woman of lower caste is **Anuloma,** the reverse of it is **Pratiloma.**

GROUP PREJUDICES IN INDIA: SOCIAL AND RELIGIOUS

V. S. AGRAWALA

Indian Life-Unity in Diversity

The basic truth of India's social and religious life is an idea of underlying unity in the midst of diversity. Peoples, languages, religions, manners, customs exhibit an endless variety. Even the physical features partake of this manifold expression of life in India. The overpowering fact of diversity, however, did not daunt the human mind in India. At the very outset of thought there was evolved here a formula which frankly admits the great fact of diversity, but still more courageously points out the truth of an underlying unity or spiritual oneness. The Rigveda sums up this basic approach in the following words:

एकं सद् विप्रा बहुधा वदन्ति

"One Being, the Sages speak of in manifold ways". It is fortunate that in a country where so much of racial, linguistic, religious and geographical diversity is the gift of nature, human genius rose above the obvious differences and discovered the immortal formula of spiritual oneness that has been the source of mutual tolerance, synthesis, forbearance and goodwill. Synthesis in all spheres emerges as the supreme fact of Indian history through the ages. Synthesis is the firm foundation that supports the edifice of Indian culture. Mutual tolerance is the law of life that has contributed to the onward march of life in India. Amidst all the clashes and conflicts of history, time and again, the basic genius of synthesis has reasserted itself and made foreign and indigenous elements come closer by the process of mutual assimilation and a broad-based give-and-take operating in a very subtle manner to the advantage and happiness of the constituent parts.

In the social field, India is a veritable museum. This fact is, however, not at all frightening or embarassing, backed as it has been by a living faith in the truth that God is one and however different be the manifestations or forms in which the wise men realise or speak of Him, the essential unity of all beings remains the one and the only ideal to be realised. This idea was not an abstract philosophy, but inculcated in hundred and one ways by an array of saints and poets in all periods and parts of the country. The Aryan and the Dravidian, the Austric races comprising the Mundas, the Shabaras, the Santhals and a number of other less developed peoples still inhabiting the Indian villages and jungles over an extensive area, the Hindus and the Muslims, all have their social and religious forms of life. But there has been an implicit understanding in the hearts of men that each should be free to pursue his own way of life and that each is journeying along different paths that lead to the same summit. "Just as the rains that fall from the clouds reach ultimately the ocean, similarly whatever deity you adore, you attain one supreme Divinity," thus says the Pandava Gita. "There are many systems of thought which divide the tracks that lead to perfection, but like the floods of the Ganges collected from many different sources mingling ultimately with the ocean, do the different tracks converge in one supreme Godhead," thus announced Kalidasa, the best representative of Indian thought during the golden age of Indian history under the Guptas. Greatest of all the exponents of this point of view was Asoka, who lent all the force of his dynamic personality and the resources of his State for bringing together the different castes, creeds and communities and inculcating amongst them mutual concord and amity. His doctrine of religious harmony was based on two cardinal principles, namely, restraint or regulation of words (*vachogupti*) used by the followers of one sect in respect of another and secondly knowledge by the followers of one sect or religion about the others (*bahusrutata*). He says : " One should not thoughtlessly extol his own sect and condemn that of another. He who holds up or glorifies his particular sect, because it is his own and disparages the sects of others, does more harm to his own sect by bringing to it discredit." As a practical statesman he was not content only with the preaching of precepts, but gave effect to them by taking appropriate administrative measures, by appointment of special officers to promote in the country, and among the masses, a spirit of tolerance. Asoka's immortal words continue still to be the supreme motto of our national Constitution and the new State :

समवाय एव साधु

" Concord alone is right ".

Harmlessness to each constituent unit, safeguarding of its individuality and freedom to develop its own way of life—these were the principal guarantees under which life has evolved in the social and religious spheres under the Indian sky during the last four thousand years. To use a Vedic phrase :

स्वे क्षेत्रे अनमीवा विराज।

" Be you harmless in your own sphere ".
This was the basis of life for each cultural unit, whether in the field of social institutions, religious beliefs, language, forms of dress and other habits, each extending its hand of friendship to seek coalescence and subtle interlacing with the life fibres of others. Similar to the life-pattern of creepers and shrubs, plants and trees growing in unfettered freedom in the midst of a forest, the various cultures in India have been nurtured in the vast sanctuary of national culture, each retaining its individual pattern, yet mingling wih others, moulding and modifying itself in the freest manner and finally contributing to the enrichment of the nation's life-texture. Many different trends have become interminably mixed up in the pattern of Indian life imparting to it a soothing and pleasant effect. The cultural fabric of the country being the outcome of its past history should be considered as of inestimable value for the freedom of mind and the democratic way of life that we are now aspiring for. Regimentation has been against the creed of Indian culture. Freedom of growth according to one's own genius has been the law of life in Indian society. Side by side with this there also has operated a binding influence working imperceptibly and from within to direct the various elements of social and religious life to knit together into a harmonious pattern.

India, its Assimilative Genius

Time and again it has happened in our history that foreign peoples have come and settled in India making the country their land of birth and culture. The new group settled at first as an island in the midst of the indigenous population. Gradually the subtle influences of national culure began to operate and assimilate the new elements into the body politic. The process is somewhat comparable to what happens in the body of the mother oyster which from out of its own self exudes a milky secretion to surround the minute grain of incoming foreign matter. The result is a new prized pearl of resplendant effect. The earth or the genius of the land permeated thoroughly the exotic cultural and racial elements that came to it from time to time. This process has been continuous and unending during the course of Indian history. To enable the genius of the land to cast its subtle spiritual net, there should be an essential background in our mental make up. It is the conception of the earth as the mother and the people being her sons.

माता भूमि : पुत्रो अहं पृथिव्या : । (अथर्वा)

The miracle of assimilation begins as soon as this relationship with the land is accepted. "Earth is the mother, I am a son of the soil". Each group can be knit together in thought and action only if each adheres to this common creed. It is said that in the primeval ages this land of ours was concealed under the ocean. It manifested her form for those who are children of the soil or sons of the mother.

(आविरभवन्मातृमद्भ्य : अथर्व)

The relation of mother and son is the most sacred and basic relationship known to mankind. Each group must subscribe to this fundamental truth in order to find its proper place in the body politic. The milk in the mother's breast is only for those who are her sons. Out of this devotion spring all our rights as citizens of any country. Any individual or group that fails to live truthfully to this ideal forfeits the right to enjoy the fruits that flow from the motherland. On this point there is no compromise or half-way house. Unalloyed loyalty to the mother alone entitles her sons to enjoy the full fruits and rights of citizenship. Truly speaking the process of physical and cultural assimilation and synthesis amongst the various groups of social, religious and political life depends on this fundamental attitude. The vast masses of Austric peoples became one with this soil. In our ethnical terminology they are the Nishadas. They had their distinctive social life marked by an earth-bound religion devoted to the worship of trees and stones, Nagas and Yakshas, spirits and godlings, all rooted in the soil. Their group individuality was maintained not only in the past but has continued even today. They have contributed enormously to the development of Indian thought and religion. A whole host of tree and serpent deities, of Yaksha and Naga spirits, of gods and goddesses has been freely incorporated into Hinduism from the Austric peoples. Religious anthropology is laying bare in a most surprising manner the extent of Austric borrowings in Hinduism. Even the followers of the higher philosophic way subscribed to a religion in which the primitive deities of the earth and the forest freely mingled with the gods of higher religion.

A synthesis between the Vedic and the Austric way of life and religious doctrines was brought about by Veda Vyasa. In the ancient annals of a dim past where factual historical intimations are few, the name of Vyasa stands alone as the symbol of a mighty cultural synthesis. He compiled the three Vedas (Irayividya) on the one hand, and admitted to an equal sanctity the Austric beliefs in the compilation of the Atharva Veda, also reckoned as the fourth Veda. The Mahabharata viewed from this point of view is a document of social and religious synthesis which brought together the Aryan and the Austric peoples subscribing to a common cultural heritage. This process of acculturation went on for hundreds and thousands of years, so that ultimately most of the primitive tribes were weaned from their tribal life and occupations. In the eastern parts of U.P. we still have a substantial portion of the population designating themselves as Nishadas, but who are intrinsically now Hindus.' Their traditions, religious beliefs and social institutions are made up of several strata partaking both of higher Hinduism and primitive religion. The Puranic Hinduism represents the type of culture which was the product of a synthesis between the various social and religious groups. There is hardly any part of the country in which this process of cultural synthesis has not been witnessed. Almost everywhere do we find small social groups with their limited horizons so far as individual life and cultural interests are concerned. Within that orbit they share a feeling of compactness and of homogeneity. In many respects they still retain their allegiance to the clan. The New Democracy that is evolving in India today will certainly dissolve their narrow affiliations and mental partitions, building up in the long run a national consciousness which makes people live in terms of the whole nation.

Group Prejudices, their Varieties

Amongst the various prejudices in the minds of the people the most flamboyant is that due to geographical limitations. Regional, and national prejudices are born out of our inability to extend our loyalty beyond a limited horizon of a particular region, province or country. Men have to be positively taught that birth in a particular area, province or country is an accident, which does not confer upon the individual any mark of distinction. Pride on this basis is a false doctrine. While a citizen should train himself to observe his duties or *dharma* in respect of the immediate surroundings in which he is placed, he must not make it a reason for cutting himself off from his fellowmen. Provincial prejudices are the bane of our national life. They divide us into compartments and we usually withdraw ourselves into narrow grooves, thinking only of narrow loyalties in place of giving off ourselves freely for greater services. It is one thing to derive inspiration for patriotic duty on the basis of our birth in a country, it is quite another to allow hatred, pride and isolationism to take root in our hearts under the guise of unhealthy patriotism. The destined goal for humanity is to realise its oneness in the process of evolution. Spatial distinctions are bound to disappear with the growth of world consciousness. Science is annihilating distances and the mutual understanding of mankind is increasing—both these factors will relieve us of our narrow geographical prejudices. Half of the ills of humanity today would disappear if the great ideal of the " World as one Family " (*vasudhaiva kutumbakam*) become a reality and not a pious wish. Territorial religious prejudices originate almost from the same psychological factors. Just as a man is excessively devoted to one god and becomes blind to the truth that there are other manifestations of the Divine by whom his other fellowmen may swear and that both of these are but forms of a single godhead, one without a second who is indivisible and universal, similarly a man steeped in narrow nationalism thinks only in terms of limited loyalty to this or that country and forgets the truth of One World. The success of our social training in the modern world depends on our capacity to reconcile local loyalties with greater interests and develop an approach of amity and harmony between the two, not treating them as sources of conflict. A true son is he who loves not only his own mother, but also shows regard for those of others; similarly a man with true patriotism cultivates a wide love for all peoples and all countries although his power of service and his material resources are by nature of a limited extent. In the modern world the motherland is a great symbol which moves men to the depth of their spiritual being and inspires them to great sacrifice, devotion and human love. This new basis of patriotism for the spiritual training of mankind in the modern world should be fully utilised to ennoble the group prejudices from which men suffer. There is no doubt that one's devotion to motherland can be converted into an ambrosial tonic to metamorphose one's whole being.

A second variety of group prejudices is rooted in racial differences. These are made the cause of much mutual dissension and bitterness. Almost the whole of humanity is suffering today from the poisonous effects of racialism. Man forgets that he is after all a human being and not a specimen of this or that racial type. In India the historical processes have much blunted the edge of such distinctions. Unfortunately racial animosities have of late been excessively fanned as a technique of power-politics. A large part of our group prejudices can be traced to such propaganda. Whereas at one time people's minds were calm and passionless and their hearts full of human love and understanding, racial bigotry has now filled them with hatred and made them blind even to ordinary human duties. Under its influence all restraints are forgotten and men begin to behave like beasts. The rule of the jungle where gory claws and tearing teeth reign supreme is now operating among human beings, who should be possessed of at least some intelligence and fellow-feeling. The pernicious doctrine of the Hindu and the Muslim, the Aryan and the Semitic, the Dravidian and the Mongoloid, the Negro and the Austric, has made humanity both spiritually and culturally bankrupt. Men have forgotten their primary duties. Even the stage of head-hunting was perhaps actuated by reasons which could be better understood than those which operate in the case of our blind recial massacres. It is an axiom that the motherland perhaps in each country bears upon her bosom men and women of different denominations and of diverse racial groups, but this should not make us forget the basic unity of men. In the Prithvisukta of the Atharva Veda we find a noble utterance, which speaks of the motherland as the bearer of different peoples:

जनं बिभती बहुधा विवाचसं नानाधर्माणां पृथिवी यथौकसम् ।
सहस्रं धारा द्रविणस्य मे दुहां ध्रुवेव धेनुरनपस्फुरन्ती ॥

The earth, bearing upon her many different peoples (*Jana*), speaking many languages (*Vak*). following different religions (*dharma*), as suit their particular regions. Pour upon us a thousand-fold streams of bountiful treasures to enrich us, like a constant cow that never faileth.

(Atharv. XII, 1, 45).

Such noble utterances can be traced in all great religions and literatures. They are the common legacy of mankind embodying the everlasting ideals of human love and mutual goodwill. Differences of race, language

and religion, very often the causes of distressing racial group prejudices, have always been there and must remain with us up to the end of time. The greatness of human mind consists in transcending these differences and discovering the basic unity of men. Although we speak different tongues, the Word behind them is One. Great minds and great peoples in their epochs of glory speak this One Word. It is the language of the spirit which binds us together, overriding the material differences of castes, creeds and languages. The Divine Essence is the same in all human beings. To the extent we discover this oneness, we ourselves march on the higher path and fulfil the destiny intended for us. Great ages in human history are distinguished by the great spiritual truths they discovered and put into practice. We in India today are on our trial, as many others also are on trial in their respective countries. We sink or swim by our failure or success to solve the group differences. We must release forces of harmony which alone will conquer the blinding vulgar passions. Spiritual truths seen in full glory inspire us to offer our lives for them. They are the veritable springs of faith and courage. Great actions require great courage. Humanity cannot simply afford to think in a dwarfish manner on the spiritual plane, when science has conferred upon it giant powers, both for evil and good. Mankind today stands in need as much of great scientists as of great spiritual thinkers, whose vision must be clear, hearts bold, and courage unflinching in the face of trial and risks. Mental pigmies cannot solve the mighty problems of human crisis, whether in India or outside. It is false to think that India alone suffers from group prejudices today. It is a world crisis. As we co-ordinate our efforts in the solution of economic and scientific problems, so also should we husband our resources to solve the spiritual problems of humanity. What is the good of science and of power and plenty conferred by it, if a tide of hate overfloods the nations, if our acquisitive greed keeps half the world famished and starving? The problem is very vast. It relates to the creating of a world conscience. Wise men in all countries must discover a way to rid mankind of their narrow passions and and prejudices. It may be called the technique of self-introspection. Each nation must learn the lesson of auto-scrutiny. It has to discover for itself to what extent it can shed away its own weaknesses. It has to be a struggle in self-purification-just the reverse of that sorry spectacle of mutual recrmination and fault-finding in which nations indulge in world assemblies. Such a course for conquering our inherent prejudices of evil can be administered at each centre and even now. Each country, each caste and narrow group must adopt it in the light of its own truth. We have to search our hearts for the wrongs done by us to others and we must take effective steps ourselves to get rid of such failings. Some may whisper that this is the way for saints and not for worldly men, who take a practical view of things. Such a statement reflects defeatism. It amounts to admitting that truth as we see it is beyond our application. The attitude is rather unscientific. That which we believe to be the truth must become a reality of our life;
—this is the attitude and ideal of science.

Lessons from Past History

We in India today must look to the lessons of our past history and build our future in accordance with the noble traditions of mutual tolerance and synthesis that we evolved in this country, where different peoples and cultures came into political, religious and social contacts. Let us take for example the linguistic problem. An objective study shows that Indo-Aryan is the basic language of the country. Sanskrit at one time, about twenty-five centuries ago, was the spoken speech of the people. Under the evolutionary process the Prakrits supplanted Sanskrit and they themselves were replaced by Apabhramsa as the language of the masses about the 8th century A.D. In course of time by about the twelfth century, the provincial languages made their appearance and attained maturity by the sixteenth century. During this last stage from the twelfth to the sixteenth century, the Hindi language while retaining its full glory in the form of roots, suffixes and syntax, assimilated a considerable number of words from Pushto, Persian, Turkish and Arabic. These words became an integral part of the language having been freely used by such master poets as Malik Muhammed Jayasi, Suradas and Tulsidas and also passed into the common speech of the people in cities and villages. The Muslims and the Hindus shared alike the joy of creating this new literature. Malik Muhammed Jayasi wrote the Padmavata in the purest rural speech, his language being a model of that Avadhi which the Hindus and the Muslims speak to this day without distinction in the greater part of eastern U.P. Enlightened emperors like Akbar, Jahangir and Shahjahan were not only themselves great patrons of this literature, but also composed songs in the language of the people and this tradition continued right up to the time of Wajid Ali Shah of Avadh. In the Deccan, king Adil Shah wrote the Nauras-Nama in a style of Hindi known as Dakhani Hindi, which was the result of a beautiful synthesis between the speeches of the Hindus and the Muslims. A close study of the Hindi idioms shows to what extent this language is indebted for its idioms to the Persian language. They are now the adornments of our speech, being the products of a natural assimilation. This style contributed to the enrichment and expressive power of Hindi and we must maintain and develop this process of evolution still further.

In the domain of culture this process of synthesis and mutual borrowings was no less remarkable. The court culture of the Mughals derived freely from the traditional institutions of medieval Hindu kingship. In the details of court paraphernalia they no doubt introduced many new features, but retained numerous elements of traditional court life and culture. For example, in the sphere of fine arts, the Mughals created much that was new, but grafted it on traditional styles. Hindu painters were employed by Akbar in large majority, who evolved an independent Indian style by mingling the Persian and Indian elements together. In the fineness of drawing, beauty of colours and vigour of expression, Mughal painting exhibits the best points of both the traditional Hindu painting and of Iranian pictorial art. Very soon it became a national style and such great illustrated works as the Mahabharata, the Ramayana, the Harivamsa, the Panchatantra were executed in several editions along with others of Persian inspiration like the Darab-nama, Babar-nama, Taimur-nama, Hamza-nama, etc. The history of painting under Akbar furnishes strong proof of the fact that whenever India has tried an experiment in cultural synthesis, it has emerged richer and its own genius has blazed brighter being called upon to absorb and transform the foreign elements. The same phenomenon happened in the case of art and architecture. The beautiful blending of Hindu and Muslim elements in the palace architecture of Akbar gave birth to what constituted our national style of building until under British occupation it was disowned and replaced by a foreign style unassimilated to the soil.

A similar experiment was witnessed in the domain of music when the classical Ragas and Raginis were amplified and a new style of both vocal and instrumental music came into vogue. A comparative study of Ain-i-Akbari of Abul Fazal written at the court of Akbar in the middle of the sixteenth century and the Varna-Ratnakara of Kavi Sekharacharya written at the court of Hari Singh of Mithila in the early fourteenth century, shows how much Mughal institutions and court life depended on earlier traditions even in such matters as their tent equipage, adornments, arms, musical instruments, etc.

The healthy traditions of tolerance, synthesis and assimilation initiated by Akbar and followed by his enlightened successors, although interrupted for a time by Aurangzeb, did much to build up a common basis of life in which group prejudices of a social and religious character were subordinated and all people shared in a common pattern of life taking the best of their free will. In the sphere of religion and philosophy, the growth of Sufism on the one hand and of Vedantic Bhakti on the other, put the people in an accommodating frame of mind in which each group approached the problem of the Divine not from an angle of hostility to the other, but in a spirit of mutual understanding and sincere quest. Akbar's Din-Ilahi was nothing but a Muslim counterpart of the Nirguna-cum-Saguna movements, which were uppermost in the people's minds in the 16th century and a process of adjusting the two opposite points of view in a rational approach to spiritual problems. We find the same problem of the Absolute Divinity and of the personal God posed with much intensity of feeling in the Surasagar of Suradas. Akbar's reverence for the sun as a visual symbol of the deity and of the twelve signs of the zodiac, his invitation to Parsi, Jain, Christian and Hindu teachers and to Muslim divines to discuss the problems of religious philosophy in a detached but a sincere manner free from prejudice and his cardinal principle to treat all his subjects whether Hindu or Muslim in an impartial manner, marked not only a triumph for his political genius, but also solved the mighty problem of medieval India when unassimilated exotic forms had created a vacuum which required to be filled up. He gave a positive direction how the incoming cultural institutions and forms could be naturalised and become part of the national heritage as 'children of the soil'.

Dara Shikoh may be reckoned as the best fruit of the cultural synthesis initiated by Akbar. Himself a great master equally of Persian Sufi thought and the Vedanta of the Upanisadas, which he had read in original and translated into Persian, he wrote a remarkable work under the title *Majmua-ul-Bahrein,*-Mingling of the Two Oceans'. He regarded the Hindus and the Muslims as the two oceans and considered the rapproachment of their higher thought as was being witnessed in the seventeenth century as the mingling of the deep waters. These healthy traditions continued uninterrupted throughout the eighteenth century and up to the middle of the nineteenth century. Political factors operated in their own way to cause group alignments of kings and potentates, but neither religion nor culture suffered narrow segmentation on that account. These were the two great unifying factors which cut across all divisions. From Maharashtra to Bengal and from Tanjore to the court of Lucknow and Ranjit Singh, the vast masses of the people, the aristocrats and the rulers, both Hindus and Muslims, all were interested in the culture of each other. Group prejudices were non-existent or were completely eliminated from our social and religious life.

In the political upheaval of 1857 we find both Hindus and Muslims and every section of the population mingling their blood for a common cause. Begum Hazrat Mahal, queen of Wajid Ali Shah on the throne of Lucknow, entrusted the direction of the struggle to her Hindu generals and financiers and Rani Lakshmi Bai on the throne of Jhansi had a number of Muslim advisers and helpers and soldiers in her army. It indicated a common urge for freedom from foreign domination and is proof of the fact that both the leaders and the masses in the Hindu and Muslim society were psychologically balanced and integrated towards each other.

The history of the last one hundred years as it developed after 1857 shows that the natural channels of cultural synthesis and mutual tolerance which the genius of the land had nurtured through past centuries was sadly interrupted. The powers that controlled India's destiny during these fateful years manoeuvred to sow the seeds of dissension in all fields of life. The Hindus and the Muslims, the Brahmans and the Abrahmans, the Sikhs and the Adivasis, became the pawns in a political game and the whole process of cultural evolution was upset and reversed. Instead of broad-based loyalty to the motherland, group loyalties were encouraged and all people fell a victim to fostering the claims of one particular group against the other. These pernicious tendencies culminated in the partition of the country. The fire of hatred once enkindled is difficult to quench. It flares up again and again consuming together with the hearts of the people all that has been held as sacred and noble and built up as a result of centuries of common effort.

Need for Cultural Synthesis

The problem has to be approached not from the political point of view, but as a crisis of culture. The time-old forces of mutual adjustment and assimilation, of cultural synthesis and amity must be restored to renewed functioning so that they may redeem us, both the Hindus and the Muslims, and all other groups inhabiting the great Indian continent from mental and material wreckage. The soul of this great country was fed by an inexhaustible fountain of spiritual and religious truths that saturated the hearts of men with overflowing love and fellow-feeling. That soul must reassert itself once again. All thinking men and women, to whatever group they may belong, should listen to their inner voice which is also the voice of the motherland beckoning us to sink all differences of race, language and religion in a common brotherhood and humanity.

WOMEN AND GROUP PREJUDICE IN INDIA

HANSA MEHTA

Woman, Stabilizing Force of Society

Woman is considered to be the stabilising force in society. Man by nature is a nomad. Had he been left to himself he would perhaps never have settled down in one place, but would have continued his wanderings. The woman on the other hand, because of her strong maternal instinct, needs shelter to protect her young ones and finds it convenient to settle in one place for that reason. The primitive man lived on his hunting which kept him on the move and encouraged his desire to wander. The discovery of agriculture as a means of livelihood, and it is believed that a woman made it, was a landmark in the history of human society. From nomads men and women became children of the soil and tied down to mother earth for their subsistence. Civilised life, one may say, began from that date.

Her Conservative Psychology

Desire for stability which is so strong in woman leads to a desire for no change. Woman therefore is by nature a conservative. This conservatism is good in so far as it preserves the best in our traditions. On the other hand it is positively harmful if it tries to preserve what is not good because of lack of discrimination of judgment.

There are many social institutions in this country which have outgrown their use and are, therefore, not necessary. But they are still kept up because of this conservative tendency. The slightest deviation from the beaten track raises a cry of the community or religion in danger and women are the first to raise the alarm. The recent opposition to the Hindu Code Bill gives a good illustration. The Code, that will benefit women most, has found some women opposing it. Take the caste system or the problem of untouchability. In spite of all the legislation, the public are slow to recognise the evil. Mahatma Gandhi has described in his autobiography the feelings of Kasturba with regard to the untouchables. It was his firmness, however, which slowly weaned Kasturba from her prejudice against them. There are many Kasturbas in this country but few Gandhijis, who would convert their partners rather than be converted; and that is how the social evils perpetuate.

Group Prejudices Rooted in Fear

The group prejudices are a result of conservative tendencies among men and particularly among women; and these tendencies are born from the instinct of self-preservation or self-protection. If we examine these prejudices we shall find some fear or sense of danger at the root of them. These prejudices can be classified as prejudices against a group in the community itself or prejudices against another community.

In the first category comes the prejudice against the untouchables. Whatever may be the origin of untouchability, it is believed and wrongly too, that Hinduism sanctions it. Any attempt to remove untouchability, is therefore considered a danger to the religion of the Hindus. So long, therefore, as the wrong belief persists, this prejudice is bound to continue.

In the second category come the communal prejudices i.e. prejudices of one community against the other. There also the sense of danger to the community is at the root of the prejudice. Take the prejudice against the Muslims. Its origin is not recent but can be traced to the advent of the Muslims in this country. The Muslim raids in the country; their destruction and desecration of temples; the coercive conversion of the people and the shameful treatment of women, had a cumulative effect in building up this prejudice. It is true that there were many honourable exceptions to this general behaviour of the Muslim conquerors. While there were Mohmed Begada, who destroyed and desecrated the Somnath Temple and Aurangzeb who levied the 'jazia' on the Hindus, there were also Emperor Humayun whose chivalry towards the Rajput queen he captured is well known and men like Akbar who respected all religions. "But the evil lives after the man" as Shakespeare says "and the good is oft buried with his bones". The prejudice against the Muslim community is built on the evil done in the past and it has been strengthened by the recent occurings at Noakhali and the Punjab. The people feel and rightly that their religion is in danger, their homes are in danger, their very existence is in danger. For women, the Muslim rule was considered unsafe. Whatever the prejudices are there to-day, they are the result of an unhappy past.

Compared to the prejudice against the Muslims, the prejudice against other communities is not so strong. Take the Christian community. Christians too believe in proselytising. To that extent they are a religious danger and to that extent the prejudice against them exists. But the Christians have more subtle methods of conversion than the Muslims. One appeals through the stomach while the other uses brute force. The Christians have not shown any disrespect towards women. Being monogamists they have not indulged in wholesale abduction of women. This is an additional reason why the prejudice against the Christians is so much less than against the Muslims.

Then there are Jews and Parsis in this country. They have lived in harmony with other communities. They do not proselytise and, therefore, are not a threat to the religion of the country. Their behaviour on the whole has not aroused any feeling of fear or distrust. There has been, therefore, no prejudice against these communities.

There are communities which are prejudiced against the Hindu community. But this prejudice is due to the fear of the numerical strength of the Hindus. They are a majority community and naturally are considered a potential danger. But this prejudice is of recent origin, and enhanced after the brutal way in which the Hindus retaliated in the Punjab and elsewhere.

I have no desire to discuss the provincial prejudices in this article. They are mostly due to economic reasons and not due to any fear complex. Women are not directly affected by them.

So far as women are concerned my thesis is that the group prejudices have grown out of an instinct for self-preservation or self-protection. Their persistence, however, is due to two reasons viz. (1) ignorance; and (2) fear. If these two factors can be removed, there will be no justification for them and they will die out in course of time. The problem before us, therefore, is how to remove them.

Remedies

For ignorance the remedy is education. Women in particular need education. They are so steeped in ignorance and religious superstitions that it is difficult to convince them how unreasonable some of their beliefs are. We should give such education from primary stage onwards so as would discourage communal prejudices. They must begin to realise that such prejudices have no place in the changing circumstances of a new world. The education in short must be such as to enable them to use their judgment and make them distinguish between fundamentals and non-fundamentals. It must make them realise that the stability of a society or of civilisation depends on the preservation of its fundamentals and not of non-fundamentals which are bound to change from age to age. For instance untouchability which is basically wrong can never be fundamental to either Hindu society or Hindu religion. And to cling to such practice is to perpetuate social injustice which is bound ultimately to undermine society rather than stabilise it. Knowledge of what is fundamental and what is not, will go a great way in removing social prejudices.

With regard to the removal of the second factor viz fear that is a more difficult task. Unless a feeling of confidence is created and there is an assurance that no danger exists either to themselves or to their community it will be difficult to remove fear from the minds of women. The only way to bring about feeling of confidence is for the communities to seek more opportunities of coming together. A closer contact will make them understand each other better. Seclusion of women on the one hand and the religious prejudices on the other will not be helpful in solving these difficulties. Women will never feel reassured till they know that they enjoy the respect due to them and that they are physically and morally safe. It is, therefore, upto the community itself to give this assurance by its own behaviour in its dealings with others. To promote mutual respect, one must endeavour to protect the dignity and worth of the human personality as the charter of the United Nations lays down. Where there is mutual respect there fear does not exist. Freedom from fear is a fundamental human right and if we succeed in promoting it we shall have conquered all the prejudices that are born of fear.

GROUP PREJUDICES IN RURAL INDIA

MANILAL. B. NANAVATI

Rural and Urban Life: Study in Contrasts

It is commonly believed that the simple, unsophisticated life in the village communities in the country is less affected by the virus of group prejudices, that is so much in evidence in the currents and cross-currents of the more complicated and variegated aspects of life in the towns and the cities of India. In a way and to a certain degree, this is so, but only on the surface that life presents to a casual observer or a temporary visitor. Apart from the major seasonal changes that bring about changes in the occupational contents of the lives of the people in rural India and major upheavals like floods, famines or epidemics, life flows more placidly with hardly anything more noticeable than a few ripples on the undisturbed and even surface along a more or less set course

But if the surface is smoother, it is so only because the depth is greater than in the urban communities. Here in the villages, the lives of the individuals and the groups are more intimately related to each other. The contact, the interplay of social, religious and economic forces that operate in the village communities, is very much closer and more prolonged with repercussions extending over generations than in the urban areas with their life patterns cut more clean and separate from each other and running along their individualistic grooves.

In big cities, after living as neighbours for five years, often under the same roof, one may know no more than perhaps the name and occupation of one's neighbour. In the village, on the other hand, you know the smallest details of all that happened in the course of half a century or more involving three generations in the life of a family that lives at the other end of the village from you. And this is not due merely, as is very often erroneously imagined, to a lack of vulgar curiosity in the case of the town dweller and too much of it in that of a villager. The villager in essence is no more interested in the lives of his fellow beings than a townsman. In the mass, he is ever so much more indifferent to what happens to others than the better informed and more imaginative city man.

The fact is that in the case of a member of the rural community, the impact of his life both in time and space is more extensive and more penetrating. This is a result partly of the circumscribed, narrow and numerically less variegated patterns of life that a villager can lead in relation to his fellowmen in the same village or the surrounding villagers. But it would be a mistake to attribute the whole of the force of this effect or of all the effects that flow from it to this cause alone. Not only are the points of contact in the case of rural communities greater or their interplay more intimate, but the roots of group and individual contacts, the roots of life itself and their pattern of relationship apart from their contents go deeper in an old country like India, in time, to the feudal ages and even beyond those to the stage where men lived on a more communistic level, far below the present social organisation of the community, based on family as a unit and the state as the corner stone or the summit of society.

In fact, the very conception of family itself in its subconsious colour and contents varies very much from what a family means to a modern sociologist. Unconsciously, but no less effectively, the more placid looking but in reality the more complicated and subtle villager, thinks of a greater part of those who live in the same village, as tied to him as a result of the force of preceding generations, and belonging to the same family. The humble but aged cobbler at the lowest stratum of society is still an *uncle* and his wife an *aunt*, to the young son of the wealthiest farmer or moneylender, in the village. This is an important aspect that nobody who wants to study a village community, be it for the purpose of gauging the operation of group prejudices or for any other specific economic or sociological purpose, can afford to forget as forming a real and effective background to the subject of his study.

Socio-Economic Groups in Village

Having thus established this basic difference in the social structure of a village community, let us now turn to the groups that hold a sway over life in the rural areas and the prejudices that have come to be attached to these groups, to the detriment of a smoother running of the social stream in these regions. A village even more than a town or a city is cut up not only vertically, horizontally and diagonally into overlapping groups, but the groups here are more rigidly defined and of longer duration in time.

By far the largest or at any rate the more important than all the rest taken individually is the group consisting of the landholders, be they actual cultivators of the soil at the present stage or not. There is a small and to a certain extent a superior group made up of the family priests, the moneylender, the schoolmaster and the ayurvedic physician or what might generally be called the hereditary professional group, which still clings to the remnants of its past glory. There are next, the superior skilled artisans, who form a recognisable group by themselves and finally there are the landless labourers who lend a hand in every piece of work that needs doing. And then, there is the Harijan group, a few of whom may be cultivators in a small way, but otherwise mostly to be identified with the last group, but living apart from it and which though in many cases economically superior, is considered socially inferior to it.

This is a very rough and ready classification. There are many more sub-groups and overlapping groups. Besides, the dividing lines are not so sharp and distinct as they were a generation or two ago. A sociological treatise, planned on scientific lines, will have to go into greater details and more intricate classification, to define the various social and economic strata at which life is lived by the innumerable village communities in India. But for our purpose, for the purpose of studying the play of group prejudices in the rural areas and its overflow into the larger life of the nation, into politics, industry, trade, commerce, education, the fine arts and culture and the composite life of the nation as a whole, this provisional and broad classification would be serviceable if not scientific. It is in the group prejudices that we are interested primarily and not in the groups themselves. A study of the latter will take a volume by itself.

Caste Prejudices a Corroding Poison

Just as proximity in space is the more important factor in the operation of group prejudices in other walks of life and other areas of the country, proximity in time and in the greater coherance of its evolutionary process plays a more important role in the interplay of these prejudices, as we have tried to outline above, in the village community. The caste prejudices, therefore, which have yielded considerably to economic competence or social and political position in the towns, are still far more rigid in the social segregation that they involve in the villages.

To make a concrete instance or two, to typify what this means in the every day social set up of a village, we shall consider an extreme contrast. What I have in mind can best be conveyed by saying that Sjt. Ambedkar or Sjt. Jagjivan Ram can live and work with no trace of social or mental friction and irritation in Bombay or New Delhi but not in their own respective villages. Even their outstanding pre-eminence might not be able to save them from mental discomfort, from an oppressive feeling of not belonging to the group. Stripped of their political position, their economic affluence and their social prestige, their great mental attainments will help them but little to enter into the corporate life of their village, if they were to return there. They will not be able to do so to the same extent as a very mediocre or even a poor specimen of a member of the main class of landholders or the village priesthood could.

I record this as a social fact, recognising fully the disgrace it involves not for the persons mentioned but for our village social organisation. To them personally, I would pay the same tribute as I would to any great pioneer who has the strength and the courage to rise far above his cramping environment. It is people like them who, in the long run, help society itself to efface and neutralise the effects of such corroding poison in the body social.

But few, very few indeed, have the strength or the mental integrity of an Ambedkar. It is an extreme instance taken to illustrate the evil effects of this prejudice. But really speaking it does not personify the constant and continuous poisoning of the communal life of the villages. An outstanding and remarkable personality can always escape the bonds of social or group tyranny. The evil is minimised in their case, except in the greater mental agony and torture that they might be made to undergo in their struggle to free themselves, because of their necessarily more sensitive natures.

The evil at its maximum of more permanent duration is, on the first hand, in the friction that it causes in the everyday life of the village itself and the impoverishment it brings about in the general mental, economic, educational and cultural level of the rural community. This comes about in two ways. The very opportunities for healthy growth are denied to a large section of the community, thus keeping them at a lower level of attainment and contribution to the general wealth and welfare of the community and the countryside in the first place. In the second, the play of this prejudice has been responsible for driving away many a man and woman, who do manage in spite of the prejudice and the disabilities it enforces on those who are the victims of such a prejudice, because of birth in a lower stratum of the village society, to rise above his or her station at birth, from the villages to towns.

The villages would not have been in the static and unhealthy condition in which they are today, if many of their mentally and morally more developed sons and daughters had not been hustled out of them by the sense of oppression and frustration that a society whose growth has been arrested imposes upon persons who are alive. Their very presence and their work would have let loose ideas other than which there are no more explosive forces in the world. They would have seen to it that the villages did not drift into isolated relics of the past as asylums for the aged, the infirm and the mentally defective.

I recognize that there have been other forces too, that have helped in this self-stultifying process in the life and growth of many of our villages, apart from this operation of the group prejudice against the lowly born. But this is neither the time nor the occasion for studying them. It has, however, to be recognised that this cause has been a very potent one for the mental and economic impoverishment of our village communities.

But the group prejudices, that operate in a village, are not all confined to those arising from the caste system and the rigid divisions it imposes on communal life. The economic necessities of life, the common dangers and the equally common natural calamities, that communal life in the rural areas have to face, do go in a certain measure to bring the castes together on a common platform and a more evenly shared basis of existence. The religious festivals, the social celebrations such as marriages, the Dewali, the New Year, etc., do go to create a sense of a common life. Were it not so, the villages would have developed into armed camps poised at an unstable equilibrium and always liable to run into strife and conflict at every turn.

Role of Village Officials

An important group prejudice that operates in the villages is that of the creation of a class that has been or is in more active association with the administration and its machinery. At every turn, the life of a villager comes into contact with the administrative machinery—the land revenue system, the police, the law courts, the village panchayat and the co-operative society, the school, especially where education is compulsory, the health authorities and the eternal question of dung heaps, the irrigation authorities, the state transport and a hundred other things, each small in itself but important and impressive in its total and cumulative effects.

The *Patel* and the *Patwari* or the *Kulkarni*, the school master to a lesser extent, a group of capable, pushing and often intriguing persons form a coterie in each important village, that finds it to its interest to create or perpetuate group and personal prejudices in the life of the village. Every village has its ancient and smouldering feuds and hereditary enmities. These are fanned into flames or scorched and laid under ashes, according as this powerful group happens to be of a constructive or destructive nature. The activities of this group or the sub-groups within it, have an important bearing on the operation of group prejudices in any given village. With the coming of democracy its importance and influence has increased tenfold.

Economic Group Prejudices

While the social group prejudices in a village could be more or less confined to its hierarchy of caste and to the status that a given profession or occupation ascribes to the group engaged in it, the economic group prejudices, while they have always been there, have been more accentuated in recent times. For instance the feud between the farmer and the professional cattle-breeder or even a landless labourer with a couple of milk cows or buffaloes has always been there. It is purely due to economic reasons in its origin, due to the destruction that the latter causes to the crops of the former. But in course of time it has come to be stabilised as between two classes. These classes are economically interdependent, one needing bullocks and the other requiring customers for the stock that it raises.

The new agrarian legislation has brought about a new class consciousness on the one hand between the money lender as a class, and the agriculturist as another. In the old days there was more co-operation and a greater harmony in their dealings. The former acted, apart from making advances, also as a middle man for the sale of the latter's produce and the purchase of his requirements. The prejudices on both the sides are now, however, taking deep roots, and have been responsible for breach of peace and crimes of violence or incendiarism in some parts of the country. It has now come to a stage where the money lender does not consider his life and property quite safe, where for generations he was a virtual power, and he is migrating to the towns and cities. If we can replace him as an institution, it would bring wealth and prosperity to the countryside and there would be nothing to lose. But if we fail to do this on an extensive scale, the quality of agriculture and the net yield from the soil are bound to suffer.

The relations between the farmer on the one hand and the agricultural labourer on the other, though not free from class or group prejudice even in the past, were at least better adjusted and in many cases merged in the long run, into social and emotional relations also. The worker did feel a kind of loyalty to his farmer employer and knew that he could depend on him to help him in his times of difficulties. The farmer felt a kind of responsibility towards his more permanent workers and even to the members of their families. The harmony on the whole was greater than the mutual prejudice and so the village economy had a kind of permanence and durability.

Today the group prejudice is growing powerful and operates to the detriment of both the classes. Agriculture and village life as a whole are of a paculiar nature and make, special and extra-legal demands, on all the elements that go in their composition. Any elaborate legislation to regulate this might, if the parties fail to adjust their relation on some fresh but sound basis, ruin agriculture and bring new burdens on village communities that they may not be in a position to shoulder.

It is the same with labour legislation as with social legislation. Too rapid or radical an advance might not only overshoot the mark and leave things unimproved but it might create fresh group prejudices, which might prove more deadly and destructive in their effects, for the economic life in the villages than the old ones. A wise government would always temper its enthusiasm with practical considerations, without sacrificing the essence of social justice. In trying to bring about greater social justice to an oppressed or undeveloped group, we should not harm the social fabric itself or destroy it in our haste.

All the agricultural work on a holding, however small, cannot be done by the farmer and his family. He has to have some one to work for him. For an economic holding a farmer will have to have many more persons at least for seasonal operations. There will, therefore, always be a class or group that will have no land, though it will be working on land. You cannot turn the whole of rural India into co-operative or communal farms within a short time, except through a violent and bloody revolution.

Greater Need for Group Harmony in Village

Agricultural work by its very nature cannot be so clear cut and amenable to legal definitions as work in a factory. A sense of group harmony alone can secure smooth and timely work in the many millions of fields in the country. Remove this harmony and you will have class and group prejudices, each group or class trying to harm or get the better of the other. Final adjustment may or may not come, but it is quite possible that agriculture as such in the meantime may be ruined or rendered uneconomic for anybody to undertake. In trying to secure a fair or a minimum wage for the farm workers, let us not destroy the fair or minimum yield from the land. You cannot control all the uncertain factors in agriculture. Science may come to control some. But for a long time in India there will be many an uncertain factor affecting the crop. It is only to the extent that you can control these that you can control wages.

Group prejudices in the rural area are a source of greater danger to the life of the nation as a whole for a very peculiar reason. As in the U.S.A. or in the United Kingdom, or in the West generally, there is not a clear line of demarcation here between the townsmen and the villagers. Whether you take business or industry or the learned professions, politics, letters, arts and the administrative or defence services, the perrenial source of supply for all these, is not from the offsprings of the town dwellers but in a large measure from the villages. Even a large section of your permanent town dwellers itself has one foot and one eye in the towns and one in the rural area. His relations and early associations often enough are in the countryside.

If the source be contaminated, the towns and cities are bound to be so. The migrant to town has not only a heritage of all the ancient group prejudices in his blood and mental make-up, but he adds to it at times a kind of bitterness and venom of his own, especially if he come from one of the groups lower in the social scale in the villages. He is more group conscious, because he is forced to abandon his native soil and his native group, because of disabilities that are heaped on him. He knows what awaits him if and when he returns to his place of birth, whatever eminence he might achieve in his new surroundings. He carries this burden all through his life, however well life might deal with him in his new habitat. And an embittered man is an unsocial man. An upper strata of embittered men will not give us a healthy or smooth running social organisation.

Remedies

The remedy therefore lies in removing the pollution at the source. If not for any other reason, let us turn our eyes and efforts to the villages, to remove as many causes of social injustice of class and group prejudices, as also to remove or renovate the old institutions that have served their purpose and are today sources of social prejudices, retarding progress and enlightenment to the countryside. If those who are boys and girls there today can be made to feel free and unfettered in their growth, they may not want to or be driven to migrate to towns. If even an urge takes them there, they will not come with a load of discontent, dissatisfaction and bitterness against prejudices, the force of which they have experienced there. They will enrich the towns and the cities, life and literature, professions and politics, instead of polluting them with their heritage of hatred.

We have tried to indicate a few of the main class or group prejudices that operate in rural India. There are others as well. An analysis of all these and a search for their removal is a task that cannot be compassed in the course of a short paper. They would take a volume by themselves. After a sleep of centuries, we have awakened to the awareness of many an evil. This awakening in itself is responsible for some of the old group prejudices giving place to new ones.

A planned rural economy, when it comes to replace in course of time, the present subsistence economy of rural India, will remove many of these prejudices. Groups there will always be. Even a classless society has and will have groups. Human nature is selective in its associations and this creates groups for various purposes and for varying ends. Likes and dislikes cannot be ruled out. Groups will follow in their wake and possibly some prejudices as well.

But if men and women are better educated, more enlightened and broader in their outlook, they will keep these group prejudices under a restraint and not let them affect their conduct and attitude towards the other group, if not in their actual relations. It is after all only a matter of social and civic education and the lessening of the points of friction.

A stray word, a chance utterance, that might emphasise such prejudices and create positive cleavage between groups, as they often do today in the more remote rural area, will not be there when we are more rationalised and less subject to instructive reaction and behaviour. Our only hope is in the right type of education that will coalesce existing groups and not create new ones. Today, education, the little of it that is there in the villages, has created fresh and at times bitter group prejudices between the two groups—the so-called educated and the unlettered groups.

Section IV
Politics and Prejudices

GROUP PREJUDICES

B. PATTABHI SITARAMAYYA

Nationalism, a Modern Phenomenon

It is the tendency of modern times for the people of any country with its clear-cut geographical boundaries and age-old historical traditions, with its particular civilization and its peculiar cultural background, with its hoary customs and current manners, with its civic laws and social institutions, with its ancient arts and modern crafts, with its uplifting religion and established form of worship, to function as a composite nation owing their allegiance to one writ and one Law, one currency and one postage stamp, one state and one government. The concept of nationalism itself is not fully a century old. France has passed through three Revolutions and witnessed three Republics alternating with three Monarchies beginning with the guillotining of Louis XVI on January 21, 1793 and of Marie Antoinette on October 15, 5 months later. America itself was not welded into a nation in spite of her declaration of Independence (1787) at Philadelphia by 12 out of 13 States, till after the termination of the Civil War (1860-65). The German confederacy became a Federation only after the defeat of the French at Jena in 1871. The Ionian Islands and Greece were brought together a century and a decade ago, but they continue to be in an incohate condition still. The first world war added Latvia, Esthonia and Lithuania, to the nations of Europe and brought into being by a reshuffling of old Servia, Montenegro, Bulgaria, Rumania and Eastern Roumalia boundaries, new nations like Czechoslovakia and Jugoslovakia and reunited the Austrian, German and Russian Polands into one integrated whole. The basic difference amongst the component factors of these new States was of language and culture, of different groups if we may so describe these tiny little tracts of territory compared to India with its vast varieties of climate and soil and continental dimensions of area and population.

Nationalism in India

The variation of language and life so clearly visible in different parts of Europe are all reflected in India while the latter remained a single country as a subject nation under the overlordship of a foreign power. In a country where religion has always formed a powerful tie and a still more powerful fissiparous force, it is no wonder that the modern conception of nationality, hardly a century old even in Britain, should have struggled ever so hard to establish itself as a vital and operative force in bridging the wide chasms that have existed for centuries in language and literature, in religion and worship, and in culture and civilization. Left to themselves the Indians would have absorbed these ever multiplying differences easily enough for they had thus absorbed the Turanians, the Mongols, the Rajputs, the Jats and even the Moghuls, and the Christians of Europe, the most ancient of whose settlers and converts are well over sixteen or seventeen centuries old. It was true that when Man Singh gave his sister to Akbar and his daughter to Jahangir, the Moghul line of Kings produced Vedantins like Dara Sikko and philosophers like Akbar himself, but the process of assimilation which naturally takes centuries was interrupted by the appearance of the European races one after another on the Indian soil,—first the Portuguese, then the Spaniards and the Italians, later the French and the English, the last of whom became the lords and masters of the continent of India.

India, a Cockpit of Conflicting Groups

The appearance of a foreigner on the scene of Indian politics and his political domination, whether it be by the Turks, the Afghans and the Moghuls from the North or the Europeans from the West, was always made possible and encouraged by internal differences and even internecine warfare. The seeds of mutual animosity so sown fell upon favourable soil, for the religious exclusiveness of the Hindu charged with an element of self-righteousness of the Pharisaical type, fostered the growth of a spirit of aloofness in him bordering upon a spirit of even contempt, not only for the neighbour but also for his faith and philosophy, his materialistic outlook and machine civilization.

Already there had been for centuries even apart from political trends and influences, hundreds of divisions congealed and consolidated into castes and sects, schisms and schools of thought which had isolated themselves through prohibition of commensality and intermarital alliances and taken wanton pleasure in keeping the ring inviolate. While contact with the West, through Christian missionary teachings and general mental awakening, sought to broaden the vision and widen the outlook of the people at large, the growth of English education, the vested interests, the sense of abjectness and servility incidental to and inevitable from foreign rule, the ready response to the policy of *divide et impera*--all promoted group formations particularly along long standing and well-established lines of socio-religious and socio-economic classification. The group leaders who rose to power made a point of conferring posts and preferments in public offices, favours in business and prizes in general on close relations, people of one's own village, tahsil, district or province or members of one's own caste and creed. Nepotism soon came into being and multiplied the groups. The groups in turn fostered a sense of nepotism so establishing vicious circles operating in concentric rings.

British Policy of Divide et Impera

The sudden departure of the British on the 15th of August 1947 could not obliterate the stigmata long implanted on the face of Indian Society. When the British came to rule India direct through their sovereign, the Muslims who had till then been in high favour with the British, felt the injury and insult caused to their de jure *King* at Delhi by the truimph of British arms in the Mutiny and therefore boycotted the courts, colleges and councils established by Britain in India in the first four years of that Mutiny. They sulked and sat in their tents, but there were not wanting groups—notably, the untouchables who were long suppressed, and some even among the Muslims who began to be recently depressed, who joined hands with the latest conqueror who had thus been initiated into the famous policy of Divide and Rule. Once the process of fission began, the organism of Indian Society broke up into innumerable units or groups by the same simple process of fission by which the amaeba multiplies. The Hindus took full advantage of the situation and began to fill places of authority and positions of influence in the Halls of Honour of the British Court and it was not till 1875 that the Muslims, realizing that they were being fast left behind, woke up and established the first English High school at Aligarh. But there was a time lag of 17 years between the Universities established in 1858 and the High School opened in 1875. It was a race between a chaise and pair and a single-bullock cart. That was why in 1906 the Muslims frankly called themselves a separate unit and asked for separate electorates which were conceded by Lord Minto. In 1916 the Indian National Congress itself swallowed the bait hook and string and conceded weightage in addition to separate electorates. Once a group was formed and began to be rewarded, appetite grew with eating so that in 1931 residual powers were conceded to Provinces and in 1945 parity in the Central Executive and finally in 1946 double majorities in Legislatures. But nothing short of partition satisfied the group and the Muslims in the Muslim minority provinces having worked for and rejoiced over the partition, began even after partition to claim special and separate Electorates and Reservation of seats for the Muslims in their Legislatures. Though for the time being, these demands are held in check, yet there is no cartainty that the old trends have disappeared altogether.

The moment that the British saw their policy was forestalled at Lucknow (1916) and took shape as a Hindu-Muslim concordat, later accepted by Mr. Montague with slight changes, they turned to the far South and to the far North in 1917 and created the Brahmin-Non-Brahmin movement in Madras, C.P. and Bombay and the Sikh—Hindu movement in the Punjab. These both are still at work for the Brahmins, no more than 3% of the population in India, are driven out of all fields of competition and are shown their place and proportion in colleges and public services. The Sikhs who are no other than Hindus claimed special weightage and reservation so long as the Muslims enjoyed it. Later came the Depressed Classes movement and the Tribal Classes agitation.

Group Prejudices; How they Work

What is the position today in the Provinces and what is the legacy in administration of British Rule? At Railway stations, dining halls for Brahmins and Non-Brahmins are separately arranged in the South India, while Hindu Pani and Muslim Pani are separately served and stocked in Central and Northern India. It is unfortunate that when you give evidence in a Law Court or write out your description in registering a document, you have to mention your caste. This has just been relaxed in Orissa. Thus what is required to be overlooked, was emphasized according to British regulations. This only added fuel to the fire of communalism which had always been there for the very names of Indians bear suffixes which indicate their caste and sub-caste. Let us study a few examples. The *Kayasthas* of Behar, U.P. and Bengal are easily identified by the suffixes of Srivatsava, Saxena, Asthana, Mathur, Bhatnagar, Kulsresht, Gowd, Hamisht, Valmik, Nigam, Surajdhwaj and others. The Brahmins of U.P. are divided into Kanyakubj, Sarayupari, Gowd, Sanadh, and Saraswathi groups, some of these have titles which run as follows and help to identify them : Misra, Shukla, Trivedi, Dube (Dwivedi), Chaube (Chaturvedi), Tripathi, (Tiwari), Pathak, Pande, Bajpai, while the Banyas are Agarwals, Guptas, or Maheswaris. The Khatris (businessmen) are known as Melhotras Tandons, Kakkads, Seths, or Bhallas. The Kshatris are Thakurs, Puris, Kapurs, Chopras and Dhavans.

In the South the titles of Ayyar and Ayyangar, indicate two categories of the Tamil Brahmins, while Pant and Achari indicate the Brahmin in Andhra and Maharashtra. Mudaliars, Pillays, Naickers, Gownders and Settis are caste titles in the Tamil area, while Nayudus, Chowdhuris and Chettis are current in Andhra. Nayar, Menon, Pillay, and Puduval are caste titles in Malabar and so are Shetty and Bhandari in South Canara.

So far as our Sikh brethren are concerned, the very title *Sardar* which precedes their name indicates their religious affiliation except where it is a personal title, while the additional titles Namadhari, or Akali, Udasee, Grihasthi, Nihangi, Vasthradhari—all indicate sub-sections. The Sikh Harijans or the Harijan Sikhs bear the denominational titles of Mazhabis, Ramdasis, and Sikhligars.

Amongst the Harijans of the South, there are 84 divisions or groups recognized by Government and the warfare between the Malas (farmers and weavers) and Madigas (Cobblers) is proverbial. These groups observe untouchability amongst each another, while they are all "untouchables" to the caste Hindus. In Bombay and C.P., the rivalry is between Chammars (Cobblers) and Mahars (weavers and farmers). Today the rivalry has gone to the extent of obtaining court injunctions against leaders presiding over Conferences of Depressed Classes being held, in Gwalior and Tittalgarh which are sponsored by respective groups. In South India (Madras) at the time of the choice of candidates in 1946, the Madigas (Cobblers) claimed a turn for themselves as the Malas (Farmers) had had theirs already. I readily agreed to the proposal but asked them to ponder over as to when they would get their next turn. They blinked and I answered the question for them by saying "420 years hence". "How please?" was their query. You have 84 groups recognized by Government and if *Madigas* should follow *Malas*, then other groups will equally claim their turn for five years each and yours will get your second turn after 84x5 or 420 years. They withdrew their request for they knew not what they spoke.

All patriotism works in concentric circles. The man in power is apt in general to think of his family, relations and people of his sect or group, village, tahsil, district and province. In London we think of India, in Delhi of Madras or Bombay, Nagpur or Cuttack and so on. In the Legislatures of each of these cities we think of our Districts, and in the Local Boards of Districts we think of our Tahsils, while in the Tahsil Boards we think of our Mandals or Firkas, our villages and in the Village Panchayats we think of our streets. So far the circles run on a territorial basis, but concurrently or intercurrently we have our biases running along religious, caste and sectarian channels. These centrifugal tendencies have struck deep roots in the administrative and what is worse, in the educational world of India today. It is sufficiently bad that high placed people should be accused of parochialism and provincialism, but when to this is added the charge of nepotism based upon consanguinity or sect bias, the position becomes intolerable.

Diagnosis

In considering the remedies to a malady which offers no difficulty in diagnosis, we have to appraise the present-day social conditions and evolve principles of treatment based thereon. Shall we, or shall we not, recognize the age-long social, socio-economic and socio-religious distinctions and disparities that have penetrated society and coloured the life of the whole nation. Let us face facts. Indian Society is a well-developed organism which has transcended the crudeness and savagery of tribal times and clannish conditions. The Indian village is a miniature cosmos which is self-contained, self-sufficient and self-complete, in which are represented all the arts and crafts that subserve civilized human life and wherein the functions of each are discharged for all on a co-operative basis run by the Village Republic. Service Inams are granted once for all for the Patwari or the Patel, the former is variously named as Shanbhog, Kulkarni, Kurnam or Menon. The carpenter and the smith, the weaver and the printer, the dyer and the dhobie, the barber and the potter, the cobbler and the farmer—are all endowed with lands and so are the smaller village servants and equally the priest and the physician, the teacher and the pujari. Each has his caste or sub-caste and the calling is hereditary in each case, a fact which accounts for the unsuspected skill, dexterity of hand, resourcefulness and originality of the man on the dung heap and the dustbin, who has attended no school but is put to *learning* by *doing*. Each cottage is a College, each parent is a professor, each child is a pupil, each craft is an Art. In such a scheme of mundane equipment the Brahmin alone is left to minister to the spiritual needs of society living on the precarious assistance rendered by his fellow-villagers. When, therefore, the British started the Universities, he became the first recruit to colleges, the first graduate of the University, the first lawyer in the High Court, the first Councillor in the Legislature. The rest of the population was slow to abandon their hereditary and reliable occupations and callings in favour of this new and unfamiliar and equally uncertain commodity called English Education which it was said had a remunerative value. Property and vocations had a rare charm for them but as decades passed and education found its reward in positions of power and authority which became enviable objectives, the Brahmin, who had led the van was blamed for leaving behind the rest of society, the critics little knowing that the beneficiary was not responsible for the benefits which were thrown open to all. It was thus that a new consciousness dawned upon castes and sects and groups of the neglect they had suffered, which operated along two channels, one of hatred of those who were held responsible for such iniquity and the other of love of oneself and one's own group. Group instinct for utter self-preservation in the first place and self-advancement in the next, came handy to the Rulers as well who could thereby prevent concerted action and foster divisions that kept asunder those whom God hath united. Hatred of one's neighbour more than love of one's kith and kin became the vital and operative force in modern life. Consciousness of group life became the order of the day in offices, and population was classified in the South India with the ratios fixed in public services for each of the major groups and likewise in regard to admission to Colleges. The more forward among the latter soon became the object of envy and presently the more backward groups claimed priority and proportions as against the more forward amongst the protestant major groups. Representation in Legislatures was added to the services as an additional factor to be reckoned in the race of life and finally has come the admission of students into colleges based upon the exclusion of the progressive and intelligent sections. No wonder if all this made for a certain fall in the standards of efficiency! But this was deliberately sought, not accidentally found. For over a quarter of a century these distinctions, selections and exclusions have prevailed in the Southern Province of Madras and they had their reflections in the rest of the provinces in India where the warring groups were either Muslim and Hindu or Hindu and Sikh with of course the sub-castes emphasized in this game of hatred. In Behar it is the warfare between Kayastha Khathri and Bhumiar Brahmin. In U.P., it is the Kashmiri vs. the native of U.P. The Brahmin is practically nowhere in this province of Pilgrimages and Pandas. In Bengal the race is amongst

Kayasthas, Vaids and Brahmins. In this manner, group instincts are being perpetuated and one of the causes of the degeneracy that has infected the Congress is this group virus to which an antidote must be discovered.

Antidote

The remedies are obvious, if they can be drastic. Government's share in perpetuating the distinctions must be done away with at once. In spite of a declared order, Dining Halls "for Brahmins only" continue on the M.S.M. Rly. The Courts and the Registrar's offices must be directed not to ask details of caste, of parties. The obnoxious communal circular must be put an end to. The University Commission's report has been published not a day too soon. It is the examinations of Universties as criteria for admission to the public services that have put up the Brahmin in the South and made him an object of jealousy and a victim of ill-will. With the declaration that University examinations and public services must be divorced from each other and with the additional reform of introductnig "objective" tests to test knowledge and achievement alike, the priority of the Brahmin in memorizing feats and intellectual gymnastics will not continue any longer. The virus of group hatred will not have a favourable nidus in the University or Public Services and therefore cannot spread to the region of political positions or power. Above all names of persons should stand unsophisticated as they were named by their parents and not be embellished by prefixes and suffixes indicative of castes and sects. A careful watch must be maintained over the exercise of patronage by officers high and low and Ministers in the Provinces and at the Centre in giving appointments, in granting permits and licenses and in assigning contracts with a sense of partiality to men of their province, their district or their caste.

A new code of equality should be inculcated from the primary school upwards which discourages the consciousness on the part of the urchins, of distinctions of caste and creed, and the whole atmosphere of schools and colleges should promote harmony and concord amongst pupils. Hostels should be cosmopolitan. In 1898 when I joined the Madras Christian College, I was assigned to a Students' Home where no caste distinctions were observed, except one between meat-eaters and non-meat-eaters. The Y.M.C.A. and the Y.M.I.A. have done much to wipe out this pernicious group consciousness. But the pity of it all and the point to be always remembered is that it is after young men and young women enter life that they become overborne by the prevailing ideologies of society and become *first* willing victims, *then* proud propagandists of the same. The after-care of scholars and students, of apprentices and artisans, goes a long way in preparing the ground for intercaste and even interprovincial marriages. Commensality alone may be practised with thoughtless ease but inter-marriages may kill group consciousness the better. A sustained and serious campaign of socio-economic reform and an indefatigable crusade against nepotism and provincialism, coupled with a discriminate study of the faiths of religions without falling a prey to 'their dogmatic schisms and schools of thought and due emphasis on the moral values of things that count, —are the cardinal principles by which alone, it may be possible to renovate Indian Nationalism on a catholic and cosmopolitan basis in a decade or two for the new seed takes time to sprout and the new plant to grow into a tree bearings flower and fruit of economic justice and racial equality, of the innate worth of man and woman recognized by virtue of manhood and womanhood and not on birth or breeding.

GROUP PREJUDICES: ADMINISTRATION

S. V. RAMAMURTY

Role of Leaders in National Rebirth

Administration is the implementation of the policies and plans of the Government of a country. Before achieving a Government of its own, a country has to fight for power. In order to get strength for such a fight, a nation has to equip itself with a philosophy of vision and faith. One can draw a parallel between the rebirth of Italy in the 19th century and the rebirth of India in the 20th century. Mazzini was the philosopher, Garibaldi the warrior and Cavour the statesman of new Italy. In India, the roles have not been so clear cut. Gandhiji was the philosopher and warrior and Nehru and Patel both the warriors and statesmen of new India. The mixure of two roles does not necessarily strengthen both roles. Gandhiji has been a philosopher of significance not only to India but to the world. Pandit Nehru has not only been a warrior of India but a world figure. His statesmanship shows its strength primarily in vision while Sardar Patel's statemanship shows its strength primarily in action. In the stature of the central figures of the Indian and Italian rebirth, India retains a scale of significance which her size and the immensity of her human material and even its priority in history justify as compared with Italy.

Feeling of Frustration

The Government of India in the last two years since India won her freedom in August, 1947, is under the dominant control of Pandit Nehru and Sardar Patel. Many great problems attendant on a national revolution of the importance of the Indian political revolution have been tackled with vision and firmness by these two great leaders. In spite of this, it is true that there is a growing feeling of frustration in the country in the economic and social fields with which administration is primarily concerned. Men are asking, "Is this the India of which we have dreamt and for which we have prayed?". Why has such a revulsion of feeling grown so soon after the enthusiasm with which the freedom of India was sought and won?.

Inefficiency of Administration

Some twenty years ago, I was talking in Rome with an Italian diplomat who was one of Mussolini's able lieutenants. He said to me, "It is easy to get power. Have you men to administer power when you have got it?". My answer then was a confident affirmation. We had Indian administrators as able as any of the British administrators ruling the country. The former had the advantage of a new vision and a new faith through the rise of a new flood of national consciousness while the latter could only safeguard the ramparts of a sinking imperialism. I did not recognise however that administrators were needed not only of adequate quality but in adequate numbers.

The answer to the Italian diplomat's question has been given anew by Dr. John Mathai, when he was Finance Minister of the Government of India. Speaking in the Constituent Assembly on the present economic situation in India, Dr. Mathai is reported to have said that the need in India is not so much more proposals as more willingness, ability and readiness to implement the proposals. He continued thus: "The question of implementation is really the most vital question that we have to face to day. The more I think of the economic problems with which the country is faced to day, the more I feel that at the bottom they are not really economic problems in the sense of technical economics. They are really problems of administration. Deep down they resolve themselves into problems of efficient and honest administration. What we are up against today is a slowing down, I was almost going to say, a breakdown of our administrative system, a gradual disintegration just at the point where the administrative system comes into direct contact with the masses of our country. If we are to make a better contribution than we have been able to do so far, what is required is not intellectual analysis, not more planning of big things but to settle down to the drudgery of good, honest administration".

Dr. Mathai has rendered a public service in stating with courage what in his view is the cause of the sense of frustration which the mass of the people have begun to feel in this country, so that the statesmen in charge may reexamine and rectify the measures they take to give effect to their policies and plans.

Some months ago, I had occasion to speak to Dr. Mathai about the implementation of a large scheme of irrigation and power development which both he and the Prime Minister were satisfied was sound and the execution of which both of them considered would not only benefit the country but also raise the prestige of India in the world. Yet both Dr. Mathai and Pandit Nehru were unable to prevent the scheme from being sabotaged. I asked Dr. Mathai, "Is there no one in India who, when a thing is good, can get it done?". He then said that it was a big question. He has now given the answer. Good schemes fail to be implemented in this country because of the slackening or even the breakdown of honest and good administration to which he has referred.

Group Prejudices, its Causes

I suggest that the reason for the growing inefficiency of administration is group prejudices. It is true that they existed under the British rulers of India too. Indeed they were to some extent fostered by the British rulers on the principle of divide and rule. But the play of such prejudices was kept under control so as not to affect the overall efficiency of administration. The prejudice of race, religion, caste, language, province, opinion or property was all played upon before and allowed to operate but within limits. Now that British control has ceased, these group prejudices are running riot. It has always been evident that with a few honourable exceptions, members of Government in India were provincially or communally minded and in their day to day administration whether it be in the selection of personnel or schemes tended to favour their own provinces or communities. This tendency has if anything been accentuated under the present sysem when unless the voice of a member representing a province or community is heard in councils or committees when decisions are to be made, the province or community has no chance of its interests being secured. One is forced to form a group as a defence against the prejudices of other groups. What the heads of ministries do, so also the heads of departments or persons under them in authority do too. In the region of provincial differences, the extent to which they operate is greater under a national Government than was the case before. In the region of caste differences, the extent to which they are allowed to operate is greater under a professedly impartial Congress Party government than even under a professedly communal government. The prejudice of the Congress group based on the common experiences of the fight against foreign domination is shown towards non-Congress groups in the administration of national affairs. The prejudice of non-property class groups is shown against propertied classes. While policies and plans are made under the influence of group prejudices, they are implemented by administrative staff who tend to be yes-men and as such become servants of group prejudices. The loosening of administration is due to the loosening of control from an outside force without such force being replaced by that of an inner unity. What then is the remedy for such a situation ?.

U.N.O. Charter Shows the Way

The remedy to group prejudices is the rise of unity among all the members of such groups. Each group in a nation consists of the individuals of the nation. A group needs an additional qulification but the basic qualities of the nation must continue, if the members of the group are to continue as members of the nation. So too, the existence of nations in humanity does not do away with the nationals being all human beings. While politics governs the activities of nations, ethics governs the activities of individuals. Nothing is more hopeful in the working of the United Nations Organisation than the provision that the basic rights and fundamental freedoms of each human being irrespective of race, religion, sex, language, political opinion or economic status should be safeguarded without discrimination. In pursuance of this provision, a Declaration of Human Rights has been prepared and transmitted to the General Assembly of the United Nations Organisation, so that a covenant on the basis of such principles may be prepared and on acceptance by nations become a part of international law. If the unity of India is not to be interfered with by the presence of groups, there is need for a similar declaration and firm and courageous implementation of the principles of such declaration. Security of life, right to equality before law, freedom of thought and religion, freedom of information and opinion, right to a government based on the will of the people, right to work and protection against unemployment, right to a standard of living, right to free and compulsory elementary education and to equal access on the basis of merit to higher education—all these principles which are recognized in the Declaration of Human Rights prepared for the United Nations Organisation should be accepted as valid and firmly implemented among all people in India. It is notorious that education is denied to people because of their birth. It is notorious that employment is denied to people because they do not belong to the group of the people in authority who make selections. It is notorious that persons of property are denied right to equitable compensation as legally determined. It is notorious that regions of the country are neglected in development because their representatives do not belong to groups in power. Group prejudice finds its extreme form in individual selfishness. A combination of selfish individuals or mutually prejudiced groups cannot form a nation. Only an organic nation can dream and plan and take effective action. A combination of discrete individuals or groups is amorphous and lacks direction in life. India which was unified under external rule has not regained unity through the rise of an internal cohesion of quality, when the external rule has been removed. Administration which is the implementation of policies and plans is therefore slackening. Two years of freedom have left people generally in India with a sense of frustration. The hope that life in India would with freedom gain a quality of adventure is receding. India indeed seems to be in danger of becoming an unfinished adventure.

I would not however end on that note.

India has for four thousand years kept her heart fresh and strong so as to be a beacon light to men. She partakes something of eternal life. Her life. is an adventure. It is an eternal quest, a quest for the common man, the man that is common to all men, the man who holds spirit but does not limit it, the man who is not contained even by his wife and children, his nearest and dearest, the man who reaches *sanyasa* and loves all men because he is all men and all men are he. India whose true genius lies in her quest for the selfless man can attain the unity and freedom from group prejudices wherewith she will administer her dreams, her plans and her targets. May the Indians of this generation rise to the height of eternal India!.

GROUP PREJUDICE AND POLITICAL PARTIES

ASHOKA MEHTA

Political Parties; their Varied Patterns

How far, if at all, do group prejudices influence political parties and their ideologies ?

Do social and religious differences affect the alignment of political opinions in the country ? What, in brief, is the relationship of group prejudices, that this symposium seeks to uncover, with political parties ?

Political parties do not conform to any uniform pattern. In the United States of America two big traditional parties hold the sway. Various regional and sectional interests have sought expression through these parties. The Democratic Party in the Southern States is basically different from the Democratic Party in, say, Minnesota State. But these diverse elements nationally sail together under a common flag. Third Party movements have so far failed to rally significant and sustained support.

In Great Britain two big parties have held the sway. These parties, Tory and Liberal before, and Conservative and Labour now, are based upon different interests : land-holders, and merchants and industrialists before, men of property and working people now. Single member constituencies, that prevail in the two great Anglo-Saxon democracies, favour two-party system as against multi-party system fostered in countries that have adopted one or the other form of proportional method of representation.

The difference in two party systems in Britain and in the United States is well marked : in the former country the parties have been organised on distinct ideologies, in the latter country the parties have been more traditional than ideological. The old bottles serve to carry new wines !

In Europe, parties have been organised on religious, regional, class and ideological bases. Christian Democratic parties, drawing their strength from the devout support of the Catholic masses, are in power in three leading countries of Western Europe. Well marked regions, like Bavaria in Germany and Catalonia in Spain, have developed regional parties. The parties of industrial workers and of peasants in some countries of the North and of the South-East Europe are classic instances of class basis given to political parties. The world-wide schism between the Socialists and the Communists testify to the strength of ideological divisions.

Whatever be the forms of political parties, in determining their contents group feelings play a large part. The forms are determined by historical accidents, but the contents reflect the different social and economic interests and pulls in the society.

Political Parties in India

In India, uneven social developments have made the society rich with group loyalties and group antipathies. The political policies pursued by the British rulers encouraged these divergent interests. The electorate, under the British, was split up on the bases of religion, class, race and sex. Under limited franchise such divisions led to a multitude of parties and perpetuated a variety of group solidarity and group prejudices.

Communal electorates were meant to foster religious as against national or general outlook. If in advanced countries like Germany, Italy and Holland religion plays an effective part in articulating political opinions, if in a country like the U.S.A. a candidate like Al Smith loses the Presidential election because he was a Roman Catholic, is there anything surprising if the Muslims and the Sikhs organised powerful communal parties and even the Hindus leaned towards veiled communalism in a less developed country like India?

It was a triumph of the nationalist forces that prevented the total break up of Indian political opinion into a multitude of conflicting sectional groups. All the other differences were ultimately enveloped into the larger folds of the Indian National Congress and the Muslim League that gave birth to the Indian Union and Pakistan.

The two big parties, the Congress and the League, developed the envelope character that distinguishes the Republican and the Democratic parties in the United States of America. Within the envelopes varying contents were put at different times and in different places.

Muslim League, an Analysis

The Muslim League was built up through exploitation of religious prejudices of the Muslims. Within that group, and therefore in the League, other tensions found reflection and were ultimately balanced. Different sections of the Muslim community, such as Bohras, Khojas, Memons had their own solidarity and their traditional prejudices. It was not easy to coalesce these groups into a homogeneous whole. Beating the opposition to the Congress Party and the Hindu community to the white heat enabled the League to cover up the kinks in its organisation. But within its folds, the various sub-groups jostled one against the other.

Apart from the prejudices of a Bohra against a Khoja, there were the provincial prejudices. The Sindhi Muslim never welcomed the hegemony of a Punjabi Muslim. The rice-eating Bengali Muslim felt himself apart from the sturdy wheat-eating Punjabi Muslim. The alchemy of Islam has not dissolved the differences and prejudices of provincial groups.

Differences in religious ideas have acted as another irrational factor. Chaudhary Sir Zafrulla Khan, because of his allegiance to Kadiani school of thought in Islam, has failed to rise to the stature his talents entitle him to.

Within the Muslim League, itself based upon religious exclusiveness of a community, there are layers of group prejudices, mostly based upon the stubborn facts of India society that have survived conversion and defied the democratic climate of Islam.

These tendencies are better brought out in the analysis of the Congress Party as the Hindu community suffers from social rigidities and social antipathies to a greater extent than the Muslims.

Scheduled Castes Federation

Caste is a strong force in the Hindu community. Its influence on politics is well-marked. The division goes deep between the caste Hindus and the outcastes. The latter were brought together in the Scheduled Castes Federation. The Federation took advantage of the caste solidarity as well as of the strong antipathy the untouchables felt towards the high caste Hindus. The political favours, shown to them by the British rulers, encouraged such a tendency. Even in the organisation of the S.C.F. the Mahars, one of the Scheduled Castes, played an important part. They form the key-stone of the Fedration's arch, while other caste groups like Chamars and Mangs have hesitated to follow Dr. Ambedkar, the leader of the S.C.F. and have not unoften gone with the Congress Party.

Non-Brahmin Parties in South India

In the South, the Brahmins have enjoyed for long cultural hegemony and because of their high educational qualifications a special position in the administrative services. The so-called Backward Castes, including various groups of Non-Brahmins, have combined to fight the Brahmin predominence. Originally the non-Brahmins were organised outside the Congress Party and in the period of 1923-35, provincial ministerships in Bombay and Madras were in the hands of Justice Party and other non-Brahmin groups. The sweeping victory of the Congress Party at the polls in 1936-37, brought about a shift in the politics of the non-Brahmins. They trooped into the Congress and ere long the party machine, in some of the provinces, passed into the hands of the non-Brahmins.

The caste solidarity of the non-Brahmins, the antipathy towards the intellectual and cultural predominence of the Brahmins and the scramble for jobs have made the conflict between the Brahmins and the non-Brahmins the axis round which politics revolve in the South.

A recent press report, for instance, reads as follows: " The Madras Government in a press note yesterday stated that no seats were allotted to the Brahmins out of 500 vacancies in the cadre of supervisors in the public works department, because a large number of Brahmins had been selected in the previous years ". The selection is thus not made on the merits of the candidates but on other extraneous considerations.

Within the ranks of the non-Brahmins different caste groups exercise their pressures and give vent to their prejudices.

In Tamil Nad, the social and cultural movement of the non-Brahmins against the Brahmins, called the Self-Respect Movement, developed into an aggressive movement for regional autonomy based on cultural exclusiveness known as the Dravid Kazhagam.

As the franchise is widened, each social group and sub-group within the generally immobile Hindu society struggles for predominence or at least a share in the loaves and fishes of offices and jobs. Democracy in India has so far been a clever balancing of different caste interests.

Provincial Prejudices

Next only to the caste loyalties and prejudices are provincial feelings. In West Bengal, for instance, there is a mounting feeling against non-Bengalis. That the non-Bengali capitalists have never scrupled to exploit the fair and rich province cannot be gainsaid. But the anti-capitalist feeling is buttressed and coloured by provincial prejudices. Efforts at joint front of all the exploited people against the exploiters evoke only a limited response. They get strength only when provincial feelings are brought into play. The demand for the inclusion of Manbhum and Singhbhum in Bengal and their detachment from Bihar have shown great evocative force. The irrationality of the attitude is realised when we contrast the opposition to non-Bengalis in Bengal with the indignation felt by the same Bengalis at the provincial jealousies shown by the Assamese. These obvious contradictions are rarely recognised and in their positive and negative forms they add to the emotional strength and the driving power of provincial prejudices.

Within a province, sub-group and sub-regional feelings are found to grow. In Bengal, for instance, there is a developing antagonism between men from the West and men from the East Bengal. The latter consider the former inferior in cultural, educational and other qualifications.

What is said of Bengal is true of other states and regions.

Group Prejudices, Determinants of Party Policies

The economic backwardness of India, the lack of social mobility especially among the Hindus and the woefully incomplete cultural homogeneity create a variety of fissures in Indian society. These fissures have developed a whole complex of group loyalties and prejudices that subtly influence the policies of political parties and distort their functioning.

Group prejudices, whether they be religious, social, or regional determine the contents of policies of political parties. Naturally these prejudices are neither openly recognised nor accepted. They are rationalised as in the case of the Muslim League or the Scheduled Castes Federation. Not unoften progressive phrases are used to cover up the group pressures that determine the shape of policy. The determining fact is what provides strength to a political party. The progressive phrases rarely bring the well-knit parties, drawing support from the religious or regional group feeling, the strength that they usually show. Even in the case of parties like the Indian National Congress, inside the general "envelope" sectional prejudices seek to obtain support and sometimes control.

English Knowing "Neo Brahmins"

A new group prejudice is slowly emerging in political parties. It is the group strength of persons uneducated or inadequately educated. The prevalence of foreign language, English in the case of India, as the official language of the country has created a special type of monopoly. Only a handful of men who know English are able to operate effectively in political and administrative matters. As a strong opposition grew up against Latin in Europe in the Middle Ages, so in India against the English knowing "neo-Brahmins" an opposition is growing up. That opposition sometimes spreads from the minority that strives to exploit its familiarity with a foreign language to the need of technical knowledge itself. Ignorance is slowly becoming a source of pride and in the next few years education and knowledge might become a handicap.

The prejudice that ignorance feels towards knowledge gives a new edge to the opposition felt by the non-Brahmins towards the Brahmins and the workers towards the intellectuals.

Middle-Class Prejudices

Another recent instance of group prejudice is the obstinate attitude of the middle-class in the country. They are convinced that during the war years the rich have become richer and the workers too have improved their standard of life. Only the middle-classes have got depressed. Even when it is shown to them, on the basis of statistics collected by governmental agencies that it is not so, they insist in believing that in a working class family there are a large number of earners and that their money wages as well as real wages have substantially gone up. But facts belie such sweeping generalizations. An average working-class family has 1.5 persons as earners and their wages are today no higher than what they were before the war. These indisputable facts fail to influence the thinking of the middle-classes. Here is a group prejudice that defies factual analysis and that is likely to determine in the years to come the political policies of probably the most significant class in the country.

With the achievement of freedom, it was hoped, that narrow loyalties and sectional prejudices would get loosened and ultimately dissolved. The post-freedom mood of frustration, brought about by a variety of reasons, has strengthened the sectional feelings, if anything aggravated the contraction of the bonds of sympathy and understanding. In place of the frank avowal of group prejudices, as in the past, such prejudices, adhered to in practice, are accompanied by sweeping generalisations and soaring ideals. The parochial persons pooh-pooh nationalism in the name of widest universal allegiance! From the armoury of Marxism, a number of weapons, including the potent one of "manifest destiny", are taken over by most groups based on religious, regional and social (or caste) considerations. A new amalgam of reactionary practices and radical verbiage is emerging as the latest expression of group prejudices. Such an amalgam threatens to discredit genuine progressivism, as National Socialism did in Germany.

Increasing Social Disintegration

In the social disintegration that is going around us, the *foci* of integration are becoming increasingly narrower. Nihilism exploits every single fissure in the society, and every group prejudice is stirred up and made articulate. The language is often deceptive but not difficult to distinguish. My friend Dr. Rammanohar Lohia has brilliantly characterised pseudo-radicalism as "Socialism of envy" as against the vital radicalism termed by him "Socialism of anger and sympathy".

Inside the traditional parties, these group prejudices are entrenching themselves. The evocative names of the Congress and the League cover up today group prejudices that belie not only their ideals but their history.

In India today political parties based upon distinct ideologies drawing their strength primarily from rational programmes and policies are either non-existent or too weak to receive serious consideration. Extraneous factors, related to prejudices connected with religious, regional or social sectarianism, provide much of the driving power of different political parties. The group prejudices are naturally covered up by ideological rationalisations but no serious student of politics can miss the hard core of reality within.

Conclusion

Rapid economic development of the country accompanied by widespread educational advancement and deliberately fostered social mobility alone can shift the keel of our politics from group prejudices to significant ideas and ideals. The world over the politics are part ideational, to borrow the convenient word coined by the American sociologist, Pitrim Sorokin, and part rooted in interest. In India the economic dislocation has intensified social tensions, expressed in a hierarchy of castes. Political democracy is powerless to resolve these rigidities and obstructions; democracy itself is in danger of getting discredited unless it is strengthened by a programme of rapid economic development carried out in the context of widening educational opportunities and general social mobility. Due to the absence of such a planned programme of development, political life in the country is in serious danger of being submerged under the passions of conflicting group prejudices.

A wise and courageous leadership can sublimate group prejudices into a creative force. The classic instance of that kind is provided by Khan Abdul Gaffar Khan. Charismatic leaders are able to evoke and organise a group prejudice, as Qaid-e-Azam Jinnah and Dr. Ambedkar have shown. But a truly elevated leader is able to transform the prejudice into a force of sympathy and understanding. In the crisis of culture we face today we are entitled to expect from the leaders this intellectual and emotional *tour de force*. A right socio-economic policy and wise leadership can save the country from the creeping ravages of group prejudices.

INDIAN STATES, THEIR FUTURE

V. T. KRISHNAMACHARI

Two Indias: Their Separate Development

When towards the closing years of the 18th century the East India Company attained its position of supremacy in India, it decided—largely on grounds of expediency and as the question actually arose in each case—whether a particular part of India should be brought under direct management or permitted to be an "Indian State". The map of India—its division into "British India" and "Indian States"—was not the result of any long-term policy but was due largely to historical causes. When the Crown took over the Government of India, the division as it then stood was accepted and perpetuated. The picture that emerged was that of over 550 States scattered in patches throughout the sub-continent—15 large ones with populations ranging from 16 millions to a million; over 80 'medium' States with populations from about 100,000 to a million; and the rest, more than four hundred in number, hardly distinguishable in size and resources from private estates.

In the decades that followed, "British India" and "Indian States" developed on parallel lines. There was no meeting point except at the Centre and that in a specified list of matters. The Provinces were under the Central Government which laid down policies for application in all important sectors of the national life—education and other social services, landholding and tenancies etc.,—and also possessed authority to see that these policies were executed. In regard to Indian States, there was a two-fold policy. The first related to matters of common concern affecting the whole of India and the second to purely internal matters affecting the States. In regard to the first which comprised such matters as defence, railways, posts and telegraphs etc., the Central Government insisted that Indian States should conform to arrangements considered essential in the broader interests of the sub-continent as a whole. By exercising its rights of "paramountcy", the Central Government brought into existence, during this period, a network of agreements and usage relating to these matters which made it possible for policies to be formulated and executed throughout the whole of India, thus creating a sense of unity in the economic field which did not exist before. Within the States themselves, in matters which were not of "common concern", the policy followed was one of non-intervention. These comprised matters having a vital bearing on the lives of the people—education and social services, land policies, civil and criminal law etc. In all these, Indian States were free to regulate their plans at their discretion. Interference came only when there was misgovernment or oppression.

Progress Uneven

This policy had its natural results. Indian States were isolated from the common life of the country and progress was uneven. In some of the larger States where there were fairly long periods of minority during which the Government of India set up administrations directly responsible to it or where there were forceful Rulers with zeal for reform, high standards were established. For decades these States rendered useful service to India in several ways. They offered opportunities for service to distinguished Indians to whom high office was not open at the time in British India. In them were tried experiments like free and compulsory education and separation of executive from judicial functions, which public men in India pressed on the Central Government for many years, without success. Then again, the Rulers could, unlike the Government of India, enact social legislation to bring Hindu Law into accord with changing conditions of modern life. In these States, development and other policies reached higher levels than in adjoining India and they sought, along with advances on modern lines, to conserve the best elements in the ancient culture of India. These, however, were exceptions. The majority of the Indian States lagged behind the rest of India in matters essential to national life. There was stagnation.

Freedom Movements in States

It inevitably followed that movements for the extension of self-government were less powerful in States than in the rest of India. In the bigger States to which reference has been made above, there were efforts to associate the people with the Government and also to bring into existence local bodies with democratic elements. Broadly speaking, these States maintained the same advance in these matters as the rest of India until responsible government was established in the Provinces. This further step was taken in the advanced States later than in Provinces. In the other States, no serious attempt was made to bring self-governing institutions into being. The same description applied to the religious and cultural movements connected with Indian renaissance. The larger States fully shared in them and made notable contributions to the new spirit. The bulk of the States were untouched by them.

Concept of All-India Federation

In the years 1931-35, discussions took place for the setting up of an All-India Federation of which Provinces and Sates would be component parts, the aim being to bring the whole of India under a single constitutional government empowered to formulate common economic policies. Negotiations for this purpose were not successful and when the war came, they were held in abeyance.

The picture presented by Indian States at the time of the passing of the Indian Independence Act can now be briefly summed up. Provinces and States had no formal constitutional connection. They developed on different lines. While in all matters of common concern uniformity had been brought about, there was much diversity in regard to education, land policies etc., which affect the daily lives of the people and are vital to well-being. A few States kept abreast of adjoining Provinces and evolved administrations which were efficient. Generally speaking, however, Indian States lagged behind the rest of India in progress. The national political movements touched only the more advanced States and left large populations unaffected. The criticism was often heard that the existence of States was a hindrance to the national movement. There was this amount of truth in this—that large populations lived under conditions in which they never felt the influences or felt them only slightly.

States after Indian Independence Act

When the Independence Act was passed, paramountcy came to an end and with it all the links between Provinces and States that had been forged in the previous decades in regard to matters of common concern. This void had to be filled and as a result of a series of conferences that took place in July 1947, all the States, with only a few exceptions like Kashmir and Hyderabad, agreed to accede to the Dominion of India in the three subjects of Defence, External Affairs and Communications. This was an epoch-making event. For the first time Provinces and States evolved a common constitutional link which enabled the Central Government to legislate for States in these essential "federal" matters and to exercise executive authority in the States in them. Later the extremely difficult political and economic problems facing India as a result of Partition and of post-war world conditions—deficit in foodgrains, the influx of refugees, the fall in production, inflationary trends etc.,—called for a closer laison between Provinces and States. This gave rise to two inter-related movements. In the first place, the States which had no viability had to merge with adjoining Provinces or with one another to form bigger units. Secondly, all the States units acceded to the Dominion in a larger range of subjects, especially those bearing on the economic life of the country—in other words, they agreed to endow the Central Government with legislative and executive powers to the same extent as the Provinces. The only difference that remained was with regard to taxation. The States did not accept the liability to federal taxation to the same extent as the Provinces. The financial relations remained the same as before.

The representatives of Provinces and States are now sitting in the Constituent Assembly with the object of framing a constitution which would apply throughout India. According to the Objectives Resolution, this constitution is based on fundamental principles among which the follwing are important : (i) that sovereignty vests in the people of India, and (ii) that Provinces and States should join as equal partners in setting up a common Government.

When the new constitution comes, therefore, Provinces and States will be exactly on the same footing on all matters including those relating to finance. The Central Government will exercise the same authority over States as it exercises over Provinces and largely through its own officers, as is the case in other Federations like the U.S.A., Australia, Canada etc. The difference that now obtains in regard to finance will be removed then and States will bear their share of the federal burdens on the same basis as the Provinces. A scheme for this purpose framed by the Indian States Finances Enquiry Committee has been accepted by the States and the Government of India.

January 26th, when the new constitution will formally come into effect and India will take its place as a Republic, will also mark the equality of status betewen Provinces and States. Indian States reduced in number by merger and amalgamation will have the same rights and responsibilities as Provinces and their people will take their place along with the people of the rest of India in the national life. The isolation that characterised the life of Indian States for nearly 150 years will then disappear. It will be the task of the new Governments in the States to ensure that the people of the States attain higher standards of living, including facilities for education and medical relief and equitable tenancy laws and are thus enabled to make their legitimate contribution to the common life of India.

THE NEW CONSTITUTION AND THE REMOVAL OF GROUP PREJUDICES

M. VENKATARANGAIYA

Role of the New Constitution

Fear and suspicion are at the root of most group prejudices. Any agency or factor that removes or mitigates the sense of fear and suspicion will go a great deal in removing or weakening the group prejudices also. It is from this standpoint that the new Constitution of India will be examined here. It will be found after such an examination that it serves as a very important factor in removing some of the group prejudices prevailing in the country. If there are critics who point out that even after the passing of the new Constitution and after it has begun to function, group prejudices have not completely disappeared from the country and that in some respects they have even become more intense, the answer to them is that the sources of group prejudice are of a large variety, that it is only with some of them that a Constitution can deal, that even in regard to prejudices with which it can deal, a certain period of time is required before the full effects of its provisions are produced and that in any case other agencies besides a Constitution—agencies like education and enlightened public opinion—should come into operation, if group prejudices are to be completely eradicated. What one has a right to ask in this connection is whether the new Constitution of India has done all that a Constitution is expected to do for removing or weakening group prejudices found in the country.

Allays Fear and Suspicion of Minorities

To this question the answer is an emphatic "yes". The new Constitution has done all that is possible for a Constitution to do in the matter of removing the sense of fear and suspicion found in certain groups in the country and inspiring in them a sense of confidence which will grow stronger and stronger with the functioning of the new system of government. It is well known that in India many of the group prejudices are the outcome of the fear and suspicion entertained by the minority communities towards the majority community. Among these are included the Muslims, the Harijans (the scheduled classes), the Christians, the Anglo-Indians, the Sikhs and so on. Some of these groups received a specially favourable treatment at the hands of the British and naturally they were afraid that with the withdrawal of the British and with power passing into the hands of the majority community they would not only not receive the privileged treatment that they previously secured but that they may even be persecuted for the somewhat pro-British attitude that they displayed in the past. Moreover the Muslims especially had the fear that the Hindus may now take revenge on them for the alleged misdeeds of the muslim ruler in the medieval period of the country's history. The Harijans had a suspicion that the treatment that was accorded to them in the past on the ground of their being untouchables would be continued with greater rigour by the caste Hindus who would enjoy all political power in a free India. More or less similar were the fears and suspicions of other minority groups.

Means Adopted to Remove Them

It was therefore necessary that in framing the new Constitution effective provisions should be introduced for the purpose of removing such suspicions and fears. This was realised by the framers of the Constitution and they have incorporated into it a number of articles which should go a great deal in making the minorities feel that there would be no discrimination against them in future and that they would enjoy all the privileges and advantages of full citizenship in the same way and to the same extent as persons belonging to the majority community. Articles of this nature broadly fall into three categories. There are those which deal with the fundamental rights of all citizens. There are articles which provide sanctions and safeguards for the rights so guaranteed. And there are other rights which are specially conferred on particular minority groups for a short or long period, rights which will specially benefit them and protect them against exploitation by other groups of which they are afraid.

Fundamental Rights

The purpose in including a list of fundamental rights in the new Constitution is to instil into the minds of persons belonging to the minority groups a feeling of confidence that any unequal or discriminatory treatment that the majority may be disposed to accord to them will become illegal and that those who persist in such conduct will receive punishment at the hands of the State. The Constitution therefore clearly lays down: "The State shall not deny to any person equality before the law or the equal protection of the laws within the territory of India."; "The State shall not discriminate against any citizen on grounds only of religion, race, caste, sex, place of birth or any of them;" "No citizen shall, on grounds only of religion, race, caste, sex, place of birth or any of them, be subject to any disability, liability, restriction or condition with regard to (a) access to shops, public restaurants, hotels and places of public entertainment; or (b) the use of wells, tanks, bathing ghats, roads" etc. This right to equality and to non-discrimination extends to freedom of speech, of association, of movement freely throughout the country, of owning and enjoying property and so on. There is no need to give here the whole list of fundamental rights. What is necessary is to recognise its significance to the minority groups. It ought to put an end to their feelings of fear and suspicion and instil into them a sense of confidence that in free India they will enjoy equally with the members of the majority all the privileges of citizenship.

Protection to Religious and Cultural Minorities

There is another feature of the Constitution which deserves notice here. What the minorities require is not merely a non-discriminatory treatment but also some special protection for their culture, religion and mode of life. It is then only that they will have real confidence in their future. The new Constitution of India provides for this also. There are articles in it which, besides guaranteeing freedom of religion, enable religious and cultural minorities to conserve their language, script or culture, to establish and administer educational institutions of their choice and receive financial aid from the state in maintaining them. There is therefore no reason why Muslims or Christians or any other section of the people, who want to protect their culture, should have any apprehension that the majority community will not permit them to do so. These articles have an added significance in view of the possibility of the creation of linguistic provinces and the consequent emergence of the problem of linguistic minorities on a larger scale. Even today there is such a problem in Orissa as between the Andhras and the Uriyas. But these articles ought to give the needed assurance to such minorities.

Sanctions and Safeguards against Infringement

We may next refer to the second category of articles in the Constitution dealing with the safeguards against infringement of fundamental rights. There is no need to observe that where adequate safeguards are not provided, rights become merely rights on paper and cease to have force in practice. This is not however the case with the new Indian Constitution. There are three or four features of it which deserve special mention in this connection. (1) One is that the rights guaranteed are rights which no government—Central, State or local—is permitted to infringe. This is an improvement upon what obtains in many other democratic states including the United States. For a long time it was only against infringement by the federal government that fundamental rights were guaranteed in the United States. State governments were not subject to similar restrictions. It is only in recent years that the supreme court in that country had begun to put liberal construction on individual rights in their relation to legislation by States with the result that the tendency to-day is that they are safeguarded against encroachment by state laws. Here in our Constitution fundamental rights are made binding on all governments—Central, State and local. None of these can interfere with them. Moreover the Centre alone has been empowered to pass all the legislation needed to safeguard these rights from attacks either by state legislatures or private parties. There is therefore no risk here of effect being given to them in certain areas and not in others. (2) The Supreme Court of India has been empowered to declare invalid any acts of the legislatures as well as any rules and regulations made by administrative authorities which interfere with fundamental rights. This power has already been exercised in several cases. (3) We should not forget in this connection that it is a democratic government that will function in the country under the new Constitution. Adult Suffrage and Joint territorial electorates have been introduced. The result is that persons belonging to minority groups will have a powerful voice in determining who the legislators are to be and what policies and programmes they should adopt. This in itself is a guarantee against majority tyranny. (4) Minorities have freedom to organise themselves into associations and to carry on agitation and propaganda for safeguarding their interests. They can shape public opinion. From this the conclusion follows that the rights conferred on them will not be mere paper rights but will become effective in practice.

Special Advantages to Minorities

The third category of articles in the Constitution gives certain special advantages to minority groups and these ought to remove from their minds whatever fear and suspicion they have. Among these advantages a few are noted here for illustrative purposes. (1) Parliament is empowered to make provision for the reservation of appointments or posts in favour of any backward class of citizens. It is also laid down that the claims of the members of the scheduled castes and the scheduled tribes shall be taken into consideration in the making of appointments to services and posts. (2) For a period of ten years seats are reserved in legislatures to scheduled classes. Appointments of members of the Anglo-Indian community to posts in the Railways, Customs, postal and telegraph services which they have been enjoying in the days of the British will be reserved for them for a period of ten years. (3) A special officer will be appointed for watching the interests of scheduled castes and scheduled tribes. (4) Special provisions have been introduced for the administration of tribal areas inhabited by the aborigines so that they may not be exploited by people from the plains. These provisions are given here only for purposes of illustration. They are not an exhaustive list of all such provisions.

Conclusion

The conclusion that follows from this analysis of the provisions of the new Constitution is that it has done all that is possible for a Constitution to do to allay the feelings of suspicion and fear that minority groups have in the past entertained towards the majority group, that there is no reason why the former should continue to have any prejudice towards the latter and that in the years to come there is scope for a larger amount of mutual understanding among these groups and that if prejudices do not entirely disappear it will not be due to any defects in the Constitution but to causes and circumstances outside it. Let it also be noted that a Constitution lays down only the broad principles according to which relations between different social groups should be regulated. But the extent to which these principles are put into effect depends very much on the vigilance displayed by those groups. Vigilance has been regarded as the price of liberty. If minority groups are to enjoy the rights guaranteed to them by the Constitution, they must be vigilant in the matter, take advantage of the freedoms conferred on them and organise themselves in association with all liberal and fair-minded people to work for a social order where tensions between groups will be reduced to a minimum. The Constitution can at best lay only the foundations. The superstructure will have to be raised by subsequent legislation and, in shaping such legislation, minority groups should be as active as the majority.

Section V
Minorities and Prejudices

THE POSITION OF CHRISTIANS IN A SECULAR STATE

BISHOP V. GRACIAS

Secular State; its Meaning

Perhaps we had better begin by examining the meaning and implications of the phrase a "Secular State". This seems all the more necessary today when we take note of the erroneous and positively harmful interpretations given by some writers. There is a tendency in the Press to use the word "secular" in order to give religion either no place, or only a back seat in the public life of the country. By a "Secular State" we understand a civil society or nation in which no single religion is given a privileged position by the law of the land, and a government which does not officially practise a particular religion, or favour any one religion at the expense of others. But it may be observed that in this concept of a "Secular State" it is the government that is specially concerned. But since the men who form the government and its officials are, of course, free like other citizens to have their own religion and practise it, one can easily see that it will be a delicate and difficult task for them to maintain complete "Secularism" in their official acts and contact. While a secularisation policy excludes religious favouritism, legislators and administrators are naturally inclined to favour their own personal religion, or even unconsciously act under its influence.

Secular State and Christians

In a "Secular State", therefore, while Christians could not reasonably expect any preferential treatment on grounds of religion, they do expect, however, that they be given ample facilities by the law of the land to live their life completely. Now here the age-old and well-tried philosophy on which the great civilisation of Europe was built up, the philosophy which dates from the Greeks but which the Catholic Church developed and made its own, may give us some help. For the greatest thinkers of the past have studied every aspect of human life, and especially of human society, and their conclusions are such as to appeal to every reasonable man, whatever his religion.

Christian Ideal of Life

According to this philosophy—and Christian teaching says the same—" man is placed here on earth in order that he may cultivate and evolve to the full all his faculties to the praise and glory of his Creator; and that by fulfilling faithfully the functions of his trade or other calling he may attain both to temporal and eternal happiness" (Pius XI; *The Social Order*). Now man is essentially a *social* being, which is what Aristotle meant when he called him "a political animal". He cannot live a fully human life in isolation; society is necessary to him. But, be it noted, society is necessary to man *in order that* he may fulfill the purpose of his existence; it is a means to that end. Society exists for man, not man for society. It will be seen at once what a great gulf separates the traditional Christian philosophy from those evil modern systems, like Communism and Totalitarianism, which regard man as existing for the State, instead of the State existing for man.

"Natural Rights" of Man

This brings us to the question of "natural rights". From the fact that man has been created by God and placed in this world for a definite purpose, it follows that Nature (i.e. the Author of Nature, God) has invested him with the moral power or "right" to do and to procure what is necessary for him to fulfill that purpose. The authors of the American Declaration of Independence laid down as self-evident truths "that all men....are endowed by their Creator with certain inalienable rights; that among these are life, liberty, and the pursuit of happiness" and "that to secure these rights governments are instituted among men...". Citizens in a well-governed country enjoy many rights which are conferred on them by the laws of their country, but it is important that it should be recognized that every man possesses certain rights by the mere fact that he is a man, rights which he owes not to any human laws but to the law of Nature, the Natural Law as it is called. It is for the civil government to protect and harmonize all human rights, but it should be especially careful to respect the "natural rights" of its citizens, for these are logically antecedent to and independent of the State and its laws.

Christian View of Family, State and Government

The first "society" in which man finds himself when he is born is the family. This primary human society is a natural, not an artificial or voluntary, society. It has been ordained by Nature and its Author for the propagation of the race and for the protection and training of the children until they in turn are able to defend themselves and found new families. We see in the family all the elements of a true human society. Parents, again in virtue of the Law of Nature, have not only the duty but the right to provide for their children and look after their upbringing. They possess real "authority" to which their children owe "obedience", and we can see clearly from the example of the family how the purpose of all "authority" is the welfare of those who are subject to it, in this case the children. The father is the head of the family, and it is he who is ultimately responsible for its well-being and good order.

Individuals and families make up the State, in the sense of the civil society or nation. And this too is "natural", ordained by Nature and its Author. And since the State is a natural society, it must be admitted that authority in the State comes from God, the Author of Nature. Every legitimate government, then, whatever may be the technique by which it is appointed, receives its authority from God and is answerable to God for the use it makes of its authority. The purpose of the civil government is, of course, the wellbeing of the citizens, and the protection of their rights. These principles of the Natural Law are firmly held by all true Christians, and it is on that account that they are invariably conspicuous for their loyalty and good citizenship, whether they are ruled by a Christian government or not.

But here we must enter a *caveat* against an error that is unfortunately widespread at the present day, namely the idea that a legitimate government or a duly elected Parliament is entitled to make any laws whatsoever that seem good to it, and that whatever is thus made legal is therefore morally right. This is by no means the case. As we have seen, every civil government receives its authority from the Law of Nature, i.e. from God, the Author of Nature. It is, therefore, bound to see that its laws and administration are truly just, that they do not infringe upon the rights which Nature itself has conferred on individual men and women, or on that other natural society, the family, and that in general they are in conformity with the Natural Moral Law, which finds expression in the universal conscience of mankind. From the most ancient times, writes Dr. Fairbrother in his book, "The Philosophy of T. H. Green" (1896), "men have consciously appealed from the laws that they are bidden, as citizens, to obey, to higher rules even more valid and binding.... Any rule or institution which can be shown as tending to weaken or destroy the true nature of man, to hinder the development of his 'natural' capacities, to put obstacles in the way of the realization of that ideal of character which is his true self, is *eo ipso* condemned. The phrase, Jus Naturae—Law of Nature—has often been misused, but, understood rightly, it bears witness to fundamental truth ; for

'There's on earth a yet auguster thing

Veiled though it be, than Parliament and King',

Viz. Humanity itself. Civic responsibilities, as well as moral, or rather because they too are moral, must be deduced from the essential nature of man." Even "a secular government" cannot evade the responsibility which is implied in the very nature of human government, of upholding what the universal conscience of mankind considers right-doing and discouraging what the universal conscience of mankind considers wrong-doing. The word "universal" is especially important here, because it is the universal conscience that testifies to the Natural Law that is in all men. A nation's moral judgments which are not those of the generality of mankind will be due to a particular religion, and should, therefore, not be allowed to influence a "secular" government.

We may seem to have wandered somewhat from our subject, "The Position of Christians in a Secular State", but in fact the point we have stressed regarding natural human rights, the rights of the family, and the limits which Nature itself places on the authority of the State are very pertinent to it, for they explain what Christians look for in the government of their country. As is well known, Christians as a whole are loyal, peaceable and lawabiding citizens. There is nothing in their religious life or worship which can be in the least offensive to any other body of citizens, and much that is highly beneficial to others besides themselves. They are entitled, therefore, to ask that they may be given ample facilities by the law of the land to live their life completely, and not be required to do anything which their religion forbids them to do.

Catholic Church and Indian Government

If we are to go into greater detail, it will be best to confine ourselves to the Catholic Church, first because it constitutes the largest single body of Christians in India, and secondly because it has a written law, the Canon Law, in which the specific requirements of Catholic life and worship are clearly set down. Canon Law legislates only for Christians, and that only in matters where religion or morals are concerned. Catholics, therefore, make no arbitrary or unreasonable demands. The Church does not impose any obligations on its members without good reason, and it is perfectly easy for the legislator or administrator to ascertain what Catholic requirements are. To take the simplest example, the Catholic Church requires institutions in order to carry out its mission, such as churches, convents, schools, hospitals, dispensaries, cemeteries and so forth. These are all works of public utility and many of them extend their benefits to large numbers of non-Catholics. Catholics will reasonably look for sympathy and help from the civil authorities in establishing and augmenting such institutions. Happily, it is fully recognized in this country that those who run Catholic institutions do not do so for personal gain, and that all money given to such works is spent in India and for the people of India.

There are some who object to Catholic charitable works on the ground that their ultimate aim is to make converts. This objection can only be raised by people who have no personal knowledge of the way our institutions are run. You never hear of any actual beneficiary complaining of annoyance in this matter, for the simple reason that there is no such annoyance. The propaganda value, so to speak, of Catholic charity lies in the force of example and in contact with Catholics themselves. "Let your light shine before men", said our Master, "in order that they may see your good works, and glorify your Father in heaven." Certainly, every Christian should wish to help others to share in the immense privilege of belonging to the Christian family, but this can only be attained by internal conviction of the truth of Christianity, and that cannot be imposed or forced.

Catholic Schools

A special word is necessary regarding Catholics and education, because one of the things which Catholics consider essential is that their children should receive their education in a Catholic school and indeed the Canon Law of the Church obliges Catholic parents to send their children only to Catholic schools. Childhood is the formative period of life; as the saying goes, "the child is father of the man." We are constantly told that the most important aspect of education is the training of character. Need it be wondered at, then, that Catholics insist upon this training being given in a Catholic school, by people who are able to instil sound religious and moral principles. Earlier in this article we have seen that according to the true and traditional philosophy, from which modern democracy sprang, the individuals which make up a nation are not mere chattels belonging to the State, but human persons possessing rights as men and as parents which are anterior to and independent of the State. Communist and Totalitarian States may ignore the rights of parents and treat children as State property, but a democratic State cannot do so without being false to its own principles. Since our "Secular State" is professedly democratic and utterly opposed to Totalitarian methods, it must, therefore, respect the right of parents to decide what kind of education their children are to receive, and should not in any way penalize Christian parents who wish to give their children a Christian education. If public money, for which all citizens are taxed, is spent on education, Christian schools should receive a justly proportionate share in the shape of grants. To be sure, if the State spends money on a school, it is entitled to see that its educational standards are adequate, but in this respect we can safely say, speaking generally, that Catholic schools are second to none.

Secularism : its Implication

As we said at the beginning, to give full effect to a "secular" policy of government must needs be a delicate and difficult task, because while a secular policy excludes religious favouritism, legislators and administrators are naturally inclined to favour their own personal religion or even unconsciously act under its influence. It has already become apparent that not all the governments subordinate to the Government of India have as yet realized the full implications of its "secular" policy. In some places, serious disabilities have been placed on Catholic educational agencies; in others, Catholic mission work is threatened. But we are confident that the declared policy of India's first national government will eventually be accepted in every part of the country and given full effect to, so that India may indeed become a model to all countries both of civil and religious freedom. The clear guarantees given in our Constitution are a splendid indication of the goodwill of the government towards one and all in the Republic of India. For this, the Christian community has been very grateful and will ever strive to safeguard in the best and most constitutional manner its rights by respectful representations to those in authority. Thus will the community continue to make, as it has done in the past, a worthy contribution to the progress and happines of the country.

PARSIS IN INDIA

R. P. MASANI

Were They Ever Victims of Group Prejudice

Thirteen hundred years ago, successive waves of Arab invaders brought about the collapse of the once mighty Sassanian Empire of which, at one time, pre-Maurya India was in a sense the eastern boundary, Iran the heart and Greece the westernmost limit. It was generally believed that the Muslim conquerors offered to the vanquished people the choice between the Quran and the Sword. Recent studies and research have, however, shown that the victors were not such bigots as they were represented to be. The evidence of the history and literature of the times is against the presumption of inordinate intolerance. The Prophet of Arabia regarded the followers of the creed of Zarathushtra as the people of the Book. He rejoiced and took pride in the fact that he was born during the reign of so good and great a Zoroastrian monarch as Noshirwan, the Just. After the Arab conquest the bulk of the population, no doubt, embraced Islam but a large section continued to cling to their ancient faith in the mountainous region of Khorasan and other places. We have it from so eminent an authority as the Arab historian Masudi that till the time of his writing (A.D. 916) the "Magi" worshipped fires of different kinds in Iraq, Fars, Kerman, Khorasan, Tabristan, Azarbayjan, and other regions. The very fact that there is till this day a population of more than ten thousand Zoroastrians in Iran as the relic of the ancient Iranians shows that though some over-zealous successors of the early Khalifs were guilty of excesses, Zoroastrians could still adhere to their cherished religious convictions and offer their prayers in fire-temples in various parts of Iran. It must have been, no doubt, a great struggle to stick to their faith unmolested by the Arabs and by their own co-religionists who had become converts to Islam. A band of Zoroastrians, therefore, migrated from Khorasan to the island of Hormuz at the entrance of the Persian Gulf and thence to India.

Two Kindred Peoples

Where the "Pilgrim Fathers" first landed in India and when, are still matters of controversy. The traditional date for their landing at some spot near Sanjan—716 A.D.-may, however, be accepted for our present purpose. Since that date, neither the immigrants nor their descendants, known as Parsis, have ever been victims of racial antinathy or group prejudice. Students of early history of Iran and India do not need to be told that that was not the first contact of Iranians with Indians. But neither the refugees nor the Hindu ruler whose permission they sought for landing had any idea of the relations which had subsisted between the two countries—commercial, cultural, political—for more than a thousand years before the time of which we are speaking; nor were they aware of the fact that in the dim old days the ancestors of the people of both the countries lived together as one race, spoke the same language, professed the same faith, performed the same ceremonies, followed the same customs and worshipped the same deities. To appreciate clearly why the question of racial, communal or group prejudice ought never to arise as between Hindus and Parsis, it is necessary to relate briefly, at the outset, the story of the kinship of these two branches of ancient Aryan Stock.

Where did these people live together as one family? According to the sacred books of the Parsis, the homeland of the people with whom originated Zoroastrian civilisation on the lofty plateau of Iran was *Airyana Vaejah*. "the cradle of the Aryans." It was the first of the land created by God. Here it was that a joint conference of the heavenly angels and the best of men was convened by the Creator under the leadership of King Yima. During the reign of this king, surnamed the Shepherd, there was such a large increase in the people that *Airyana Vaejah* could not contain them. Thrice the illustrious king led his subjects southwards, "on the way of the Sun." But their troubles did not end with these migrations. Angra Mainyu, the Evil Spirit, contrived to inundate their country with an icy deluge. However, a timely warning from Ahura Mazda of the coming catastrophe enabled Yima to retreat with his subjects and their flocks and herds, before the storm burst over their heads, to a temperate clime further south. To that new home, too, they gave the same beloved name *Airyana* **(Iran)**.

Society was then still unsettled. There were constant migrations in search of new lands and constant warfare with the aborigines whom they displaced and who became their inveterate enemies and unceasingly pounced upon them from their mountainous homes. About 2,000 B.C. we find the Indo-Iranians settling down in the neighbourhood of eastern Iran but finding group after group of their kinsman leaving them and turning south eastward, entering India by the passes of the northwest and thence spreading towards the Gangetic valley in which developed famous civilized Hindu Kingdoms.

Such, in brief, is the story of the separation and reunion of the two branches of ancient Aryans which, of all the people pertaining to the Indo-Germanic stock, lived the longest and the closest together. Had those refugees from Iran been aware of this ancestral history, they could have asked for protection from their brethren in India on grounds of blood relationship. But although they sought shelter as foreigners professing a different faith, no racial antipathy stood in their way. Nor has communal or group prejudice in any form or guise marred their even tenor of life or hindered their progress in their own way.

Neighbourliness

It is a remarkable episode in the history of India that the handful of immigrants from Iran were received with arms outstreched by the population of India and that since that date they have lived as good neighbours with the varied sections of the people in Gujerat and other parts of the country to which they spread in course of time, acquiring importance and influence out of proportion to their number. As pointed out by me in one of the Oxford Pamphlets on Indian Affairs, *The Cultural Problem*, the settlers in India readily adopted the Hindu way of life and customs and allowed even some of their religious ceremonies to be influenced by corresponding Hindu rites to such an extent that a Parsi could hardly be distinguished from a Hindu by name or by costume, by religious rite or mode of life. Whether the rulers were Hindu, Muslim, Dutch, French, Portuguese or British, the two communities lived together in harmony for centuries as good neighbours on friendly terms. It used to be said with legitimate pride that the two communities had blended together as milk with sugar.

The tide of nationalism had not yet set in, it mattered little who ruled. What held the two groups together was their healthy sense of neighbourliness and civic brotherhood. It was only after the apple of discord was thrown in their midst during the middle of the nineteenth century, in the shape of an official appointment, or membership of a legislative assembly or of a local body, that people began to hear, although mostly in whispers, of Hindu-Parsi jealousies. The Muslims were then out of the picture, as they took to English education long after their Hindu and Parsi brethren had begun scrambling for posts and positions in the public life of the country. Such jealousies and rivalries as were fomented between the two communities during that era had, however, nothing to do with racial bias or prejudice.

The ears of the chronicler who records such outbursts of hostilities and discord, which are not uncommon among members of the same community, should not be deaf to the notes of friendship and harmony. For centuries together Hindus and Parsis have fraternised with one another and lived in peace in towns and villages as did Muslims and Hindus untill recently, conscious of the essential unity of their civic and cultural life and tolerant of the differences in regard to matters admitting of diversity. Out of numerous cases of life-long friendship a few historic instances may be noted. The partnership and friendship of Motishah Seth, son of Amichand Shankersheth, the famous jeweller of his day, with Wadiaji Bomonji Hormusji and his family was the theme of many an interesting anecdote durng the latter half of the nineteenth century. When Hormusji Wadia died, he entrusted not only his business to Motishah, but also the management of his private estate and household affairs, his sons being minors at the time. Motishah faithfully discharged the duties entrusted to him. He made it a point to pay a visit daily to the members of the family of his deceased friend and continued such visits even after the minors had attained the age of majority.

Motishah was also Sir Jamsetjee Jeejeebhoy's partner, as were Jivraj Baloo and Maganbhai Karamchand. Another esteemed Hindu citizen, Damodardas Sukhadwalla, the founder of the People's Free Reading Room in Bombay whose name will ever be remembered with gratitude as the Andrew Carnegie of India, was an intimate friend and associate of Dinsha Wacha, Khurshedji Rustomji Cama and Sorabji Bengalee in their activities for Civic and Social reform. But for his spontaneous, munificent donation of Rs. 1,00,000|, to perpetuate the memory of Khurshedji Cama, the K. R. Cama Oriental Institute might never have been founded.

Among numerous Hindu friends of Dadabhai Naoroji was one Karsondas Madhoji. When Dadabhai had his business firm in England, he had large business dealings with Karsondas. Even during the hectic days of the Share Mania he gave credit to the constituents of Karsondas and agreed to honour bills drawn by Karsondas himself to the extent of £60,000. Frantic cables were sent to Dadabhai by friends in Bombay informing him that Karsondas was on the verge of insolvency and advising him not to honour his bills. But Dadabhai had given his word and he honoured all the bills, even though it meant and actually turned out to be his own undoing.

Evolution of Races Through Migration and Inter-breeding

Are we, then, to suppose that the two communities we are speaking of had no racial feeling or group prejudice? Both the ancient Iranians and their kinsmen in India during Vedic period held very strong notions indeed, concerning purity of blood and purity of race. Neither was immune from what are called national or racial prejudice against people believed to be of impure blood or unclean habits. They believed that the well-being of the commonwealth depended on ceremonial purity and this gave rise to exaggerated notions of defilement. But as between them there could be no such aversion. On the contrary, their common beliefs, traditions and customs concerning personal as well as ceremonial purity served as a cament.

Even in the case of people having no such common origin or common fund of conceptions and traditions, in the light of modern knowledge and the teaching of the Science of Man concerning the origin of mankind and the oneness of the human race, there should be no reason for estrangement between them on grounds of racial inequality or incompatibility. The word "race" is so loosely and indiscriminately used by politicians and people generally all over the world, creating needless barriers between man and man, that it seems desirable, indeed, to avoid the term in social surveys. There is only one species of man the world over, though the variations are many. Diverse groups comprising mankind have, no doubt, certain well-marked differences, physical as well as mental. For instance, those who have made their homes in the countries in Northern Europe, such as Norway and Sweden, are commonly tall, their skin fair, their hair wavy and their heads more like an egg than a sphere. Their eyes are generally blue to grey and their noses straight. On the other hand people living in Southern Asia or the Far East are of medium to short stature, round-headed and have brown or yellowish skin. Their hair is black, coarse and straight and the noses small and round. Among some of the typical mongoloid peoples a small fold of skin is seen arising above the free edge of the upper lid of the eye and passing down and almost covering the inner canthus. Then there are the Negroes in Africa and other countries, tall and dark-skinned, often almost black. Their hair is also black, eyes dark and the noses flat and broad with wide nostrils. The old Indo-European, the East-Asiatic and the African constitute the main divisions into which mankind is divided, but they all branch off from the same primitive stock and although diverging from one another for hundreds and thousands of years they all form one human race.

Even as regards the three principal varieties or types, various limitations to the use of the word "race" have to be noted. The individual differences between various members of one and the same group are often so considerable, movements and migrations of people century after century have been so numerous, intermarriage so frequent and the crosses between one group and another so prolific that it is often extremely difficult, if not impossible, to say to which type specific individuals may be said to belong. In the circumstances, to use the term "race" indiscriminately and to talk of purity of blood and superiority or inferiority of nations is to ignore the history of human evolution. The most notable among such mixed groups are the British and German peoples and the heterogeneous elements constituting the population of the United States. To assign them to any "race" is to confound the word "race" with "nation," which means a group of persons born in a community living in an era having certain geographical boundaries and sharing a common fund of traditions and conceptions of social obligations and owning allegiance to a common set of regulations and enactments. It was well urged before the Universal Race Congress held in the year 1911 at the University of London that the question of the number of human races had quite lost its *raison d'etre* and had become rather a subject of philosophical speculation than of scientific research. It was, said Dr. Felix Von Luschen, " of no more importance now to know how many human races there are than to know how many angels can dance on the point of a needle." He pointed out that the great majority of modern authorities claimed a monogenetic origin for mankind and rightly observed that the aim of the Congress should be to find out how ancient and primitive races developed from others, and how races had changed or evolved through migration and interbreeding.

Pseudo-Scientific Theories of Inequality

So much for physical appearance. As regards mental traits, the same dictum applies. Although the differences in respect of mental endowment are stil numerous and enormous, they are by no means innate and inmutable as they were taken to be according to the theories which were enunciated by early anthropologists and exponents of the psychology of peoples with an air of scientific knowledge but which were actually based on a fragile framework of sophistry. One such author, whose works were widely read fifty years ago, was Gustave Le Bon, author of " The Crowd." It was his belief that the idea of equality of individuals and races propounded by earlier authors was illusory. "The point that has remained most clearly fixed in my mind after long journey and through the most varied countries," says he in another book of his, "*The Pyschology of Peoples*." " is that each people possesses a mental constitution as unaltering as its anatomical characteristics " and he concludes his Introduction to this book with the observation that the irreducible differences and inequalities in the mental constitution of different peoples are, together with old age and death, " a part of those iniquities of which nature is full and to which man must submit." It was strange that such an exposition of the subject despite the evidence of eminent anthropologists to the contrary, was then regarded by the reviewers of Le Bon's books as careful and profound.

Just as tall and short, fair and dark-skinned, long and short-headed come from one stock, so are intelligent and primitive, enterprising and unenterprising, refined and coarse, superior or inferior in inherited capacity, belong to the same species of man. The fundamental structure of the human mind is uniform in all people and human nature is also the same everywhere. Man's emotions and feelings, his intellectual ideas, his love of beauty, his longing for harmony, his striving for perfection, his attachment to his country are the same everywhere. The core of every culture is the same—the fundamental humanity of man. The differences in educational, hygienic, economic and ethical standards are easily accounted for. Favourable circumstances and surroundings, advantageous geographical position, favourable conditions of trade and contact with the outside world, cause one group of people to advance more quickly than another, while some groups remain in a primitive state of development. One type may be refined, others may be coarse ;

but all are adapted to their surroundings and the backward ones are not necessarily inferior to the more advanced or refined   The differences that exist between them can be traced to historical circumstances, passing social conditions and arrested stages of development. All the branches of the human family, according to recognised authorities, seem to be equally good or bad, equally improvable or susceptible to deterioration. Given a number of generations and favourable circumstances, the savage may equal, or even surpass, the civilized man of to-day.

"The only savages" in Africa are certain white men with "Tropenkoller," said Dr. Felix Von Luschen, Professor of Anthropology in the University of Berlin, during the early years of this century in one of his University lectures. A few years later, he declared emphatically that he adhered to that opinion. Paradoxical though it seemed, he said, "I am still seriously convinced that certain white men may be on a lower intellectual and moral level than certain coloured Africans." He knew, no doubt, that what he was stating could be upheld only in theory.

Fortunately, for the fugitives from Iran, no pseudo-anthropologist was abroad thirteen hundred years ago to propagate theories of racial differences, none of those unscientific exponents of the science of man to vitiate the minds of the people inhabiting different parts of the World with his theory of division of the human race into two types, one superior and the other inferior, and to disseminate beliefs concerning the innate inequality of different groups of people, their irreducible differences, physiological divisions and psychological limitations. The Hindu ruler whose protection was sought by the immigrants from Iran was blissfully ignorant of all such racial problems. Nor had the refugees any idea of the barriers that have since divided groups of people and kept them apart.

Warm Welcome

While, however, all accounts agree concerning the cordiality with which the emigrants from Iran were welcomed, there is a good deal of confusion regarding the date of landing of those "pilgrim fathers", the spot where they landed and the name of the Hindu ruler whom they approached for permission to make India their home. The only available source of information on the subject is a poetic composition in Persian, *Kisseh-i-Sanjan*, written by a Parsi Priest of Navsari, Behman Kekobad Sanjan, in the year 1599, after the traditional date of the arrival of the refugees. The authenticity of *Kisseh-i-Sanjan* has been challenged by competent scholars but until more light is thrown on this episode this traditional account may be accepted in broad outline. According to this account the Dastur, who expounded to the Hindu Prince the principles of the Zoroastrian faith and the social customs followed by the fugitives, added: "*Do not be afraid of us* for no harm will come through us to this country; we shall be the friends of India; we shall destroy your enemies."

What harm could a handful of Iranis do to the people of Gujerat? Did the Dastur think that the king had reason to be afraid of the immigrants from a country whose kings, in days when imperialism was not considered a crime and a curse, had gloried in warfare and had extended their sway to India and extorted tribute from her princes? But none of them, as pointed out above, had any knowledge of that strife. Perhaps the Parsi prelate was thinking of the fear of aliens so common in those days.

Be that as it may, the story of the rise and fall of the Empire of Iran has for the war-mongers of to-day a lesson which is worth recalling. The Parsis pride themselves in tracing their descent from ancestors who in pre-historic days brought demons and giants to their knees and who in the sixth century before Christ founded a mighty empire. Vanquishing the Medians, Cyrus the Great occupied Kashghar and Yarkand, subdued the whole of the Babylonian Empire, conquered Palestine, set the Jews at liberty, and allowed them to establish themselves at Jerusalem and to rebuild their temples. His son Cambysses brought Egypt within the orbit of his empire and his successor, Darius, penetrated India as far as the Punjab and annexed the valley of the Indus. Conquering Bysanthium and Macedonia, he overran the south of Europe, but was repulsed by the Greeks in the famous battle of Marathon. His son Xerxes was successful on land but met with reverses at sea. Shapoor, the renowned Sassanian king, then led an invasion of the Roman Empire and his successor Noshirwn the Just obtained several signal victories over the Romans. After him, however, there were no heroes left to keep the flag flying.

The curse of conquest comes home to roost. The fall of Babylon, the decay of Egypt, the disintegration of Greece and the decline and fall of the great Roman Empire bear testimony to this fact. What happened in the case of these countries happened also in the case of Iran. The demoralising influences that flowed from tribute levied by them degraded the conquerors and undermined the basis of integrity of the empire as well as the social structure of the Iranians. Living a life of ease and luxury, indiscipline and insubordination, they left Iran an easy prey to the simple, sturdy and disciplined Arab invaders.

The Fog of Eight Centuries

The early history of the Refugees from the time of their arrival in India down to the fifteenth century is shrouded in obscurity. There are no authentic records to show how the refugees fared in India after their arrival ? What were their pursuits ? What was their economic condition and standard of living ? What was their status in society ? What were their educational and intellectual activities ? What was their contribution to the prosperity or good government of the country ? No research scholar has hitherto had any glimpse of the history of these settlers during those early years. One looks in vain, however, for any importance concerning them in authentic annals of the times. It is related, however, in Kisseh-i-Sanjan that when Muslim invaders penetrated into the Province of Gujerat during the fourteenth century, the Parsi residents in Sanjan fought valiantly by the side of the Hindu Chief. The Muslims were repulsed but they returned in large numbers and succeded in the second encounter. The Parsis were killed in large numbers. Thise who survived had to abandon their settlement in Sanjan. There is, however, in this account, a confusion of dates and places and the identity of the Muslim invaders is not yet established. One can therefore, infer that during that long era of unenlightenment the Parsis in India must have led an uneventful life as cultivators, domestic servants, or petty traders, sunk in ignorance and poverty.

The earliest specific reference to their activities in Bombay in the year 1584, is found in *Colloquios* (Conversations on Drugs and Samples of India) by Garcia da Costa, a Portuguese physician and botanist. This devotee of Saraswati, the goddess of learning, was also a great favourite of Luxmi, the goddess of wealth. Bombay was then owned exclusively by him. From his book it appears that the Parsis had by that time established themselves as traders in that city which has since become their stronghold.

"There are other shop-keepers", he says," who are named Coares, and in the kingdom of Cambay they call themselves Esparcis and we the Portuguese call them Jews."

He questions, however, the popular impression and points out that "the Parsees are not Jews but gentiles who came from Persia". In support of his contention this erudite son of Aesculapius produces some very interesting facts and arguments.

"When one dies", he observes, "they take him by another door and not by that they serve themselves, have separate houses where they are laid down when dead and placed here until dissolved; they look to the East, are not circumsised, nor is it forbidden to eat pork, but it is forbidden to eat beef. And for these reasons you will see that they are not Jews."

It is generally believed that the Parsis in India began to flourish with the advent of the British but their rise may be traced to the days when the Portuguese were in power in India and employed them as agents or middle-men. Since those days they have availed themselves of the opportunities available to them to distinguish themselves in various spheres of public usefulness. For a handful of people to attain the position that they have attained in a country inhabited by millions is, indeed, an inspiring example for the students of human evolution looking forward to a better association of individuals and nations and better social organization and co-operation than what subsists in this madly disorganised, divided and distracted world of ours. It would need a separate volume to do justice to that theme. All that is necessary to say for our present purpose is that if during the past four centuries the Parsi community has grown in strength and influence, it is due no less to the spirit of brotherhood and neighbourliness of the sister communities·among whom it has lived as to its own capacity, resourcefulness, adaptability and sense of obligations of citizenship

HINDU-SIKH RELATIONS

G. D. KHOSLA

Aim of Sikhism

When three hundred and fifty years ago Guru Nanak spread his message of peace and unity throughout India, and evolved a creed which was intended to bring together the factious elements of Hinduism and Islam, he could not have anticipated that with the unfolding of events Sikhism would provoke a sharp conflict with Islam and to a lesser though regrettable extent bring about a schism between the Sikhs and the Hindus. What were the aims that Guru Nanak set before himself and the hopes he entertained? The founder of the Sikh religion was anxious to unite the Hindus and the Muslims of India on a common platform where they could stand together and resist the invasion of the foreign Mogul. The followers of this new religion formed a united brotherhood forswearing untouchability and practising service and sacrifice. But religion has a curious way of developing into a unifying and at the same time a disrupting influence. As it grows and gathers vigour it begins frequently to travel beyond its proper domain, and aspire to political power. Christianity and Islam did not confine their activities to the emotional content of the individual but drove their followers into wars of aggression and conquest. In our own day there is a danger that the mutual mistrust and prejudices of the Hindus and Sikhs might drive a wedge between them and jeopardise the safety of our society. Fortunately the two communities have so much in common and the differences between them are so narrow that they can be easily bridged. All that is required is a little imaginative thinking and an earnest desire to understand the other's point of view.

Hindu-Sikh Relations before and after Partition

For nearly four centuries Hindus and Sikhs have lived together as brothers and neighbours. Their religious creeds have many points of contact. In the Punjab, at any rate, many Hindu families look upon the Granth Sahib as a sacred book and visit the Sikh shrines. Their religious and social customs are similar and in many cases identical. And, most important of all, intermarriages between the two communities have made them of one flesh and blood. A Hindu or a Sikh may look upon a Muslim as a stranger, who does not understand his point of view, for he is an interloper who came from foreign lands and, so far as his emotional loyalties are concerned, continues to be an alien; his company is not always welcome, there are certain mental reservations which are accepted on both sides, certain subjects which are not freely discussed, some social barriers which are never crossed. But Hindus and Sikhs have come to look upon themselves more and more as members of one community, as two branches of the same family, two distinct entities arising from a common stock and practising the same customs, manners and culture, speaking the same language, intermarrying one another and, to a large extent, professing the same political beliefs. It is only recently and, more particularly since the partition of the country, that differences between the two communities are beginning to assert themselves and threaten the integrity of the people of the Punjab.

Group Prejudices, their Origin and Dynamics

The prejudices acquired by a group are really nothing more than defensive barriers of self-protection. The minority community surrounds itself with a number of taboos because it has fears that it may cease to retain its distinct entity. Whereas religion should be nothing more than an emotional complex of personal beliefs and convictions, it is frequently called into assistance to achieve economic and political aims. Then we hear complaints of the language, culture and religion of the minority community being in danger, of the majority imposing its will upon the minority by brute force and by the argument of sheer numbers. On the other hand, the majority turns a deaf ear to the legitimate claims and aspirations of the smaller group and accuses it of exploiting religion for selfish and material ends. Soon we find neighbours, friends and relations taking sides and organising themselves into hostile camps, and because the appeal of the leaders on both sides is to religious sentiment and emotion, reason finds no place in the arguments advanced and feelings reach the point of exacerbation. If only there were a real attempt to understand the other's point of view in a spirit of sympathy and generosity and if only men realised that it is more important to give than to take.

Hindu-Muslim Conflicts

The events of the last forty years culminating in the recent disasters witnessed in our country should teach us a lesson unless like the cynic we are content to say that the only lesson we learn from History is that we never learn from History. The fulminations of some Sikh leaders and the lack of sympathy displayed by many Hindus are reminiscent of what happened in 1937 when Congress ministries took office for the first time in eight out of eleven provinces of India. The Muslim League felt itself faced with political frustration and made a rapid retreat to the religious pulpit whence a bitter campaign against the Congress was launched. It was alleged that under Congress rule, Muslim culture, the Muslim language, Urdu, Muslim customs, the Muslim personal law—in short Islam itself was in danger. In Uttar Pradesh where the complaints were loudest, Muslim and non-Muslims spoke the same language and had the same culture. Congress rule did not threaten to change the personal law of the Muslims or make assaults upon their religion. But the real grievance was the Congress refusal to form coalition ministries and include Muslim League ministers in the Cabinet. This was done in the name of political solidarity and governmental cohesion, but the unwisdom of this parliamentary orthodoxy soon became apparent—the differences between the two communities rapidly increased and became irreconcilable.

Congress-Sikh Conflicts

The grievances of the Sikhs in the Punjab are not dissimilar. They want Punjabi to be the official State language, there are demands for a Punjabi-speaking province, a homeland for the Sikhs, a realignment of administrative units on a linguistic basis. They ask for a larger representation in the State Cabinet and Government offices, more economic and fiscal concessions. They want to preserve their culture and the integral unity of their community. Religious Demands are made the occasion of political demands. The Hindus are unsympathetic and hostile. They accuse the Sikhs of adopting an anti-national attitude and introducing fissiparous tendencies in the unity of the Indian people. Hindi is sought to be imposed as the State language and the medium of instruction in schools. Communal representation is denied on grounds of efficiency and there is (to the Sikh mind) an undue and wholly unnecessary insistence on the secular nature of the State.

Language Cantroversy

The question of language has assumed important proportions and the Congress is accused of a breach of faith in this respect. It is said that when the Constitution of the Indian National Congress was framed, the principle of linguistic provinces was accepted and Punjabi was recognised as the official language of the Punjab, just as Bengali and Marathi were recognised as the languages for Bengal and Maharashtra respectively*. The realignment of the provinces on a linguistic basis may be inadvisable but (so it is argued) there is no justification for compelling the Punjabis to abandon their native language for another. A Sikh friend, while discussing this matter, drew my attention to the views expressed by a leader of the Congress Party not very long ago. Ravi Shanker Shukla, criticising the language policy of the All-India Radio in a book published in 1944, said :—

"It is preposterous that Punjabi should be ousted from the Punjab and replaced by 'Hindustani' of any sort. If A.I.R. professes to worship on the shrine of 'familiarism' and if its policy is to make itself understood to as large a number as possible as made out by Mr. Clow, does it pretend for a moment that any sort of Hindustani can ever be more 'familiar' to Punjabis than Punjabi—indisputedly their mother-tongue, the speech in which the voice of every Punjabi finds its first utterance, the language of every Punjabi home and the language which accompanies every Punjabi from the cradle to the grave? Mother-tongue is infinitely sweeter than the sweetest tongue. Punjabi literature, *geets* and folklore express the longings, joys and sorrows which Punjabis have experienced through centuries. Punjabi is an essential part of the very being of Punjabis; without it they will be cut off from their past. Without Punjabi, the Punjab will be anything but the Punjab. It is hoped that all Punjabis, irrespective of caste or creed, will unite to protect their *Matri-Bhasa* from the onslaughts of A.I.R. and of the Punjab Government. Punjabi enshrines the sacred literature of the Sikhs who rightly regard the Punjab as their home and Panjabi as their language. Punjabi does, indeed, look to the Sikhs in the last resort for protection, and if they want that their sacred language should not be reduced to the status of a dead language in its very home, they must fight A.I.R. tooth and nail for the place which rightfully belongs to Punjabi in the Lahore programmes. They should refuse to be bribed by half a dozen Punjabi talks and features which A.I.R. doles out to them per year. That Punjabi should be the only language of the rural programmes and a few *geets* is a slight, if anything, on Punjabi. Even those educated

---

* Article VI of the Constitution of the Indian National Congress, as amended at the Bombay meeting of the A.I.C.C. in June 1939.

Punjabis who pride themselves on their knowledge of Urdu and pretend as if they never knew Punjabi and are ashamed of it, take recourse to Punjabi when they give vent to their innermost feelings or when they retire to the privacy of their homes or when they want to be at ease. It is axiomatic that education or entertainment can best be imparted through the medium of the mother-tongue."

I have taken the liberty to quote a somewhat lengthy passage not because I agree with it in its entirety but because it contains the present view-point of the Sikhs on the question of language and because this categorical statement of the Congress belief is made the basis of a charge of breach of faith on the part of the Hindu majority in power. It is of the utmost importance that this grievance be examined sympathetically and a satisfactory solution of the problem be arrived at by mutual co-operation and understanding.

Communalism in Services

The mistrust and, in some cases, the open hostility witnessed among the members of the Services balonging to the two communities is another cause which has led to a deterioration of the Hindu-Sikh relations. This is really nothing more than a case of professional jealousy having repercussions in the wider field of social relations. Our newly acquired freedom is acting like a heady wine and is turning us into selfish and irresponsible individuals. We have yet to learn that to enjoy the fruits of freedom we must surrender a certain measure of personal liberty; to have good government we must learn to sacrifice and co-operate. Integrity and efficiency are more profitable objectives than personal advancement. The members of the Services must acquire a broader outlook and resolve their differences in the wider interests of the country.

Urban Versus Rural Tangle

The urban versus the rural tangle in the Punjab threatens to become a communal matter. In the newly constituted State the character of the population has changed with the arrival of large numbers of refugees from West Punjab, with the result that Sikhs predominate in rural areas and Hindus in urban areas. The contribution which the rural population makes to the State revenues takes the form of land revenue and water charges for canal-irrigated land. The taxes paid by the town dwellers are of a wholly different character. These take the shape of taxes on income, houses, the daily necessities and luxuries of life. The economy of a State cannot be split up into water-tight compartments having reference to rural and urban areas. Every department of the administration cannot be self-supporting. It is only when everything hangs together that the business of the State can be carried on efficiently. It is a false notion that the benefits which any particular individual or any particular community derives from Government should be measured in terms of the contribution he or it makes towards the State revenues. It is perhaps natural that when a new tax is imposed or the demand from any particular quarter is increased, there should

* R. S. Shukla, Language Policy of All India Radio.

be resentment against the additional burden and protests should be raised against those in power; but criticism of fiscal measures should not be coloured by religious emotions. When the Punjab Government recently increased the water rate on canal-irrigated land, there was observed a tendency to excite communal passions because the rural population on whom this burden fell had a majority of Sikhs. The Government may have been ill-advised to adopt this measure and it is possible that other sources of revenue could have been tapped with advantage, but it was never intended that members of one religious community should benefit at the expense of the other; but criticism of the Government policy unfortunately took this shape. Mischievous criticism of this type is neither helpful nor constructive, it destroys social harmony and spreads discontent, and a comparatively harmless rivalry between the rural and urban areas has taken the form of communal antagonism.

Hindu-Sikh Differences not Fundamental

These instances will show that Hindu-Sikh differences in the Punjab are not fundamental. They arise from misunderstandings created by lack of sympathy and economic rivalry. They are capable of being resolved provided the leaders on both sides approach the problem with imagination and in a spirit of give-and-take. But if sectarianism and narrow provincialism are allowed to poison the minds of the people and if ambitious men exploit religious sentiment for their own ends, the people will continue to be deluded and misled and the peace of our country will be continuously threatened.

Section VI

Miscellaneous

INDIAN PRESS AND ITS INFLUENCE

DURGADAS

Indian Press and National Struggle

The history of the Indian Press may be justly described as the history of the Press in India for the emancipation of the country from bondage and foreign fetters. In the process, right from its humble origins till the attainment of India's independence, the Indian Press had to fight for its own freedom too. That on the domestic front and the larger political one, the Indian Press had kept its flag high was clear from the very name of the men associated with newspapers and journals of the times. Behramji Malabari and Kristo Das Pal, Bal Gangadhar Tilak and Surendranath Banerji, Lajpat Rai and Bepin Chandra Pal, Phirozeshah Mehta and Madan Mohan Malaviya, G. Subramania Iyer and N. C. Kelkar, were among the stalwarts who sought the medium of the press for the expression of national aspirations. The Indian Press, till recently, was either moderate or extremist, but not communal, for communalism was a later-day growth, born of the vicious forces let loose in the country by a gradually tottering and not very scrupulous bureaucracy. Even above three decades ago there was eloquent testimony to the healthy influence of the Press, and Pandit Ambica Charan Mazumdar, as President of the United Congress at Lucknow in 1916, spoke enthusiastically of the important part played by the Indian Press in the evolution of national life, and its "firm hold", despite its chequered history, "over the public mind and the sustaining energy of a growing people". To its historic role in the fight for India's freedom in the tumultuous decades that followed, Lord Listowal, the last Secretary of State for India, paid a glowing tribute. Addressing a gathering of Indian journalists in London, shortly after the Indian Independence Bill had received the assent of the King (on July 18, 1947) he said: "The Indian newspapers have every reason to be proud of the part they have played in the great constitutional change and of the good influence they have exercised on Indian opinion." Thus the Indian Press has as much risen to the height of its opportunities in canalising the thoughts of the people, and moulding public opinion in the true tradition of the Press in more advanced countries, as it has changed beyond recognition on the purely technical side. It is not, however, without tears and toil that it has slided into a more spacious world that calls for a yet more constructive role and creative constructive role and creative endeavour.

Its History

For a wonder, the Indian Press, in its earliest years, was but the Anglo-Indian Press. The first batch of English newspapers in India—beginning with *Hicky's Gazette* of Calcutta (1789)—had on it the Anglo-Indian impramatur, and yet not escaped the unfriendly attention of British officialdom. So early as in 1798, Lord Wellesley frowned at the Press and promulgated a series of stiff rules, infringement of which meant immediate deportation. The rise of vernacular newspapers came under such suspicion that even Raja Ram Mohun Roy addressed an appeal to the King and Council against the Press regulations. It was not still Lord Amherst arrived on the scene as the Governor-General of India that there was any disposition on the part of the Government to relax the application of these rules. Even the gallant effort of Sir Charles Metcalfe whose name is linked with the crusade for the freedom of the Indian Press, was of little avail, as his liberal and far-sighted policy was disapproved by the Court of Directors, notwithstanding Macaulay's support. Successive Viceroys were rather bent upon stifling the Press, and the Vernacular Press Act of 1878 was an unmistakable pointer. Undaunted by the repressive policy of the Government and the too many restrictions placed upon them, papers like the *Amrit Bazar, Patrika* in Calcutta and *Hindu* in Madras entered the lists. At the time of the ill-fated partition of Bengal and the inauguration of the Swadeshi Movement, the Press breathed a new spirit of defiance. The bureaucrats of the day found in the Indian unrest the germs of a revolutionary movement and ascribed the manifestations on the political scene to what they characterised as the inflamatory writings in the "Native Press." Introducing the Press Bill on February 4, 1910, Sir Herbert Risley spoke of "the demoralisation of the Native Press" and said that certain journals "have prepared the soil in which anarchy flourishes; they have sown the seed and they are answerable for the crop." The Press Act of 1910 exasperated the Press as well as the public, and even so famous a jurist and sedate a politician as Dr. Rash Behari Ghosh condemned it as "a serious menace". During the First Great War Mrs. Besant, whose *New India* was penalised, put up a brave fight for the freedom of the Press. The obnoxious Press Act was repealed in 1922, during the time of Lord Reading as Viceroy, as a result of the recommendations of the Sapru Committee appointed on March 21, 1921. During the Second World War, the Press had a crop of new troubles as the Government sought to prevent the Indian Press from lending support, first to the Civil Disobedience Movement and then to the "Quit India" campaign, launched by Mahatma Gandhi. Some newspapers had to close down, but as a result of the endeavours of the All-India Newspapers Editors' Conference, a new code of voluntary restrictions was evolved, and a crisis tided over with the subsequent withdrawal of the Government's prohibitory orders. During all these phases, the conflict was essentially between Indian Nationalism and British Imperialism.

Communal Press, British-Inspired

The Communal Press in India owed its inspiration, if not its origin, to the British policy-makers who felt that it was not possible to check the march of Indian Nationalism under the dynamic leadership of Mahatma Gandhi unless they unleashed the forces of communalism and set up community against community, as, for instance, the Non-Brahmins against the Brahmins in the South, and the Muslims against the Hindus all over the country, and more particularly in the North. The Congress was split on the rock of Montford Reforms. The Councils were boycotted by Congressmen, the Legislatures became the playgrounds of ineffectual Liberals and communalist reactionaries. The hour was propitious for the Muslim henchmen of the white bureaucracy to fill the stage. The newspapers, particularly those published in the Indian languages, that were founded or subsidized by communalist parties, started spouting venom. The worst offenders were in the Punjab. Pakistan was then unheard of, but Muslim politicians and publicists were intoxicated by Pan-Islamic visions. The counterpart of the rabid Muslim press was chiefly in evidence Maharashtra where the cult of Hindu revivalism had a strange spell. The first all-India leader who sounded a warning was, interestingly enough, a Muslim Stalwart. In his presidential address at the Cocanada Congress, Maulana Mohammed Ali spoke thus :

"I am myself a journalist, and you all know that I have undergone some little suffering for the sake of securing the freedom of the Indian Press. At least, I can claim the honour, if honour it be, to have figured in the leading case under the late lamentable Press Act, and it was I who started this fox even if I could not be at the kill. The removal of these external fetters makes it all the more necessary that we should exercise greater restraint than before over ourselves. But what I have seen of the Vernacular Press in the Punjab makes me apprehend that if it is not checked by the combined efforts of all Congressmen it will make us sigh for the resurrection of that dead and damned piece of bureaucratic legislation........"

The Congress Working Committee was asked to issue a manifesto exhorting the Indian newspapers to exercise great restraint in dealing with matters affecting "inter-communal relations" and also "in reporting events and incidents relating to inter-communal dissensions and in commenting upon them." With the rise of the Muslim League and the Hindu Mahasabha, and the advent of the *Dawn* in Delhi and its Hindu counterparts elsewhere, the poison spread, till sweeping indictments of communities as a whole became the order of the day. For the Congress and the Nationalist Press, it was a double fight—a fight against official reactionaryism on the one hand and a fight against communal propaganda on the other. The tempo increased when in August 1942 the Congress came into deadly conflict with the Linlithgow Government, and was at its height when Pakistan became a live issue. It suited the Government of India to enjoy the fun; and it was more concerned with the issue of war abroad than with the possibilities of civil strife in the country. It was only when the Interim Government came into being during the Mountbatten regime and the Congress was installed at the Centre that the leaders of the Indian Press could, with the help of the Government, formulate suggestions for the guidance of the Press, from time to time, in respect of news and comments on communal disturbances and communal distemper. Sardar Patel, as the Member for Home, Information and Broadcasting Departments, offered unstinted support to the Press in the exercise of its legitimate functions.

Struggle against Communalism

Long before the Partition became a reality and when communal passions rose high on the question of Pakistan, there was enough realisation in the more sober circles of the Press that the political situation in the country would further deteriorate in the absence of a code for the guidance of the Press. The Central Press Advisory Committee formulated certain suggestions. These were :—

1. During riots, reports should not contain anything to indicate the community of either victims or assailants.
2. While every endeavour should be made to ensure that reports are factually correct and are received from sources known to be reliable, such

reports as give details in defiance of the law, or are calculated to inflame public feelings or to create communal hatred should be treated with the greatest circumspection.

3. Reports of speeches, statements of news directly inciting people to violence should be avoided.

4. Care should be taken in editorials to avoid expressions calculated to encourage or condone violence or arouse communal bitterness.

It soon became clear that the above had not fully met the requirements of the situation. So, the A.I.N.E.C. at its meeting in February, 1947, revised the Communal Code and laid down for communication to all newspapers:

"That it is the duty of the Press at all times to exercise restraint in comment and report and especially at times when communal difficulties are likely to excite passion and that voluntary conventions should be respected."

The subject again came up at the A.I.N.E.C. at its sixth session in Madras, in April, 1947, and addressing the Conference as its President, Mr. Devadas Gandhi said :—

The AD HOC Committee is unanimously agreed that as long as the present emergency created by widespread communal disturbances lasts, the Press should not only refrain from publishing matter calculated to aggravate communal tension, but should contribute in a positive way to the restoration of peaceful conditions in the country. To this end, the Committee recommends the following 'code' for adoption by newspapers and news agencies throughout India.

News of communal disturbances will continue to be received from the following sources:

A. The Central and the Provincial Governments or the local authorities concerned.

B. The recognised news agencies.

C. Newspapers' own correspondents.

In publishing news received from the above sources editors should take steps to ensure that the following principles are observed:

(i) That the presentation is factual and objective.

(ii) That the communities of assailants or victims or casualities in particular incidents are not indicated either directly or indirectly.

(iii) That casuality figures are neither mentioned in headlines nor otherwise prominently featured.

Casuality figures received from any of the three sources indicated may, however, be mentioned in the text of messages, giving the source in each case. When official figures regarding a particular incident are not available, it should be clearly stated that figures given from other sources have not been officially confirmed.

Things, however, became very difficult when Pakistan became a *fait accompli*. The aftermath of partition made conditions well nigh impossible. The Communal Press grew hysterical and threatened to endanger peace further. At its meeting in Bombay (October 1947) the Standing Committee of the A.I.N.E.C. drew up the following code : "to be uniformly observed in the present emergency by all newspapers throughout the dominion of India". The resolution of the A.I.N.E.C. which was shortly afterwards approved by the Government of India runs as follows :

> The Standing Committee of the A.I.N.E.C. is of the opinion that the present multiplicity Codes and Conventions obtaining in the Centre and the Provinces should be replaced by a general uniform convention to be followed throughout the Dominion of India. In pursuance of this and while the present emergency lasts and until the position is again reviewed in the light of experience, newspapers and news-agencies shall be guided by the following conventions in the treatment of news, comments and other matter, bearing in mind the need for the cultivation of harmonious relations between the various sections of the people and the paramount obligation of the Press to contribute in a positive way to the restoration and maintenance of peaceful conditions in the country.
>
> (a) All editorial comments, expressions of opinion whether through statements, letters to the Editor, or in any other form, shall be restrained and free from scurrilous attacks against leaders or communities; and there shall be no incitement to violence.
>
> (b) News of incidents involving loss of life, lawlessness, arson, etc., shall be described and reported in strictly objective terms and shall not be heavily displayed.
>
> (c) Items of news calculated to make for peace and harmony and to help in the restoration and maintenance of law and order, shall be given prominence and precedence over other news.
>
> (d) The greatest caution shall be exercised in the selection and publication of pictures, cartoons, poems, etc.
>
> (e) Figures of casualities and names of communities shall not be be mentioned in headlines.
>
> (f) The source from which casuality figures are obtained shall always be indicated and no figures shall be circulated or published without the fullest possible verification.
>
> (g) Nothing shall be published that is in conflict with the safety of the State.

Among the subsequent developments nothing has made persons and papers more sober than the assassionation of Mahatma Gandhi. Understanding was arrived at a higher level to foster good feelings, between the two communities as well as between the two Dominions. The Indo-Pakistan Agreement of May 1948 was conceived in that spirit. It said:

> "Both Governments recognize that the whole-hearted co-operation of the Press is essential for creating a better atmosphere and, therefore, agree that every effort should be made in consultation with the representatives of the Press, wherever possible, to ensure that the Press in each Dominion does not :
>
> (a) indulge in propaganda against the other Dominion ;
>
> (b) publish exaggerated versions of the news of a character likely to inflame, or cause fear or alarm to the population or a section of the population in either Dominion;

(c) publish material likely to be construed as advocating a declaration of war by one Dominion against the other Dominion or suggesting the inevitability of war between the two Dominions."

The President of the A.I.N.E.C. also issued a personal appeal to secure "the whole-hearted co-operation of the Press in its implementation."

A definite advance in promoting harmonious relations between India and Pakistan (inter-Dominion, theoretically, and inter-communal, in a sense) when in February, 1949, the Government, agitated over the breaches of the Calcutta Agreement committed in the two Dominions, issued a Press Note emphasising the necessity to honour the agreement. The President of the A.I.N.E.C. (Mr. Devadas Gandhi) nominated on the Inter-Dominion Information Consultative Committee, Mr. Tushar Kanti Ghosh, Editor of the *Amrit Bazar Patrika* and Mr. Durga Das, Joint Editor of the *Hindustan Times* to represent the Press of India and appealed again to the Press of India to advance the cause of communal peace and inter-Dominion goodwill. Since' prejudices die hard, the task of the inter-Dominion Committee is by no means asyesy.

Its Task in Free India

With the attainment of India's independence, the Press in India may be said to have entered on a new phase in its history. Its energies are no longer dissipated by the observation of alien domination, though in the earlier years it is bound to be preoccupied with the liquidation of a past legacy. The Indian Press is alive to its new responsibilities, such as those of (1) educating the people for the wise exercise of adult franchise, (2) emphasizing the constructive side of national life, (3) keeping the country on its guard against totalitarian ideologies, (4) interpreting the mind of India to the world, and (5) advancing the cause of universal peace and good-will.

Unto this end, the Press is expected to develop a new faith consistent with India's ancient heritage, and become the instrument of a new civilisation which makes every man a true citizen of the world and takes him nearer the long-cherished Federation of Mankind. There is every hope that the new leaders of the Press of India will so fashion it as to convert it into a most powerful agency for the enlightenment and advancement of the masses.

GROUP PREJUDICES IN INDIA

LAKSHMIPATI MISRA.

India : A Land of Extremes

India has sometimes been described as a land of extremes—climatic, religious, social, economic and intellectual. Such a description is really not very far out of the mark when one begins to consider the extent of knowledge and ignorance, wealth and poverty, religious tolerance and fanaticism and a number of other vices and virtues of opposite extremes existing side by side in many groups in the country. Needless to say that such a state of affairs persisting for any length of time was bound to create serious group prejudices in society. At the same time, it cannot be ignored that in a country aspiring to be great, there is no place for such group prejudices. They have to be completely eliminated or at least reduced to the minimum possible in the prevailing circumstances if India is to rise to heights expected of her. A discussion of such prejudices would be very opportune at this stage of development of our society for, it will focus public opinion on the fundamentals of the problem and thus enable the people to see for themselves what harm such prejudices have done in the past or are likely to do in future if left unchecked. After all, it is upto the intelligentsia of the society actively to foster the agencies, factors or forces which are working for the eradication of these prejudices.

Railways : a Solvent of Group Prejudices

Railways in India have to some extent played a major part in this connection as they have acted and will continue, from the very nature of their activities, to act as an effective solvent of many of the prevailing group prejudices in India. It may be a surprise to many in this generation to know that in one of the earliest despatches from the Government of India to the Directors of the East India Company about the middle of the last century, the Board of Directors were formally warned that on account of the prejudices of the people, very little Railway passenger traffic may be expected in the country. There is no doubt that the caste and religious prejudices then existing were really such as would have easily convinced a foreigner of the impracticability of persuading high caste people to travel with those of lower castes or even to sit in compartments cleaned by sweepers or to drink water supplied from taps on Railway platforms. The present overcrowding on Railways—even travel on the footboards— would be adequate proof, if proof was needed of how the original group prejudices have gradually been overcome in India through sheer necessity.

It is true that a strong Central Administration also created a community of interest and produced in consequence a coalescing effect on the residents of different areas and members of different communities. It is, however, very doubtful if the development in this direction would have been what is today if the Railways had not, by providing the cheapest, quickest and most comfortable form of transport, compelled the members of the various groups to resort to Railway travel. A journey extending for hours in a Railway compartment cannot but create among travellers a feeling of companionship which is after all the best solvent of group prejudices. It is the daily experience of persons associated with Railway work that many of the passengers looking askance at their fellow—travellers at the commencement of the journey soon settle down to the inevitable and develop in course of the journey a feeling of fellowship or at least a desire for conversation and once the ice is broken, the conversation leads frequently to exchange of ideas even on most controversial subjects and eventually to a tolerant understanding of the point of view of the other party. This has not occurred on any particular occasion but may be said to have gone on in all compartments of all Railway trains since the very commencement of the train services.

It should not, therefore, be difficult to appreciate the cumulative effect of such adjustments between the points of view of billions of passengers who have travelled on Railways in course of a century. It has been the writer's recollection that even as late as the beginning of the present century, the majority of the passengers travelling never took any food during the Railway journey and even avoided, as far as they could, drinking water out of Railway taps. Such prejudices, if they have not yet been completely eradicated, are at least rare these days. It would therefore not be an exaggeration to say that Railways, more than any other Agency in India, have prepared the ground for Mahatma Gandhi to sow the seed which is so rapidly killing untouchability or rigidity of caste system in India. It is true that reservation of compartments for Europeans created or rather intensified group prejudices of another type but it was no fault of the Railways. These reservations had to be done to meet the political exigencies of the times. Fortunately, these too have vanished. On Railways today all passengers of a class have the same rights and privileges and are expected to show the same sense of responsibilities towards their fellow—passengers.

Unfortunately for us Railways have not been able to render the same service to India as they have done in other advanced countries in the West or in America for, in India they were planned and developed on rather unnatural lines. By the middle of the 19th century, the utility of the Railways had been fully established in practically all advanced countries of the World. In India, the East India Company had consolidated its power practically over the whole country. There were no roads worth the name and the river traffic was very slow. The Government, on the other hand, was getting more and more centralised. The administration of such a vast country could not be carried on without a quicker means of communication. However, as Railways required initially a huge capital expenditure on construction and equipment and the resources of the Government of India were limited, the construction of the Railways had perforce to be confined in these circumstances to big centres of population or Industry or Administration with the result that the Railway facilities provided in areas already developed were fully utilized and more and more was asked for to meet their growing requirements. The result has been that, during the last 80 years, some areas got comparatively overdeveloped while others continue to remain undeveloped and neglected for lack of railway facilities; e.g., practically in the whole of northern India embracing the Punjab, the U.P., Bihar and Bengal, railways are over-developed while the huge block of territory like that enclosed by Raipur, Kharagpur and Bezwada remains almost untouched.

Another factor which militated against a more uniform development of Railways all over India was that Railways in India were divided into two classes—Commercial and Strategic. Commercial Railways were the responsibility of the Central Government and built only when there was a prospect of a decent yield after a certain number of years on the capital invested while strategic lines were built for military requirements of the country and on requisitions from the Defence Department. If any province or Indian State asked for a new Railway line, the first question asked was 'will it pay'? If the answer was in the negative, the applicant was asked if he would be prepared to guarantee interest on the capital expenditure involved. If the Province or the State provided the capital or produced the guarantee, the Railway was built. For Railways in undeveloped areas, no return could of course be expected for a long time and consequently the Local Governments or the Indian States asking for such a line were not in a position to give the guarantee asked for with the result that these areas had to remain neglected.

The political set up of India was also responsible to a very great extent for the uneven development of Railways in the country. There were British India and Indian India. It will be noticed from a glance at the Railway Map of India, that British India consisted mostly of the strips of territory—fairly wide—but only along the coastline or at the foot of the hills in the north and the great mass of hinterland in the centre except the territories grouped in the Central Provinces belonged to Indian States. Out of the Provinces in British India, 5 at least were so small and had such scanty resources that they could not be expected to find the guarantee or the funds necessary for Railway development, commensurate with their needs. In case of Indian States the position was still worse. Except three or four, none of the 600 and odd States were even as big as our smaller provinces. In fact, practically all except 15 to 20, eked out a bare existence and were hardly in a position to do much for Railway development in their territories. There was also a time when the Rulers of Indian States were not generally inclined to agree to Railways being taken through their territories. An even development of the country was thus retarded not only through lack of funds but on account of politics as well. Fortunately for the country all this is now past history. The Government of India will in future be masters of the whole of the Indian territory now left over after partition. The States have either been integrated or merged in the various provinces. So, the difficulties arising from clash of interests have practically vanished but those resulting from lack of funds still remain.

Railways, Still Best Form of Transport

There is a school of thought which considers that the Railways are now an out-moded form of transport and that the country can be opened up equally effectively with roads and development of water transport; also civil aviation. It is true that with the development of Internal Combustion Engines, transport on road, river and in the air has become as quick as that on Railways but that does not nullify or even detract from the utility of Railways. Roads may be able to divert Railway traffic within a zone of 50 miles and Airways can come into the picture after 400 to 500 miles but for passenger journeys over 50 miles and less than 450 miles Railways cannot still be beaten for comfort, economy or speed. In fact, Railways will, in spite of these developments, still remain the best form of transport for third, inter and second class passengers for long journeys as well. So far as goods are concerned, Railways cannot be beaten for low-freighted traffic to be carried over long distances.

Suggestions for Their Expansion

In short, if the country is to be properly developed, more Railways should be built and particularly in the neglected but potentially rich areas like the one referred to above. The difficulty as mentioned above is, however, of the return on the capital expenditure incurred. As long as the Railway Board are expected to earn adequate returns on the Railway capital invested by them, they cannot afford to fritter away their financial resources over projects in undeveloped or underdeveloped areas. Some other method of financing such constructions must be evolved in the general interests of the country. For example, the Irrigation Department Works have been divided into two classes—Productive and Protective. Productive Works are supposed to yield enough revenue to pay for their maintenance, depreciation and interest charges, while the deficit on similar charges on Protective Works used to be met out of some other funds such as *famine fund*. A similar procedure will also have to be adopted for Railway constructions in undeveloped areas. A number of alternatives are available but, the most practical solution of this problem is to divide the Railways in India into three classes—Commercial, Strategic and Development. The loss on working of the 'Development' lines should be financed out of the share of the Central Government in the net earnings of Indian Railways under the present convention. Such Railways cannot but develop the territories they pass through and will therefore directly benefit the provinces. The loss suffered by the Central Government on such Railways should, therefore, be considered as part of the financial assistance which the Center annually gives to the Provinces in some form. It must not be ignored that such assistance to the Provinces will not be an entire loss to the Central Government for, the development of the backward areas in a Province will progressively increase the yield from taxes creditable to the Central Government and eventually make up the loss incurred by the Centre in the initial stages of the development. It has been found that with 5000 miles of new Railways in undeveloped areas, there will be very few places left in the country more than 30 miles away from a Railway. Even with the present high cost of labour and materials, 5000 miles of new Railway Construction should not cost more than 150 crores of rupees which if spread over a period of 15 years should not involve an annual expenditure of more than 10 crores on such Projects. Such an investment will however be a very powerful incentive to the development of the areas potentially rich but which have so far remained neglected and which cannot be adequately developed with less expenditure. Needless to say, once these territories have been opened up, there will be the same liquidation of group prejudices there as has occurred through the agency of Railways in the most advanced areas of the country. To summarise, the pressing need so far as Railways are concerned is to extend Railways to undeveloped areas and make Railway travel generally more comfortable and safer. It will inevitably lead not only to further increase in passenger traffic but will increase Tourist Traffic, both foreign and local, to places of cultural interest in the country.

GROUP PREJUDICES IN INDIA

SHRI V. V. GIRI

Group Prejudices: Their Genesis

The idea of bringing out a symposium on the problem of group prejudices in India and the ways and means for its solution indeed deserves every encouragement and appreciation by the leaders of all schools of thought in India. In my short article below I have first dealt with the problem in so far as it affects the society in general and the measures that are being taken by our National Government to get rid of these social evils; and later I have attempted to show the causes for the prevalence of group prejudices among the working class population in particular and have indicated some of the steps that will help in their eradication.

At the outset it is my definite view that the present fissiparous tendencies that prevail in the country are a passing phase in the transition between England giving up its hold over India and the people of India taking upon themselves the responsibility of acquiring complete sovereignty over their country. Such tendencies have their root cause in the administration of our country in the past by foreign vested interests who kept alive some of the group prejudices in their own interest. The rallying of one section as against others appeared in their view the only safeguard for the maintenance of their rule. The Britisher and his satellites in India were responsible in setting up class against class, creed against creed, colour against colour and in my view this has given a fillip to some extent to the group prejudices of our time. We always knew that for a time they rallied the Hindus against Mussalmans and *vice versa* and when these two groups united, they encouraged the untouchables as against the rest. 'Divide and Rule' was the basis of their policy and the group prejudices were encouraged for nearly a century and a half and if we think that we can do away with them in the course of a few years, we are indeed in a fool's paradise.

Gandhi's Crusade against Them

It must be remembered that even during the time when India was under subjection, Mahatma Gandhi's arrival in this country from South Africa and his taking up the leadership effected a new orientation and ultimately resulted in the East trying to lift up its head, for the first time after many centuries, politically and economically. He created a revolution in the minds of the caste Hindus that their treatment of the Harijans as 'untouchables' would no longer be tolerated and that India would not have any right to demand political independence when the majority of the Hindus subjected the untouchables to untold miseries. The opening of the temples to the Harijans was the first knock-out-blow to the Hindu orthodoxy. Now, after fifteen years since provincial autonomy was established in the year 1935, a stage has been reached when we can say that in the shortest possible time there will be no distinction between Harijans and non-Harijans. Our new Constitution which is being forged and will soon be the law of the land has rightly emphasised and put the legal stamp on the great social revolution brought about by Mahatma Gandhi by his desire to uplift fifty million untouchables of India from their age-old low social status. It lays down that untouchability is abolished and its practice in any form is forbidden. The enforcement of any disability arising out of untouchability shall be an offence punishable in accordance with law. There is already a great tendency for interprovincial and inter-caste marriages and a greater tendency for inter-dining among all classes, which have resulted in cutting down caste barriers. For instance, in the workshops in India, during the working hours, to whatever caste, creed or colour the workers may belong, they do not mind taking water from the same pot. The extension of such usage and practice in other spheres which can easily be achieved in due course will also help to an extent in doing away with prejudices.

Classless Society, Government's Goal

The tendency today is for a new world order based on socialism and a classless society. Our present Government in India have already taken steps to achieve these objectives. The States Ministry under the able leadership of Sardar Vallabhbhai Patel has completed the liquidation of the princely system. The abolition of zamindaris throughout the provinces is also a move in the right direction. At the first session of the Constituent Assembly its President, Dr. Rajendra Prasad, spoke of a classless society for India, which was to be a co-operative commonwealth, and the foundation of its constitutional character was laid by the Objectives Resolution moved by the Prime Minister, Pandit Jawaharlal Nehru. It emphasised and guaranteed the securing to all people of India justice—social, economic and political; equality of status, of opportunity and before the law: freedom of thought, expression, belief, faith, worship, vocation, association and action, subject to law and public morality.

Economic Equality : Basis of Real Democracy

There is everywhere a talk and attempt at planning in all its aspects for the well-being of humanity. It is the belief today of everyone that democracy should not merely be a form but a reality and that economic equality must be the basis of it. It is now admitted on all hands that the guaranteeing of the interests of the common man alone will justify a State calling itself an effective democracy. Then alone dictatorship of any kind will not find a place on earth. Social security is a dynamic conception that must influence social policy as a whole and likewise economic policy. In its widest meaning it seems to coincide with freedom from want. The community must possess the financial strength necessary to enable it to honour all claims that experienced foresight can expect to be presented. Its membership must be numerous enough to keep the average risk fairly stable. These conditions are fulfilled only by social insurance schemes applying to a large number of workers in a wide variety of occupations and by social assistance schemes, the solvency of which is guaranteed by the State or other powerful unit. Social security is being sought as an objective to be attained for society as a whole by society as a whole. Thus the creation of social security services brings great advantages to a society, raising its moral value, relieving directly the physical and mental distress which afflicts a vast proportion of the people, helping to reduce the causes of those evils, and cementing the structure of the society itself. The social security services promote the effective conversion of the mass of the population into a genuine society. It is therefore natural that an important provision has been made in the Constitution itself to guarantee the fundamental rights, such as adequate living wages; fair distribution of wealth; equal pay for equal work; prevention of exploitation of child and adult labour; the right to work, to receive education, including free and compulsory education for all citizens up to the age of 14; public assistance in case of unemployment, old age, sickness, disability and other cases of undeserved want; the right to a living wage; conditions of work assuring a decent standard of life and full enjoyment of leisure and social and cultural opportunities.

Role of Religious Prejudices

Religious susceptibilities have also been the cause for group prejudices and these were responsible for the ghastly incidents of loot, riot and rapine in the provinces of Bengal and the Punjab, which resulted in the migration of millions of people from one part to another. Mere palliatives, while they may be necessary to ease the situation, will not be a final remedy for these ills. We have to go to the root of things and nip the poisonous elements which have a tendency to increase these prejudices. Since it is the policy all over that Governments should be democratic and, above all, secular, whether it is the Government of Pakistan or the Indian Government or any other Government, they should persuade the people to come to the conclusion that religion is personal and has nothing to do with the politics of the State or the individual. There should be a realisation that Providence who represents truth, justice, charity, goodness, fair play, patience and perseverence can be the same God for all people, in whatever different forms the different sects may worship Him. Every individual must have the right of freedom of worship in his own way. For instance, in Ceylon I have observed many cases where in a particular family one of the sons may marry a Hindu, the other a Christian, the other a Buddhist and so on, but that does not in any way affect the harmony in the family and the Christians can go to the Church, the Budhists to the Vihara and the Hindus to the Temple and therefore communal passions never ran high to the detriment of the peace of the population. It is also a fact that we rarely hear of communal troubles and fracas between one community and another in Ceylon. In India we have to develop that spirit if we want to eliminate riots based on group, class or caste prejudices. This can be done by consistent and persistent propaganda engineered by governmental authority, non-official and semi-official opinion. After sufficient work is done in this direction, later if necessary it should be made penal and punishable if any individual mixes politics and religion to the detriment of the State. While caste system cannot be wiped out by a stroke of pen, everybody must be made to realise that all are equal and have the same rights, responsibilities, liabilities and privileges, to whichever creed they may belong.

If communal prejudices and passions had not existed in India, in all probability India would have continued to be one united whole and Pakistan would never have seen the light of day. The root cause therefore for all our troubles lies in the fact that we had allowed inter-connection between politics and religion. Therefore the rigours of castes and the prejudices following them should be reduced to the minimum. It is a matter for gratification that the Indian Constitution Bill that is being debated upon in the Constituent Assembly is opposed to communal policy and contemplates a Secular State for India. Equality of citizenship will be assured to all irrespective of religion, caste, colour, creed or sex.

Group Prejudices and Labouring Classes

I have no doubt that caste or group prejudices mostly originate from among the labouring class of people who form a major proportion of the population, because they have always been looked down on as low-class. With the experience of the labour problems in India and as a student of international labour problems I have always held that if labour, agricultural and industrial, is rightly organised, that itself will give an everlasting blow to these social ills. That will ultimately result in encouraging the idea of a classless society. But classes are bound to exist so long as there is a disparity between the rich and the poor in an appreciable degree. The workers in the field and factories are realising that they are not merely wage-earners but citizens who have a right to be associated with the administration of the industry. Therefore, if a national plan for developing industries is to succeed, workers must be given such conditions as will place them in a position to devote to their work all the intelligence, physical skill, energy and enthusiasm they possess so that their work will be efficient and the output of production both in quality and quantity will be the highest. Therefore, the industrial system, besides providing good conditions of work, should also guarantee labour the higher satisfaction that, by doing their work well, they are rendering service to the community not as slaves of the system but as free men. In order to give them greater satisfaction and to remove their fear of the future, workers should be given a voice in the control of the industrial system. The aim of democratic governments today is to put an end to all exploitation and monopoly interests of every description and they intend that production shall be for use and not for profit. The attempt of Governments in every country is for introduction of compulsory education and the liquidation of illiteracy. Prohibition is being introduced in all prvoinces in India with a view to make homes lead decent lives.

Real Remedy

Unless the conditions under which labour works are improved in all directions, group prejudices can never be eradicated. Indebtedness is a serious evil that always harps on the well-being of industrial as well as agricultural workers. Casual demands for expenditure like funeral or marriage drive them to money-lenders' parlour. There is a swarm of spurious money-lenders, pathans, marwaris and others who hover about the environments of factories and dwelling parts of the workers and they derive interest up to 300 per cent. per annum. The majority of industrial workers are in debt for the greater part of their working lives. Indebtedness of the lowest of the population in India and even those of the middle-classes can be minimised firstly by creating employment. The farmer, the peasant and the labourer in the village must secure a living wage. This can be done by improving the standard of living. In order to achieve this purpose, not only agriculture which is the biggest industry in our country should be run on most uptodate and modern lines to secure decent wages for the labourer but we must find ways and means of creating subsidiary occupation, especially during the time when the agricultural season is over. This subsidiary occupation will give the labourer sufficient income to tide over the rainy day when there will not be enough work. Secondly, there must be a network of producers-cum-consumers societies which will secure for the population articles of foodstuffs at reasonable rates; co-operative societies dealing in all other articles and co-operative banks dealing with grants of credit to the people must become the order of the day, so that there will be no usurious interests on loans taken by the poorer persons. The shylocks, whether in village or town, should not find a place anywhere. In short, every village must be served by a multipurpose co-operative society dealing with every aspect of the economic life of the population. In this connection I am glad to mention that Panchayats are being established for a group of villages with a view to make them self-contained.

There must be a minimum wage legislation because it is admitted that the wages in India are exceptionally low. This step is not only an urgent need for the well-being of the working classes in the country but is also one of the most important measures calculated to mitigate the rigours of life in industry or agriculture. This can be accomplished by bringing into existence Wage Boards. The chief object of the minimum wage legislation is to secure a reasonably decent standard of living to the workers, whether in the field or in the factory. The only real basis for fixing the minimum rates of wages therefore would be the requirements of the workers judged from the point of view of enabling them to lead such a life.

If a worker secures employment and a minimum wage and is free from indebtedness, he will then think of other desirable necessities of existence. Every family in India, especially the poorer ones, would like to have a decent house to live in, be it in the village or town. In the absence of proper facilities, especially the working-class people are thrown on their own resources and left to find accommodation themselves. This they do by living on the pavements and occupying congested and insanitary buildings. It is the universal opinion that the chawls of Bombay, the bustis of Calcutta, the cheris of Madras and the hattas of Cawnpore are a disgrace to civilisation, which allows any number of families to stay in one-room tenements and others to live their lives under the trees. The Royal Commission on Labour, the Bihar Labour Enquiry Committee, the Bombay Rent Enquiry Committee, the Madras Sanitary Welfare League and the Courts of Enquiry appointed by the Congress Governments in various trade disputes have proved beyond doubt the necessity for immediate improvement in this direction. Good housing is an indispensable necessity for health and efficiency. The general view in which both Government and employers must agree is the following minimum standard of housing even for the lowest category of industrial workers. A two-room tenement at least 10' x 12' with a verandah both at the back and the front 6' wide, a kitchen and an independent bathroom at a little distance from the main tenement and a little compound is the minimum standard for every worker. Some employers have taken this in right earnest and a living example can be found in Harvey Patte where co-operative houses have been built on the above lines. Similarly in villages even if smaller houses are built for lesser cost, it shall be taken up at the earliest opportunity and it is a matter for congratulations that the Government of India and the local governments have taken up the matter in right earnest and are trying to provide houses even at a cost of Rs. 1,000|- for the villagers. Thus if the generality of the population succeed in having employment, a living wage and a house, they would then have to be provided with other minimum conveniences which are necessary to make life bearable.

In conclusion, I reiterate that the problem of group prejudices should be attacked at the root with a determination to solve it. I emphasise that propaganda should be carried on both in the Indian Union as well as in Pakistan and even elsewhere stressing the necessity of the establishment of a purely Secular State everywhere. The caste system and all its rigidity must be reduced to the minimum. This should be done with expedition with a view to evolve a classless society. The fundamental rights for all people must be guaranteed. Religion must be personal to an individual. Economic equality must be the order of the day. From the political aspect of things, the tendency must be to evolve a socialist democracy. I have tried to show in the foregoing paragraphs how these could be achieved; and therein lies the salvation not only of Pakistan and India but also of the rest of the world from the baneful effects of group prejudices.

PLACE OF SCIENCE IN BUILDING OF A UNITED INDIA

DR. S. S. BHATNAGAR AND DR. S. D. MAHANT

Standard of Living, The Vital Problem

India's history entered a new phase on 15th August, 1947, and from 26th January, 1950, the republican constitution has been adopted. Yet, in matters of national importance, the outlook of a large majority of people who claim to be leaders of public thought has not changed and, as in the days of British regime, they are still prone to attempt to foist the blame for all acts of omission and commission on the Government. The tendency for spoon-feeding has taken such a root in the minds of people that the doctrine of self-help appears to have been forgotten by most of them.

In the building of a United India, the most important objective is to raise the standard of living. This standard is admittedly very low but then the remedy for it is not mere redistribution of the meagre wealth that we have, as many people seem to imagine. Should such a redistribution be brought about, the results will definitely disappoint all concerned, the disillusionment being the greatest for those who are the loudest in its favour. The 'haves' will of course lose but the 'have nots' will not gain to any appreciable extent and will in the end be terribly disappointed.

Expansion of Production, the Only Means

For raising the standard of living it is necessary to have funds to spend on the beneficient activities and this is only possible by producing more wealth which in its turn can only result from increased production, whether it be in the field of industry or in pursuit of agricultural avocations. It is gratifying to note that this is now being realised by many of those in authority. The Prime Minister has emphasized the need for increasing production in all directions and his appeal has been supported and reinforced by many others.

Increased production can be arranged in several ways. One of the most important steps in this direction is harder work and increased efficiency. The British worker set an example of these traits of character during the last war and accomplished the desired results. Since the close of the war, the pace has not only been maintained but also improved to meet the economic crisis through which Britain has been passing.

Ways to Achieve It

In India, however, the old habit of taking things easily still continues and the changed political status of the country has so far been without any effect in bringing home the necessity of harder work in national interest. As the Chairman of Tata Iron and Steel Company Limited disclosed in his recent speech, in spite of appreciable increases in the wages of labour, the outturn per man hour has gone down considerably. This state of affairs has resulted in Indian Labour becoming as costly as labour in America and Europe without the efficiency attained in those regions and the advantages that this country once possessed to offset the higher costs of chemicals and other raw materials by cheaper labour are no longer available. It is necessary to remedy this state of affairs if industry in India is to develop and face the forces of world competition.

Science and Public Health

One of the essential perquisites to an increase in efficiency is provision for better health of labour and in assuring this, science has an important role to play. A scientific study of the cause of diseases and their prevention and cure is helpful in creating conditions for better health. As is well known science has been of immense assistance in finding out new remedies for several diseases and pointing out ways and means of preventing others. Medicine has always been dependent on science for its advancement and in promoting this branch of national welfare, science has as glorious a record as in any other line. Pencillin and the sulphanomides, the insecticide DDT, better vaccines and improved hygienic measures have all but conquered yellow fever, dysentry, typhus, tetenus, pneumonia, meningitis etc. Malaria has been controlled and the disability from venereal diseases has been radically reduced, by the new methods of treatment.

All this has become possible by the application of science to public health and in this field India too has a creditable record. Investigations by Indian medical men and scientists have helped in locating the causes of plague and cholera and prescribing the remedial measures to prevent the recurrence of these scourges. The success achieved in this direction is manifest from the decreased incidence of the epidemics and the increased confidence with which those afflicted are treated and cured.

Science and Industrial Health

In the field of industrial health, however, we are more or less still at the start and have so far relied on the experience and conclusions obtained in western countries. It is an admitted fact that conditions in India are quite different from those prevailing in Europe and America and before finalising any conclusions it is necessary to study the problems and their treatment from the local point of view. This opens out a new and important field for scientific investigations. In this connection reference may be made to the urgent need for a regular study of the diets of labour employed in different industries and in different areas with an attempt to corelate it with output. Such a study will have important bearings in indicating the nutritional deficiencies and their incidence on production. It will possibly indicate how a change of diet may be of help in increasing the efficiency of Indian labour.

Science and Agriculture

Other important steps to increase production are the rational applications of science and scientific methods both in agriculture and industry. We are apt to boast ancient Bharat flowed with milk and honey but has sufficient attention been paid to the changed conditions, the increased population, the want of attention to make up the depletion of essential constituents of soil, the eradication of pests and avoidance of depredation by rodents and wild animals? Our methods of agriculture are still the same as they were centuries ago and the result is that in the case of both food crops and cash crops, the yields in our country per acre are low even when compared with such countries as China and Japan. Our knowledge about the condition of soils in different parts of the country is very meagre and a country-wide soil survey is essential for a proper assessment of the possibilities in different parts. Such a survey, which will demand the employment of many soil analysts will be of assistance in locating the deficient constituents and the ways and means of making good the deficiency.

Besides mechanised cultivation, use of fertilizers to supply the deficient constituents, treatment of crops and fields to kill and eradicate vegetable and animal pests, better control and prevention of ravages of wild animals, improved methods of storage to reduce losses due to rodents, and rotation of crops are some of the methods where science can be of considerable assistance in increasing production and preservation of agricultural commodities from damage. Increased control of floods and extension of irrigation to arid tracts are two other fields where the application of scientific methods can assist in becoming independent of the vagaries of nature. Agricultural wastes are at present used mostly as fuel but some of them are potential for existing and new industries and an efficient utilisation of these, as a result of scientific investigations, can make substantial contribution to the production of new wealth. Even a menace like kans-infestation, which has been responsible for reducing considerable area of land into waste land, does form a potential raw material for paper making and other cellulosic industry.

Examples of the good results obtained from the application of scientific methods to agricultural fields in this country are sufficiently well known. The evolution of new varieties of cotton to increase the length of the fibre, the famous Coimbatore sugarcane and new varieties of wheat are some of the achievements of science in this direction. But while laboratory results have received considerable attention, translation of these to field production has not been properly emphasized and has not had full consideration. It will be necessary to devote considerable attention to this aspect and evolve a machinery to educate and demonstrate to the villagers and farmers the improvements brought about by science. For this purpose the number of demonstration farms and the facilities available there will have to be considerably expanded At the same time it will be necessary to depute a very large number of agricultural graduates to the villages and fields so that application of laboratory results in field practice is accelerated and developments take place on proper lines.

Reclamation of water-logged areas is another illustration of successful application of science to promotion of national welfare. By a planned rotation of crops, the menace of water—logging has been overcome and a succession of food and fodder crops is being obtained from it in many areas.

Science and Industrial Expansion

Similarly, in industry, science is capable of playing an important role so that more and better production of industrial commodities and the production of new articles with the resultant production of new wealth, can be assured. One of the most important contributions that science can make is in the standardisation of methods of production as well as standardisation of raw material and finished good. It is a matter of extreme regret that, barring a few honourable examples, industry in India generally has exhibited an apathy to invoking the help of science and has chosen to follow methods and technical practices which can at best be described as empirical. In the lust of making quick money, the need for keeping pace with improvements in technique has generally been relegated to the background. The result has been that Indian products have, both at home and abroad, come to be associated with an indifferent quality on which people feel shy to place any reliance. This unsatisfactory position loudly calls for the application of scientific methods of controlled production on rational lines.

Industry in India is still in comparative infancy. Vast fields remain to be explored and our mineral, agricultural, forest and animal resources await exploitation and development. It is necessary in the national interest to start new industries and expand existing ones and, to be in a position to do so to the maximum advantage, it is essential to have planned development on a scientific basis. In the past our industry has grown more or less on a *ad hoc* basis with the result that we find a lopsided development with some of the industries located and even concentrated in wrong places. While it is difficult to move the existing units, it is highly desirable to ensure that the same mistakes are not repeated.

How useful development on planned and balanced lines can be, is well illustrated by the example of developments at Walchand-nagar. Primarily developed as a sugar farm, large areas of salt affected wasteland have been reclaimed and irrigation has been expanded. The area under food crops and vegetables has been increased and a dairy started. To meet the needs of organic manures, an oil mill has been established and the groundnut cake produced by the mill is used on the farm. The groundnut oil is hydrogenated and the waste products are converted into soap. The sugar cane is crushed in the local sugar factory and molasses converted into alcohol at the distillery. Research and experiments are still proceeding into the best ways of utilising the other products of the factories and the farms and avoiding waste. All this has been instrumental in increasing the volume of employment; better wages are being paid and new avenues of employment have been opened out for skilled personnel.

It is now an accepted truism that modern industry is closely connected with scientific and technical developments and Indian industry can be no exception to this general rule. A scientific study of the effects and causes and a critical anaysis of the various factors involved in production so as to improve the quality of the product and the efficiency of the process along with a possible reduction of costs, is a vital necessity for any industry to be able to sustain itself and advance in the modern world. In the planned expansion of Indian industry science and scientific research has important part to play. So far our industrialists have been content with importing the technique and knowhow from foreign countries and have taken it for granted that the practice initiated will hold good for ever. The belief has been that the practice being imported will be such as will not call for any change at any time, the differences created by Indian raw material and Indian conditions being overlooked. The experience, of the Indian industrialist has, however, brought home to him the incorrect premise of this assumption and the rapid advance of industry in the Western countries has led to a better appreciation of the importance of science to industrial advance in India also. This, however, is only a beginning and the import of the useful role of science in increased industrialisation of the country will be increasingly felt with time.

Science and National Planning

Nature in her bounty has provided us with an abundance of raw material and the interests of a united India demand that they are utilised to the best advantage in the promotion of our national welfare. *The wide—spread nature* of these natural resources, however, calls for the utmost vigilance and care in their development on a planned basis so that this potential wealth is not wasted and the requirements of the different units are met. Self-sufficiency in every respect is a dream of the past, even in the international sphere, and, so far as the different units of the Indian Union are concerned, an impracticable proposition. The needs of each unit are so interlinked with the available resources of the other that it is impossible to conceive of a plan of development in India except on the basis of a united whole. What havoc individualistic tendencies are apt to play has already been demonstrated by the partition of the country and our salvation now only lies in future development being planned keeping in view the requirements of different units as an integrated entity. The complementary nature of the problems serves to focus attention on similarities and at the same time helps to bring the differences into bold relief and the need for a solution of all these helps to emphasize the important place that science occupies in the building of a united India.